MW00624251

THE UNSHUTTERED HEART

THE UNSHUTTERED HEART

Opening to Aliveness/ Deadness in the Self

Ann Belford Ulanov

Abingdon Press
Nashville

THE UNSHUTTERED HEART
OPENING TO ALIVENESS/DEADNESS IN THE SELF

Copyright © 2007 by Ann Belford Ulanov

All rights reserved.

No part of this work may be reproduced or transmitted in any form or by any means, electronic or mechanical, including photocopying and recording, or by any information storage or retrieval system, except as may be expressly permitted by the 1976 Copyright Act or in writing from the publisher. Requests for permission should be addressed to Abingdon Press, P.O. Box 801, 201 Eighth Avenue South, Nashville, TN 37202-0801 or permissions@abingdonpress.com.

This book is printed on acid-free paper.

Library of Congress Cataloging-in-Publication Data

Ulanov, Ann Belford.
  The unshuttered heart : opening to aliveness/deadness in the self / Ann Belford Ulanov.
     p. cm.
  ISBN 978-0-687-49466-8 (binding: pbk., adhesive, perfect : alk. paper)
  1. Psychoanalysis and religion. 2. Jungian psychology--Religious aspects. 3. Spirituality. 4. Psychology, Religious. 5. Consciousness--Religious aspects. I. Title.

  BF175.4.R44U44 2007
  150.19'54--dc22

2007006821

Scripture quotations marked (RSV) are taken from the Revised Standard Version of the Bible, copyright 1946, 1952, 1971 by the Division of Christian Education of the National Council of the Churches of Christ in the United States of America. Used by permission. All rights reserved.

Scripture quotations marked (GNT) are from the Good News Translation in Today's English Version-Second Edition © 1992 by American Bible Society. Used by Permission.

07 08 09 10 11 12 13 14 15 16—10 9 8 7 6 5 4 3 2 1

MANUFACTURED IN THE UNITED STATES OF AMERICA

For my dear friend
Catherine Frantzis

CONTENTS

INTRODUCTION

Whenever I ask anyone about instances of feeling alive—aliveness thrumming through them—they answer immediately with examples varied and fascinating: standing in a misty rain seeing the grape leaves she was picking, silver and glistening, making the whole world soft and beautiful; watching the birth of his child, stunning, incredible; the total coming of sexual orgasm; a moment of "clicking," the outer meeting the inner, a sense of I get it, I get the whole thing. To ask about deadness is harder, but examples arrive: absence of being there, no vitality; attention going in all directions, as if losing it, not able to gather myself; energy gone; something of me has gone missing.

Analysis is about renaissance of this inestimable experience of feeling alive and real, and about regenerating from its opposite, deadness. Deadness includes death, especially loss of ones we love, loss of country, loss of youth from the physical and psychological maiming of war, of famine, of mud and dust of refugee camps. But more grave still is deadness while we are still alive, as if some part of us has been driven into exile and we cannot get it back.

In keeping with the vitality of these experiences, I do not want to step back to summarize the book's chapters. Instead, I want to stay with the main theme of feeling alive and real, and with the basso ostinato of deadness, and how deadness threatens and joins aliveness in vigorous counterpoint. Circling around the major variations on the basic theme of aliveness/deadness begins with the impact on me of terrorism in my city on 9/11. Our new century opening under that shadow cast into bold relief for me the preciousness of life and what we are living for, what we love, and what we find worth dying for.

My theoretical base in addressing these questions reveals a motif repeated throughout these chapters: my analytical work rooted in Jung's approach to the psyche, though other theorists, whom I have read and taught, exert strong influence as well.

Aliveness, for me, leads to livingness, a process, not an acquisition. Aliveness, as we circle around it, named and unnamed, cannot be captured, but only symbolized. That fact delivers us into precincts of psychology and religion, two refrains that resound throughout the book.

The psychological question asks, what makes for aliveness in analysis, as that makes for healing. Sounding and resounding variations of this question do not yield a succinct answer. It remains mysterious, but the mystery of the mystery is that it shows itself; it is visible. Healing turns round and round aliveness without exhausting its power. Deadness deadens our perception of aliveness, makes it invisible to us, and us invisible to it, and evil seeks to dismantle it, to disavow its actuality, to say "nothing is there."

The religious question asks what we believe of the reality our symbols point to that makes us feel connected to the source of aliveness. What do we name it? Or do we leave it unnamed? For the clinician this is an urgent question, because that belief, whatever it is, influences what we hear, how we listen, shaping the complexities of rhythm, of interval, of voice in analytical work.

The impact of terrorism rehearses a well-known motif—that we belong to each other and to something greater that holds all of us. The familiar fugue of our dependence and interdependence recalls their vertebrate integration—that working on oneself enlarges society, and working to enlarge social space among diverse groups makes possible new depths in oneself. Even our personal faults connect, as if by a hinge, to the impersonal violences we do to each other. Thus psychological work and spiritual practice form a kind of social action.

To find a method to hear all these interconnections, these intersecting variations on a recurring theme of aliveness and deadness, yields to us a more ample consciousness capable of hearing simultaneously different ways of making meaning. We can listen to how our past causes present interpretations; how our present takes us to future aims we had not yet guessed; how our conscious and unconscious mental processes can combine to expand our awareness of the whole surround, so that all the parts can be heard as well as the whole they make up. Aliveness, then, is to make something of what we hear, and to hear what we hear makes of us. Our heart becomes unshuttered.

In ending this beginning, I want to express my gratitude to the persons who generously gave permission to cite their material, my analysands with whom it is a privilege to work.

Ann Belford Ulanov
New York City and Woodbury, Connecticut

CHAPTER 1

ALIVENESS/DEADNESS

Under the shadow of terrorist attacks on American soil, and engagement in war on foreign soil, these questions become urgent: What makes for our sense of aliveness and feeling real, as persons and as a people, a country, and as part of the whole human family on this earth? What puts us in touch with our own voice and confers a sense of finding and creating a path that is true for us, while at the same time recognizing that others take different paths? What kills our voice? What makes for deadness? What is the nature of that generative space where we enhance our capacity to be real? To what and to whom do we belong?

Those of us in New York City are still hemmed in by such questions, still in grief for those killed and in our fearful wondering if when they knew they were going to die they also knew in their last moments the reassurance that they had truly lived their life, that they had lived according to the mystery of their own vocation, and felt they belonged to a larger whole; or whether they felt unlived life, undared thoughts and actions, life they should have risked now cut off, murdered. We also feel urged by the suffering of neighbors, friends, and victims to seize the life we are given with both hands and not dawdle, not delay, not evade but live full out, with all our hearts and minds and strength, to reach to the bottom and find a foothold in the meaningful, the worth dying for, and to fulfill that meaning, fully to fill our every day living it, touching it, sharing it.

New Century and Millennium

These kinds of questions assaulting us after the trauma of 9/11 and the subsequent terrorism of 3/11 (Madrid), 7/7 (London), 7/23 (Sharm el Sheik), let alone repeated attacks of suicide bombings and reprisals in Iraq, Afghanistan, Israel, and Palestine, alert us to the changing paradigm of our new century and millennium. The overarching question of the twentieth century, I suggest, was being versus nonbeing. How could we be and go on being in the face of so much destructiveness, so much inhumanity—from the world wars, from the racism, gulags, holocausts, forced marches and starvations, the persecution of any among us and any parts within us that differed from the collective norm of being? In the face of such nothingness, how could we be and have faith in being (see Geoghegan 2002, 2-3, 12ff.)?

The paradigm I see emerging in this twenty-first century is no longer cast as the verticality of being versus nonbeing of the twentieth century, but as new horizontality. We look across the whole world and talk about it being a global village, with multinational corporations extending business across continents, where Internet and Webbed connections, let alone television, bring the far into the near, the remote and foreign into the familiar living room. The sheer mass of communications puts the spiritual question to us of how to be alive and real and linked to the center in the midst of this bustling life, no longer removed into cloister, but in the marketplace. Can we reach and dwell in the still point in the midst of the whirling world of competing countries, values, populations? Can the individual find her myth of meaning, his joyous spontaneous self-expression while contributing to the group-oriented consciousness that seeks to look into, not just at, the laws by which energies of life operate—in its subatomic particles, its nature of light, its alternate methods of healing, its intrinsic psyche-matter connections?

The new question for our new century, I suggest, is how to be committed to realness when all feels relative, to find and create an unfolding path and live it full-out with all our hearts, minds, souls, strength, in the midst of others finding different paths? Can all of us in our multicultural, multireligious, multipolitical societies live together? Can we endorse that what we share in common are our differences? Can we recognize that we all look to the same origin point?

Aliveness happens in the space between what we find and create, the space between investing wholeheartedly in specific forms of therapy, of faith, of allegiance, and simultaneously non-attaching from them. We embrace our own path and accept others' differing paths. Like spokes of a wheel, we all turn around and round the center. Circumambulation replaces linear progress; the space-in-between holds the whole.

Our question is no longer being or nonbeing, but self and other, other and self, whether we are talking about splits of psychoanalytic groups, political parties, nations, religions. Even in trauma we must learn this both-and inclusion. As a woman, whose husband and father of their two young children, killed by the plane crashing into the Trade Tower, said, the collective nature of 9/11 is what is so hard; we cannot escape its anniversary nor make it just our own. The children in anger say, but this is our grief; why must we also face all these other people marking it? They feel invaded, and are still seeking in their unremitting sorrow how to find room for their own loss in the midst of everyone's loss, the country's loss.

Clinical and Religious Perspectives

Clinical work circles around the task of rescuing us from loss that makes us go dead, of enabling aliveness to regenerate. The large question about our shared horizon of the new century is the same question within our small horizon of clinical work: What is the mutative agent, what is it that we experience when alive, with buoyancy, hope, an indefinable but definite force, energy, or presence that puts us in touch with our capacity to love, to imagine, to grow, to regenerate? The question around which all circle and what all are after is what brings us alive, promotes and sustains aliveness, combats deadness—of affect, of heart connection, yet also what role does deadness play in our being alive?

If clinical work is successful, analysands finish it linked up to what they experience as the source of aliveness, the origin point. And their relation to it is portable. It does not stay glued to the analyst, but is their very own. They are the partners in a conversation that goes on outside the analyst's office and long after treatment ends, with a center deep inside and far outside themselves, that transcends themselves. Jung talks about this relationship as that of ego to Self, which is Jung's name for that center. Other depth psychology authors intimate such a connection in their descriptions of the goals of analysis. For example, Freud's goal is love and work; Bion's, connection to O which designates ultimate reality; Lacan to the Real; and Melanie Klein to gratitude; Winnicott sees the goal as living creatively; and Masud Khan thriving from *jouissance*; for Grottstein we reach a transcendent position where our conscious I lives in touch with the Ineffable Subject of the unconscious.

For religious people, this previous relationship circumscribes a connection between an I and Other, a me and a Thee, a soul and God, a beloved and Lover. Whatever the ritual we engage in to express and continue our relation to the origin point, we know it now as portable, not stuck to one place, not our possession. In Judaism the Ark was carried from place to place. In Islam the Qur'an, as *kitab*, the living text, is not bound to a set corpus, but gives access to the divine authority responsive to every moment; the Qur'an is "on the lips" (Madigan 2001, 3, 7-8). Jesus' resurrection in Christianity takes him first back to the Father, the source to which he made a bridge for us, and thus he is liberated from one set of social conditions, one historical time and space, one set of ethical rules, and available to all of us in all times and places.

What we aim for in clinical work, and what religions describe through their rituals, is durable connection to the origin point in ourselves that links to that source point in reality. Whatever we call it, we must reify it to get it, and must dereify it or lose it. Thus we enter a great

4

rhythm of, ah, I see, this is the point, this is the good, this is the meaning, this is what makes it all worth it. In this rhythm we say, Yes, that's it, and also, No, that is not it. Through our symbols, doctrines, theories that act like cloaks protecting us, we see that the great mystery is that it becomes visible. Yet ineffable it remains, and our symbols and theories but discarded cloaks that we have outgrown.

The clinical work between analysand and analyst aims to reconstitute a space where both can trust that the integrative forces of the psyche will bring forward the areas of distress and suffering. These are communicated by symptoms, by the way the two people get arranged by the field of emotions between them, the transference and countertransference, by the analysand's story told and created between the two as their relationship unfolds. The analyst is trained to be alert to the way he or she gets pushed into certain roles, marshaled to match and accumulate what this new person brings and unconsciously asks of the analyst. This "being arranged" makes for excitement in this work. An analyst never knows ahead of time, unless one's work has gone dead, fallen into clichéd repetitions, what this new work will be. Each analysis is an adventure, unknown territory, with all the precariousness, even danger, that the unknown inspires.

One new analysand, for example, was an intelligent woman of poised containment. After the first few sessions, I was not at all sure we could get anywhere down to business. There was no way in; all was spoken of freely but gathered up into the superior functioning of her graceful intellect. We were talking about her experience but not experiencing it. No mess anywhere. And mess always provides an entry point. The third session I found to my horror I was arranged to make the mess. I had scheduled two people for the same hour, something that had never happened in nearly forty years of practice. This new patient and another who had seen me a long time were both seated in the waiting room. The latter graciously accepted my apology and offer to make good by not charging her for the next session and I went to see the new person in the face of whose ordered intellect, I made disorder. Then, to compound it, entering the office where she was now calmly seated, all my papers went flying out of my hands and off my desk, making another mess on the floor. Mix-up of times, jumble on the floor, the analyst got arranged to disrupt the poised intelligent conversation killing the space between us. My distress became the entry point and I was eventually able to use it to reflect back to my analysand how we were getting arranged together into a space where things could happen, surprise us, change expectations, and admit the new.

Another analysand arranged me unconsciously to be stupid. Stunned by his vociferous rage in the context of a legal situation in which he was fighting not to be annihilated, I would say stupid things, or things he found stupid. Then the laser ray of his wrath would swivel to discharge itself onto me. His rageful contempt did what contempt always does, rendering its victims helpless, unable, without resource, which is the way I felt in the presence of his suffering. But that was the point. Until I met him where he was living, or rather not living but desperately fighting for his survival, anything I offered was, from one point of view, stupid, technically above the level of conflict and hence irrelevant, which was his endless chant at me. I was ushered into his suffering firsthand. As he felt treated as contemptible, of no account, irrelevant, persecuted, and hounded for trying to do something useful and worthwhile, so did I feel now in relation to him. The collapse of the space between us into a defensive venting made me feel firsthand his necessity to fight, which for me was to recover the space between us, between himself and the outer persecution, and between his inner life and his devastating rage. As he fought for his life, I fought for the space of the treatment between us.

The space of clinical work pushes the two people around to make space for the work to be done. Jung calls this the archetypal field and we feel it as a force, a current, a placement in psychic reality. Jung names the Self the organizing pattern of energy in this field that gathers all the parts of the psyche around a center. I am always asking, What is the Self engineering? (See chapter 8.) How is it maneuvering us, indeed shoving us, pulling us, wooing us into positions where we can experience the reality it connects us to here and now? The Self is the process of the analysis, or the process of the analysis is how we experience the reality the Self discloses through the totality of the psyche. By assembling both our consciousness and what we are unconscious of around a center, making us feel all of the psyche in us and between us and the analyst, the Self gives access to both people as they are positioned, arranged, to witness the reality the Self brings into view. Jung calls this actuality the *unus mundus*, meaning the whole reality, inner-outer, self-other, individual-world, psyche-matter.

This space for conversation between our conscious ego and the unconscious Self is not just an individualistic indulgence which critics of depth psychology aver. Jung's notion of individuation cannot be accomplished except with other people in concrete settings of social, political, and daily interaction. It occurs in the midst of living, in the body literally and symbolically. For body means definite form in a specific time and place in congress with others. Becoming all of ourself, including all the parts, responding to a mysterious summons issued to everyone, a vocation to create that path that has been laid out for us, requires responses and responsibilities to others. As Jung says, "One cannot individuate on top of Mount Everest or in a cave somewhere where one doesn't see people for seventy years; one can only individuate with or against something or somebody" (Jung 1988, vol. 1, 102); "the self and individualism exclude each other. The self *is* relatedness" (ibid., vol. 2, 795).

Becoming all of our being always begins in slime, in indeterminate hints, flashes, all mixed in with everything else, like a tiny plant issuing upward from a root in the mud (see chapter 9). This is aliveness coming into being. To come into our own aliveness, we depend on an other's interest in us, seeing us coming alive to the power of livingness in us. How amazing to see each analysand crafting her or his own way of relating to the unconscious. Some people are visual and images catch up their emotions into relatable forms. Others are auditory and hear a hum when things click, and a sound of jarring chalk on the blackboard when things don't. Some people do not think or pray in words. They think in the key of A-minor, or only in the color red.

The question is put to us with urgency in this first decade of our new century and millennium: Are we like a good plant making oxygen? And the oxygen each of us makes is breathing space for all the rest of us. We desperately need every citizen making her or his share of oxygen, for the planet, for creation of social space that can hold opposite views, and create enough room to find and construct peace.

Where one part of us seeks dominance over the whole, we have fallen into identification with one point of view, and split off and projectively identify any opposing view with the enemy out there. Such tyranny makes for deadness. In pathology we see addictive clinging to a part-object and hurling onto others all the other parts we disown.

Without a big enough space between the opposites, the alive question, What went wrong? turns into the dead-making question, Who did this to us? We lose the whole object and grab instead the part-object split off from the whole. Our inner neglect of all the different parts of us that press to be included to sustain a big space of conversation between them, mirrors the outer neglect of whole parts of our country, or parts of the world where citizens still do not have a blanket, or a bottle of medicine, or enough to eat. If there is no conversation with others, then there is not enough conversation going on between ego and Self. If there is no conversation between ego and Self, then there is not enough conversation with others.

Deadness

Deadness is the opposite of aliveness. Deadness bears a close relation to repetition compulsion, where trying over and over again to get into consciousness what so troubles us, so blocks us, so hurts us, that we

cannot allow it entrance to consciousness. Deadness is felt as refusal to
entertain objects, to let anyone in, stemming from painful lack such as
loss of parents to death, or loss of parents who, though alive, lived as if
dead, so no reverie, no symbolization, no zest grew in us in relation to
them. Deadness feels like destructiveness, as if the only way we can feel
alive is by dying a martyr's death, or by splitting off half of the world to
be killed, or by risking sensational danger in street fights, drug highs, sexual exploits, stock deals. Deadness infiltrates when helpless outrage
amasses against the West's films, music, advertisements that display naked
women, excessive drinking, provocative sex, violent language. This
infiltration can feel like a basic breaking of the blood-bond of human
connection and arouses the implacable vengeance that brings deadness
right into our living room.

For terrorism to be possible it requires a group and religion. We must
feel caught up in a shared vision of something bigger so that murder of the
innocent office worker becomes an offering to the transcendent. If it is
just us alone we doubt our sanity. Only the transcendent linked to a
shared worldview allows us to think ourselves agents of deadness in the
name of a living God.

We see deadness in actual murders, in violence of rape, cheating,
lying, defrauding, let alone collective annexation of countries, genocide,
looting workers' pension funds, wreckage of water and air, of schools and
city neighborhoods.

In clinical work, and working with our own psyches, deadness feels
like no zest, crippling anxiety, a hole in us from something done to us that
should not have been done, or from something not done with us that
should have been done. One man, amazed he stayed in a bad marriage for
so long, said it was as if he turned down the volume; he muted himself to
avoid the pain. We all know about living at half strength, feeling tepid,
dull, as if parts of us are unemployed. Deadness can also feel like too
much—that we cannot get enough food, nourishment, psychic oxygen to
stay alive. Yet anything we take in feels too much, as if life has been

9

stuffed down, made inaccessible. Starved or stuffed, without enough pro-
tein to build emotional and spiritual muscles, unable to eat what is available, with no one to lend us connection to a source point, deadness can
feel like abysmal confusion, missing pieces, missing connections, having
no voice of our own.

The issue of deadness belongs to all of us. For how do we stay alive,
fresh, excited, and glad working all our lives, maintaining the same relationship, the same parenting, the same religion, or political party, decade
after decade? Do we stay awake to our dream life? To our life of worship?
Are we living in our actual body, glad for it whatever it is, caring for it
compassionately and with gratitude? Deadness is lecturing to our body to
be something else. We would not talk to our pet the way we talk to our
body, haranguing it for years to be more thin, more full, less wrinkled,
faster at orgasm, longer at erections, looking like someone else. Deadness
can feel like carrying around dead objects inside us, parts split off as too
unbearable to own. And finally in illness and making our way to the doors
of death, are we alive as we die? What news do we bring from this last
frontier to our neighbors and loved ones?

For each of us our experience has no equivalent. We need to locate
it and ask what meanings, what symbols are we generating and in what
language are they speaking—images of dream and fantasy, of words, of ritual gestures of lovemaking, of worship, of community sharing? The greatest fear is that our life passes us by unlived.

More aliveness is always possible, more fullness. Meaning is contin-
uously manifesting and being created. Our self and symbols of reality and
our relation to it mysteriously emerge all the time when we look into the
eyes of our child or to the stars on a cold night of blackness. This beholding and experiencing the space between us and the other is where aliveness springs up. We make it dead by that space not holding, and thus we
lose our subjectivity, our self agency; or we make it dead by that space
contracting to fixate on one point, and thus we lose the objectivity of
shared consciousness with others.

Deadness as Loss of Subjectivity

We lose that space that holds the depths of beginnings by closing
down from our subjective side, not making something of our experience,
whatever it is. We lose our subjective capacity to invest reality with our
energy, emotion, imagination and make meaning of what happens to us.
Jung says our ego falls into the unconscious; it gets assimilated to the Self.
When our subjective ego does not respond, we experience the Self as the
inert weight of fate.

If the space between us and the other does not hold, all our perceptions and felt meanings drift off, vaporize, fragment like confetti. No one
helps us witness the space and what happens. Either we are not there
making something of our experience, or the other is not there, having
abandoned us or having not turned up in the first place. Our dependency
is not met. We do not lean or confide or entrust to a person, a god, a society, a favorite author or artist or even pet. One of my good friends discussed her imminent death from cancer with her small black poodle.

We refuse the foolishness of our being dependent, needing an other
with whom to talk things over. Nothing holds the space, so what could
be a container feels like a sieve. Everything dribbles out. Nothing
endures. Nothing lasts. Dreams come and go and nothing sticks. And we
do not hold the space with our own agency to respond, to reflect, to imagine, to reject, to choose. We do not inhabit our own life and make no narrative thread to link the parts of our experience together.

The space becomes a gap and we fall in. The only real thing is the
gap, the void, and the danger of dying there. Symbols do not stay real,
but fade into an absence of memory. The object fails us and there is no
hope of retrieving it. We do not risk the full force of our responses of
pain, anger, demand, desire. We cease to imagine about the events that
happen to us. We make nothing of our experience. It takes on a spuri-
ous objectivity: "it's just the way it is." There is no mediating me who
interacts, reacts, and responds, says yes and no and maybe and let me

see what this means to me, what meaning can be made of this event. We do not eat what is available and then stuff ourselves because we feel empty. We do not speak to communicate but to evacuate, to get rid of pain, not inquire into its origins. Splitting off chunks of our experience nulls what is left and it feels flat, stagnant. Even our own body can be stifled, so that we do not engage its aches or pleasures, and it falls to physical symptoms to carry the sorrows of our psyches. Our egos get overcontrolled and diminish connection with others; we feel exiled from the source of aliveness.

One woman said she could not feel the terror of her husband becoming very sick. Instead she is numb, in a swirl of reactions instead of all the different responses she actually had. They mushed together like the food she had to put in the blender for him and she felt confused and ashamed, no place to sort out what was happening to her. She lost herself. Another woman struck down by grief at the death of her loved one said she felt on automatic pilot, "soldiering on." But, alarmingly, and I felt alarmed, the grief, she said, did not get any better. It just sat there waiting. The dreams showed her repeatedly fighting to survive in a crashing airplane. The space of relating to what she suffered had changed into a gap as huge as an airplane plummeting into the earth, or into the sea, or bursting into flames, or disintegrating into the air. Another analysand, when confronted with fear of her feelings in the face of her husband's rebuke, her son's anger, a reading assignment that overwhelmed her, literally held her breath. No space existed at all between her and what she was frightened of. And then her husband felt she shut him out, or her son accused her of not getting what was going on, and the reading she wanted to do defeated her because she could not take it in.

We can lose the space of aliveness when we do not bring our subjective self into responding, reacting, depending, inventing, meditating on what we experience. We restrict our reaction to stay safe, to survive. No play happens, no playing around, no inventing; we lose the fun of living. No interest is taken in our actual experience so nothing is received from it. We avoid looking at our patterns of self-sabotage and just feel randomly tossed about by what happens. We do not look into our pain to seek the depths of its beginnings. We look at our dreams as if from afar, perceive our lives as a movie reel before which we are merely spectators.

If we do not respond to the other, and accept our dependency on the other being there, whoever the other is, and hold in our awareness the space between us and this particular other, be it God or an analyst, or an idea we have just an inkling of, or a reaction of anger or fear or anxiety, but instead just let go of it so it disappears in a dissociation, still existing but we are no longer attached to it, then we never create anything or find anything creating us. We do not take care but leave our lives shelterless, allowing our unique response to be nulled. Here is where pathology and evil get mixed up, for we use deadness as a shield against livingness and thus give way to a destructive force that, as Bion says, destroys time, space, and blocks regeneration (see chapter 6).

The space between us and our God or spouse or friend then collapses into a gap, a trauma of dissociation or absence, a blotting out, a blank. The space between us and the community also falls into the gap and then the community becomes collectivity, not people sharing existence together, holding it for each other, but a mass over against us that we must ward off, defend against, or attack. We live in what Klein describes as the paranoid-schizoid position. Ogden describes it as "That which is perceived is unmediated by subjectivity" (Ogden 1999, 31). We hold no attitude to what we see or believe. We lose parts of us, our sexual passion, our aggressive energy, our sorrow. We are a blank to ourselves. We give nothing to the other.

If we can do this to ourselves, we certainly do it as well to other people. They are eclipsed from our view, because we are not present. The movie *Schindler's List* displayed a denial of the people in the Jewish ghetto by the voluminous listmakings of their names as they were taken off to be imprisoned and killed. Denying ourselves as subjects with real live reactions to what we perceive and think and believe translates into denying others as subjects. They are as if non-present.

Deadness as Loss of Objectivity

An opposite source of going dead is when the space between us and the other contracts. Afraid of drifting off into nothingness, afraid no one will be there to depend on, we grab hold of a something and cling to it with fixity of purpose. We make a something to defend against nothing. Jung talks about this as assimilating the unconscious to the ego. Then all the energy of the unconscious pours into the ego and inflates it, swells it to rigid fixed proportions. We fasten on one solution to the argument, or labor dispute. Only this view, my view, our view is right. We lose all objectivity.

We fasten on one image of God and fall into identification with it, indeed are captured by it, and unconsciously insist others identify with this image, too. Those who do not are repudiated, put outside the fold. How dangerous this view is we see from the terrorist attacks of 9/11 where all those thousands of people killed were seen as not mattering because infidel. Or the attacks in Spain of 3/11 for the same reason. We see it in any fundamentalistic sect of a religion where the space between human and divine contracts to one mediating symbol foisted on everyone else or they are condemned. We see it in the splitting of psychoanalytic schools, the very groups whose profession it is to look into wounds of the heart and soul and make a space to work on them, converse with them. Instead, our split-off groups do not hold conversation but exile each other.

In worship, or in other ritual actions, such as sexual congress, this collapse of space and fixity of symbol translates into imperative action. We can only proceed within prescribed lines. No imagination or variation can intervene. Feelings become facts, not responses to the world. No experimental combination of I and other, self and world, can exist, so no exciting new meanings generate because they feel too dangerous. We might even get caught and held fast in some perversion where we make up an object or a style of being, a kind of false ecstasy, or compelling activity, or self celebration to bridge the gap between us and other. No space exists between the unthinkable and us so no symbolic forms emerge, no little ideas or inspiring wishes or turned-over thoughts that meander around and around and breed new insight or different perspective. Everything is tacked down, cutting off life's blood.

Underneath we feel emptiness but not a fertile one, not the one of Zen, the zero-point when the ego has emptied out and the new will accumulate and make itself known, but the gravesite of Ground Zero, of lives cut short, dying in pain and fear. In clinical work, this contracted space shows in repetition compulsions of either analysand or analyst, of fixed meanings to symbols, canned interpretations to dreams, borrowed voices talking as if one were the theorist one depends upon instead of making the theory one's own. We hear stories of mind games, clichéd reactions, dead language, dogmatistic response, and dumb anonymous suffering. Life is talked about, but not lived here and now in the room. If we speak from deadness, it is a lie. And there is no rest in deadness. The sacred is described but not entered nor received.

We all know something of this deadness and we all struggle to be alive and remain alive, genuinely, with all our hearts, souls, minds, and strength. Perhaps this is what it is to serve God as the great commandment discloses. Aliveness commands a spiritual response, a summoning.

Aliveness

Aliveness comes down to one thing—consenting to rise, to be dented, impressed, pressed in upon, to rejoin, to open, to ponder, to be where we are in this moment and see what happens, allowing the breath of not knowing to be taken, wanting to see what is there and what is not there. Aliveness springs from our making something of what we experience and receiving what experience makes of us. This is the wonder of the child the New Testament always recommends us to return to, what the philosopher Paul Ricoeur calls the "second naiveté"; the goal of Zen Buddhism to live 100 percent in the present; what Jung means when he says the ego is the receiver, transmitter of the Self. In such a space we allow ourselves to depend on something greater than ourselves, to take what it gives us and respond to it. The mystery of our self mingles with the mystery at the core of reality, and from that mingling the new generates, full of the liveliness, the shock of something coming through that is exactly what is needed, what we have hoped and longed for, but in such a surprising form that we know we did not invent it. There is a there there, contra what Gertrude Stein said about Oakland, California.

Sometimes what comes through threatens to break us down, shatter us into pieces. That may be from rock-like defenses we have built that must be faced and dismantled. Or it may be outer events of war or attack by another. We are vulnerable, in some ways unprotected, but no more so than if we live in a prison of neurosis or paranoia. This time, we muster the protection of looking into the painful experience, into our avoidance pattern, into our hurting others, and we do this sheltered in the dependable space between us and an other with whom we risk dependency and witnessing.

In aliveness the clinical task shifts from, How can we be safe and secure, protect ourselves from reality, to How much lightning can we stand? How much reality can we receive?

Wanting to protect ourselves from psychic pain, we limit our imaginations, our ability to play around with ideas, our bodily sensations. We take someone else's words instead of fumble for our own. We neglect giving attention to our dreams. We fear to go down into the depths of one relationship and instead substitute ever new ones. We avoid saying the hard truth to one we love. We refuse to let ourselves depend our full weight on a symbol of reality. Fearing the pain more aliveness would bring, we restrict the range of our living (and the living of those around us, too, for we do not make oxygen for them) and thus go dead in some part of our body or feeling. We may sacrifice whole parts of ourselves in order to protect against pain, but then the whole of us loses some of its essential vitality (Ogden 1999, 18-19).

If, then, we seek to grow more alive, even seek out analysis to find and live from our true self (Winnicott 1960/1965, 148), we can expect to face pain of the deals we made to limit our animation (life force) to protect against pain. Grief will face us for the living we have lost, but gladness and excitement will face us, too, in the living to be gained.

This struggle to live all we can in the face of death, illness, loss of relationship, unbearable grief, acts of injustice, is a struggle we share in all our different circumstances of life. How much can we see what is there and what is not there and find our own voice in response to it, to suffer its inbreaking? How did those children in the walled city of Terezin, Czechoslovakia, write poems in the midst of the Holocaust (Davidson 1941–44)? How did Ety Hillesum discover theological truth, as we read in her diaries, in the deportation camp before being carted off to her death (Hillesum 1983, 36)? Living creatively, as Winnicott calls it, is not confined to economic class or educational level, let alone to race, creed, or culture. The quadriplegic, Winnicott attests, can be alive creatively in his breathing. This is not to say that working for greater economic, educational, and environmental justice is not to command our energies, but it is to say in the New Testament words, the pearl of great price is what we sell all we have for the sake of; riches, fame, security do not ensure simple happiness in being, only this precious aliveness. What, then, is that pearl of great price? It is feeling alive and real, vibrantly the aliveness that belongs to each of us.

Here in clinical work is the mysterious moment of faith. Faith in the psyche, that it transmutes the illness, not our ego efforts however absolutely necessary they are; they do not invent the new. Our therapeutic technique is to attune to what is working through us to regenerate this aliveness spoken of in the New Testament as the abundant life, and in the Hebrew Bible as the Torah. One client described her recovery of adherence to the many commandments within the Law as channels through which we acknowledge the Oneness of things, the Holy manifesting its underlying unity in every action of daily life. Otherwise, she said, "keeping the Law is just O.C.D." (obsessive compulsive disorder). This faith in the psyche's integrative forces links up with what we might call a depth theology.

This faith allows us to believe anything is possible, that people are not reduced to their developmental deficits, or to the inevitability of lifelong damage because of trauma suffered in one's past. We are connected to the infinite within, and that grants us tiny but indispensable elbow room, illustrated by the many people in refugee camps who do not become terrorists, are not conquered by rage; and by a person's sealed-up inner life that slowly in therapy can open and integrate with their functional self. The lost sheep returns.

Because we recognize that something addresses us through and in the psyche, we see that meaning is offered generously, repeatedly right now and tomorrow. We can believe that we have the capacity, even if it is dormant, broken, in bits, to make something of what we experience, and thus participate in that mysterious creation of life in the small acts of living creatively in our lives. As clinicians we still work hard on the gaps in developmental history, the gaps in relationships, the gaps in sanity, the gaps of many kinds that condition our finitude, but we also name the One who breaks into the finite, crossing those gaps to make all things new.

This faith perspective lends energy to face the postmodern horizon we find ourselves in today where all feels relative with no fixed markers. We already know that the finitude of our lives confers a sense of being relative: from dust we come and to dust we return. Yet faith in the infinite residing in us and addressing us, in that mysterious link, as the thirteenth-century mystic Hadewijch says, between the abyss of our soul and the abyss of God, bestows on us the space of aliveness where we find what we create and create what we find (Hadewijch 1980, 86; see also Ulanov 1998/2004, 200-203). That space is multiplied again and again: we do our clinical work in the space between therapist and client; we do our mothering in the space between infant and parent; we do our loving in the space between lover and beloved; we do our healing in the space between us and the numinous.

The terrorism that marks the opening of our century describes a new pattern of threat. It dissolves or collapses that space of aliveness. No longer the clear boundaries of the twentieth century's iron curtain, but now, like the autoimmune diseases afflicting the body, terrorists can penetrate anywhere. Their organized chaos acts like the renegade pathological cells that attack the body and usurp its growing into illness.

Yet the formlessness of postmodernism where no fixed meanings ascribe to text but only locations of meaning from certain vantage points, instead of threatening our clinical work, endorse a fact we have known almost from the beginning: that our countertransference affects what we see and how we interpret. The mutative agent, that which transforms, that to which we are summoned to give all our hearts, minds, souls, and strength, unfolds in the rhythm of finding a life and creating it, receiving the infinite in every moment within the bounds of finitude. Thus an objective true path unfolds for each of us and we share our diversity within unity and a unity within diversity.

The freedom of the infinite within the finite will always pull us loose from our moorings in finite forms that describe our experiences of the infinite. Our theories of the psyche will always fall short; our religious forms will always open into formlessness because the infinite transcends all our categories and images. Pathology obscures this mystery and interferes with our freedom to respond to its freedom and its seeking us eternally. Religious life is recognizing this generative power which works in us personally, between us always, and all around us always. Clinical work aims to restore recognition of this generative state of mind where we accept this creative capacity of the self as the main part of us, and of others, too. We dig it out of the rubble of self-doubt, self-attack, despair. Deadness flattens this recognition and abandons what we construct together. In losing each other, we lose the world created out of our shared consciousness. Illness is exile and mixes then with evil which would destroy connection of us with ourselves and of others with us.

New Kind of Consciousness

To look at life and our clinical work from the vantage point of this space-in-between where aliveness springs up, issues in a new kind of consciousness. It is characterized by transcending the dualisms of subjective-objective, internal-external, past-present. It engages both primary and secondary process thinking and recognizes the protosymbolic life of the body with its sensory awareness, the organ dialect, so to speak, when the body has to carry all the psychic meaning (see McDougall 1989; see Ulanov 2001a), and, as well, the symbolic thinking that verbal and image thinking constructs. I call this synchronistic or simultaneous consciousness, to designate a bigger admittance of the whole surround that includes causal thinking: what happened developmentally to issue in this problem; and prospective thinking: toward what meaning this problem directs the person, for often the new can only come in through problems; and simultaneous thinking which means allowing anything else to come in from any source, as if to let the psyche speak to the issue at hand with associations, odd ideas, new images, even body experiences. An example would be remembering a dream a client worked on maybe two years earlier, and seeing its immediacy right now. One does not think it up; it just happens. Something jumps in.

Here we move beyond the ego as the central point of reference with its logic and patterns. We see as well other presences, what recently have been called self-states, that possess their own different kinds of logic. Here the new comes in through body nudge, psychic hunch, imaginal glimpse, spiritual surrender. The ego point of view is precious yet one of many presences, and healing arises from the space between ego and these inner presences, between self and therapist, creating what recent analysts call the third, what Jung called long ago the transcendent function (see chapter 7).

We experience this new consciousness as willingness to look into in order to explore, not to evacuate; to name in order to relate to, not to stop some horrible dread; to investigate, not to cauterize or fragment; to mull, muse over, meander, not to use thinking to exclude growth. Like the Spirit brooding over the waters in Genesis, this meditative admittance of the unknown into knowing makes growth possible. We still have our ego point of view, our conflicts and wounds, but they are not the main focus. They are put into perspective by this large view of the whole psyche. Conversation with other subject(s) within and with each person we meet and with the One who comes through all of us, this is the main focus.

A clinical example makes visible this growth being engendered, taken from a long analysis of a woman in her early fifties, white, a professional in the health field, married, mother of two children, and, she says, depressed as long as I can remember until I started taking drugs at the age of nine. We had identified her tendency to "run her life on empty," feeling always burdened by chores, rarely laughing. We had worked on resentments and self-attack, self-doubts and feeling dead. Here I want to focus on the shift, to me remarkable, from long-standing depression as a condition, an entrapping character disorder that medication had helped but did not remove, to its becoming a defense, that is, with elbow room around it, and thence to soften into a helpful symptom alerting her to preventable danger.

The shift came slowly through engaging with not knowing, and opening to imaginative encounter with this crushing depression. It began through the transference by her asking me, This depression, is it permanent? and hearing me think not necessarily so, when I asked, What does it look like? An image arrives: I live in the waiting room, she says. I may leave, but I always return there; I may get distracted, but this is my baseline. Nothing goes on there; it is not a transition to anywhere. I am blank (a kind of deadness). I saw that desire flickered even though she bartered it into a burden. She wanted warmth around her against the cold weather; it became a task to shop for a coat. She can't believe that she can turn her wish into reality, so it gets smuggled in as a chore to be done. She remembered that at seven, she made a plan "to want as little as possible" which was her way to negotiate her sense of deprivation in her family.

We lived off and on in the waiting room and another image came: a Plexiglas wall, stretching endlessly. Any way around it? Any chinks in it? I ask. No. So we stayed in the waiting room, walled off. Some time later something new happened. She brought another image but this one was drawn from actual experience of objects outside herself. Her internal world closed in depression began to converse with real objects in the external world which indicated more air circulating. She had taken her daughter and her friends to a wildlife park and baboons had attacked the car with frenzy. She saw them attacking from the other side of the car windows full of curiosity, aggression, high spirits. All this energy was precisely what was walled off in her and contributed to the sense of deadness afflicting her. Working on this image, she felt keenly this energy gone missing rather than fueling her living.

The next image displayed her distress. "A woman treading water in the ocean. She's going to die. Why does she bother!" my patient exclaimed. Then she brought to a session a small plastic cylinder of deep purple liquid soap for bubble bath, borrowing it from her young daughter. It is like this, she said, the woman is treading in this thick viscous stuff. Beautiful purple, I said. I also thought, and dissolvable, leading to pleasure when transformed by running water into bubbles (and perhaps indicative of her depression dissolving in the current of feelings and imaginative symbols [bubbles]). Then she said, My defense as a kid was, I don't need anything. I hear her inhibited desire announcing itself by confessing her disavowal of it. Then she spoke of her habit of holding her breath which she did when anxious, frightened, indeed when she felt anything, another defense now released. So we worked on breathing, breathing in and out, that led to feeling feelings which kept them from sliding into the underground depression, piling up like a viscous ocean to drown her.

The last image burst in upon her from the external world and remained there: a painting of a door ajar, a door just opening. That this image struck her from the external world and remained there, witnessed to her internal world opening up. It is not what is beyond the door, she emphasized, but that it opened. What was sealed, became unsealed. If she holds her breath now, all the unprocessed emotion can still slide down into depression, but she knows it. To the images we could put words, describing a pattern of self-protection. She sees that this holding her breath instead of feeling, this being on hold in the dead waiting room, treading endlessly to keep afloat above the thick but deeply colored, that is passionate feeling-states, is a defense, not an unalterable state of being. Depression is a defense built up over years, helped but not removed by medication. A year later she raised the same issue in a very different way. I want to talk about what gets in the way of my loving, and my feeling the love I know is there (for her husband).

Talking about depression as a pattern of defense introduces an ease-ment, a walking around all the things that could be felt if she does not hold her breath. When we talk about it, she feels overcome with wanting to go to sleep—not to see and also to yield the defense, to rest from the burdens of this endless unlived life—the chores of staying afloat—to awake to the fresh and new. She states, depression is negative numbers; life is positive numbers.

Jung's genius was to locate that search for aliveness inside us in what my late husband and I called the inner conversation between ego and Self, these two patterns of assembling psychic experience where things grow or get annulled (Ulanov and Ulanov 1994, chapters 14, 16). Alive to this inner discourse, this original conversation not duplicated by any-one else's, this very personal dialogue leads into conversing with being as such, to the reality disclosed by our symbols of the whole. That is how we make oxygen for everyone else.

A gap always remains between ego and Self, for they speak from different departure points. Wanting to be alive transforms the gap between ego and Self into a space of conversation between these two patterns of experience. A sense of engagement follows that leads into a life at once exciting and reverent. From it come enlivening images for our own sense of purpose, our capacity for loving, our image of what we believe in. We can say certain definite things about this space and this conversation, even though we each experience it differently.

Ingredients

First, we need a witness to this conversation. We need someone to depend on as we find and create our relation to Self and to symbols that body forth our experience of aliveness. For an infant it is usually a mothering one. Many schools of depth psychology analogize from the mother-infant to the analyst-analysand, seeing the analyst as the pivotal new object that inaugurates healing. I do not agree with many analysts that only analysts will do in this finding and discovering of our capacity to be alive and live with all our hearts and souls and minds and strength. Dependence may be upon a poet, an artist, a composer, a street gang, an idol like Golda Meir or Martin Luther King Jr. It may be our image of God, or a certain ritual or symbol of the unknown. It can be an historical figure. For my late husband, Augustine was as real an other in relation to whom Barry turned over his own ideas, as was Duke Ellington whom Barry knew and traveled with for a year in writing his first book about this great American musician. Dependence may fetch in an object like the child's bear, even though we are adult (see chapter 5). We must consent, indeed submit, to this dependence on an other through whom we accept the fact of otherness, that we did not create ourselves and we depend on a source outside ourselves to be at all. Religions recognize this fact of dependence and interdependence and formulate it in doctrines of Creator and creature, that we are Yahweh's bride and people, that this bigger source commands our obedience to its prophet Mohammad.

Dependence brings with it a second ingredient: ruthless instinct for living alive and real. Ruthlessness means a fierce desire to live, to submit to grief over loss and to recover and not be dragged across the line into death following the one whom we love who died, or succumbing to brokenness inflicted by another's physical or emotional attack. Ruthlessness shows itself in our desire to fight for the life right in front of us in gaining our child's health or chance to go to school, to start a group of women survivors of abuse, to go down to Ground Zero in NYC and suffer our response, to stay awake when a diagnosis is being given us, to accept we must go to AA, to take with both hands the love unexpectedly offered us. Just as much is ruthlessness daring to pray, taking a day off, allowing play and laughing, opening to sexual ecstasy. By ruthless I mean untamed energy, backed by instinct, which initially shows no concern for results to self or other, but which can transform its destructive potential in this space of conversation into recognizing others as subjects in their own right and into energy that supports imaginative living (Ulanov 2001b, chapter 4).

With that kind of strong energy flowing through us, we can face the ruthless fact that we did not originate our life, we cannot save it either. In addition, we can face that bad exists as well as good and we must find our own ways of dealing with the bad, finding its place in the larger scheme of things. Without admitting the bad—the spite, the grudge holding, the refusal to learn, the inertia, the outright attack on others—our conversation is too weak to survive the emergency trip to the hospital.

We also need this kind of intensely alive energy to face that the questions we need answered may be the wrong questions, but we never find that out until we ask them with all our heart. Our symbols for the wholeness of life, our searching for the mathematical formula, our construction of a plan for life, our need for comfort when we mourn the death of our child, our search for an answer why this terrible maiming accident or crippling rejection or mental illness happened, our efforts to find peaceful solutions to endless strife in our city, in the Middle East, in facing terrorism, all these comprise our most important questions. We must dare to ask them and insist on answers (like Job). Only by such all-out seeking do we discover that the answers given are to different questions, disclose a bigger reality than the one we represent in our most earnest question.

The feminine mode of being is a third ingredient and presides over this inner conversation which, like a river, flows forth to irrigate a whole country. As I said earlier, most schools of depth psychology emphasize the determining effect of the early child-mother relationship and pattern the analytic relationship after it. For any of us who are mothers this is a frightening emphasis, as if all goes back to what we did or did not do. Feminist criticism has rightly deconstructed this unwitting blaming. The feminine as a mode of being belongs to both sexes as a way we are human, and it cannot be reduced to one function of mothering though it certainly includes that capacity to woo the small into life. I believe in our historical time this feminine mode is the predominant mode that ushers us into recognizing the psyche in us, in others, and in itself as an objective reality, not reducible, any more than is the body, to cultural conditioning or historical determinism or to the influence of early object relations. This mode of apperception reveals the unconscious itself as a medium of experiencing reality as a whole.

In this feminine mode of being we take the downward going road into the unknowable, the slime of beginnings (see Ulanov 1971, chapter 9; Ulanov 1999/2005, chapter 10). In the midst of daily tasks and chores something new and other makes itself known through a body prompting, a hunch, a glimpse, a stirring of the loins, or a sudden perception of the eye. This is not the mode of discrimination of a subject concentrating on an object. This is a realm of indwelling, of time mixed up between past and future both entering the present. This is a being-with, a residing in the going on beingness of living, an interpenetration of part and whole.

In this place of pondering, conceiving, gestating, an affective personal knowing gets born that issues from the whole, not from the discriminations of a good functioning ego. We are led into a kind of consciousness that communicates out of being communicated to by reality beyond us. Hence we are subject to epiphanies; we are brought into right order that makes room for disorder. Such moments engender a sense of spirit moving through the psyche (see chapter 4).

This is not the spiritual practice of retreating from the world to find Spirit. This spiritual practice sponsors a creativity that conjoins with ordinary living, mixing in with it, creating us as we find it. I remember reading Ellenberger's generous description of Freud's and Jung's times of madness as "creative illness," when they made a descent from efficient living into the murk, the disorientation, the frightening, to find and fashion there original ideas which have changed the world (Ellenberger 1970, 447-48). But for these men this creative illness was time out of ordinary living while someone else, their wives, ran the house and kept the children. I remember thinking this does not work for women. For us the numinous is found in ordinary spaces and times. My "creative illness" (madness) would constantly be interrupted by having to make dinner or fetch our son from school. The feminine mode in men and women fosters the new in the thick of daily living. No time out. No special place. The remarkably new breaks into the midst of everyday life and breeds aliveness of all kinds.

References

Versions of this chapter were given to Jung societies around the United States, to the Los Angeles C. G. Jung Institute, and to the American Association of Pastoral Counselors.

Davidson, C. 1941–44. *I Never Saw Another Butterfly*. A song cycle consisting of poems written between 1941 and 1944 by the children who passed through the walled city of Terezin, Czechoslovakia. These poems have been set to music and choreographed.

Ellenberger, H. 1970. *The Discovery of the Unconscious*. New York: Dutton.

Geoghegan, W. D., with K. L. Stoehr. 2002. *Jung's Psychology as a Spiritual Practice and Way of Life*. Lanham, Md.: University Press of America.

Hadewijch. 1980. *The Complete Works*. Trans. Mother Columba Hart. New York: Paulist Press.

Hillesum, E. 1983. *An Interrupted Life: The Diaries of Ety Hillesum*. Trans. Arlo Pomerans. New York: Pantheon.

Jung, C. G. 1988. *Nietzsche's Zarathustra*. 2 vols. Ed. James L. Jarrett. Princeton, N.J.: Princeton University Press.

Madigan, D. A. 2001. *The Qur'an's Self-Image*. Princeton, N.J.: Princeton University Press.

McDougall, J. 1989. A psychoanalytic approach to psychosomatic illness. In *Theaters of the Body*. London: Free Association Press.

Ogden, T. H. 1999. *Reverie and Interpretation*. London: Karnac.

Ulanov, A. and Ulanov, B. 1994. *Transforming Sexuality: The Archetypal World of Anima and Animus*. Boston: Shambhala.

Ulanov, A. B. 1971. *The Feminine in Jungian Psychology and in Christian Theology*. Evanston, Ill.: Northwestern University Press.

———. 1998/2004. The gift of consciousness. In *Spiritual Aspects of Clinical Work*, chapter 8. Einsiedeln, Switzerland: Daimon.

———. 1999/2005. Between anxiety and faith: the role of the feminine in Tillich's theology and thought. In *Spirit in Jung*, chapter 10. Einsiedeln, Switzerland: Daimon.

———. 2001a. *Attacked by Poison Ivy*. York Beach, Maine: Nicolas-Hays.

———. 2001b. *Finding Space: Winnicott, God, and Psychic Reality*. Louisville, Ky.: Westminster John Knox Press.

Winnicott, D. W. 1960/1965. Ego distortion in terms of true and false self. In *The Maturational Processes and the Facilitating Environment*. New York: International Universities Press.

CHAPTER 2

REGENERATION

Method

To feel alive and not dead is as basic as our need for food, air, water. Fear of this aliveness lies at the root of illness. We might begin with surprise. Why should we be afraid of feeling alive and real? Isn't this truly a basic need? And don't we all hope that each day, not just at special ritual times, we feel plugged in, excited about living, spilling over with gratitude that interest stirs us to reach to others, really to speak with our children, that we know the nerve of looking for work that makes meaning for us? So why would we be afraid? Why would we cut off some of our reactions instead of engage all of them? What are the deals we make to restrict our livingness, and for what end? Do we want to be dead? Of course not; we dread deadness, which is worse than death itself, because it feels as if part of us has gone missing while we are still alive. Clinical work can be summed up as focusing on regenerating aliveness, finding, creating connection to that mysterious gift of living with all our hearts, minds, souls, and strength.

Jung's words, "As long as the animals are there, there is life in the symbol," addressed the analyst's stance in clinical work: Are we alive in each session by being there with the animals (Jung 1997, vol. 2, 699)? Jung's method recognizes the basis of the psyche in affect that is instinct-backed, tumultuous; images appear which bundle the affects, order them so to speak (Jung 1909/1960, 78; 1963b, 177). The ego engages in conversation with these images. For those of us not visual it may be a back and forth through sounds, or movements, or textures, or smells. Here we see psychologically what religious tradition calls the senses of the soul, that there are a comparable soul-sight, soul-hearing, soul-touching, and soul-smelling. A new image emerges out of this conversation between ego and unconscious, a conversation that often is more of a slanging match or a struggle. Only then can the ego translate this new symbol into living, and the ego must do so if the symbol is to be alive; it must be integrated into daily life (ibid., 1963b, 193). Evil might be understood as a refusal of this ethical obligation to others as well as to oneself.

To be with the animals pictured around our symbols means to be with the psyche as it speaks in images we do not invent. The animal in us is not under our will; it brings into awareness what André Green calls the bud of being, that instinct to living, that beginning that originates us (Green 2000/2004, 81). We affirm the animal reality by giving it attention, feeling, thinking over its presence. As Jung puts it, we must "turn back to those periods in human history when symbol formation still went on unimpeded, that is, when there was no epistemological criticism of the formation of images, and when, in consequence, facts that in themselves were unknown could be expressed in definite visual form" (Jung 1954/1967, 353).

Jung offers three approaches to psychic disturbances—causal, teleological, and synchronistic. All of them, by their emphasis on the image, mend the unavoidable judgmentalness of the *Diagnostic and Statistical Manual of Mental Disorders* whose labels of mental illness are necessary for insurance payments. Our grasping the complexity of psychic disturbances includes the method of causality where we trace present suffering back to early deprivations in our relationships to parents and others whom we depended on and loved, and to our collective settings such as living in poverty or wealth, in democratic or totalitarian societies, in nature or urban centers, let alone the influence of traumas of war or natural disasters. We need as well the teleological method that looks for meaning in where this psychic disturbance takes us, toward what shift in attitude or inclusion of what split-off part of us.

Jung goes so far as to say that discovery of the supposed cause (whether found in the past or in the unfolding aim of our problem) "is no more than an assumption or a fantasy, it has a healing effect at least by suggestion if the analyst himself believes in it and makes a serious attempt to understand" (ibid., 465). The analyst's task is to take seriously the images the psyche tosses up, to imagine the possible purpose of this disturbance afflicting the analysand. The forward growing of the bud of being is interrupted, blocked, sabotaged by some obstacle of "constitutional weakness . . . wrong education, bad experiences, an unsuitable attitude . . . ," as Jung says, and "one shrinks from the difficulties which life brings and thus finds oneself back in the world of the infant" (ibid., 473).

The synchronistic method recognizes that the psyche compensates this regressive pull by "producing symbols which, when understood objectively, that is, by means of comparative research, reactivate general ideas that underlie all such natural systems of thought. In this way a change of attitude is brought about which bridges the dissociation . . ." (ibid., 473). This last method includes and enlarges the causal and teleological approaches by admitting into consciousness that there is a Self different from the self we construct as an ego project. This unknown comes in like an animal from the forest. This unknown X might be what religions call soul, something given, there, with animal presence.

As analysts we see that the ego, though essential, is relative to the psyche's objective reality that cannot be reduced to historical causes or object relations, nor the cultural influence of shared consciousness with others. The psyche's reality, any more than the body's, cannot be demoted to being invented by ideology, social conditioning, developmental determinations, historical forces, yet we perceive its objectivity through all these individual and shared subjective constructions.

We might protest and say that Jung, and now I, are just shifting to the psyche the essence that used to adhere to eternal verities, such as truth or law, that have been deconstructed by postmodernism. I would answer no. The evidence for the psyche's reality is in the spontaneous imagery, the emergence of connections, symbols, patterns of energy that I do not know and do not author (the other side of the No-thing place in chapter 9). Ego life has a developmental paradigm, a cultural and historical one, too, and these bring relevant facts to the clinical venture, a narrative telling where we have come from and where we are going, gathered into the causal and teleological methods of interpretation. But in addition, what I call the synchronistic or simultaneous approach is to see the whole surround, including what we do not conceive. Glimpsing this totality to which we belong but do not design keeps us as analysts alive throughout decades of work. Momentarily we grasp that our obligation is to go toward this totality and offer willingly what we make of it and help our patients to make of it.

This synchronistic approach is not esoteric theory but highly practical. One man, a veteran of years of analysis with different clinicians, felt sprung out of his lifelong tendency to feel obligated to others that deadened every relationship into meeting their expectations. Desire degenerated into duty. He could then find freedom only in escape; and the other felt cheated by the absence of his presence. The new came in a total attraction to a woman, what he called a "shot of eros" that felt like a tremendous influx of energy: "it is *my* life, not a dress rehearsal for something else. I saw the shot. It was meant for me. I can't get out of it. The psyche is real and brought an inward eye, a vision. I don't hang around looking for auras. I trust I see what I am meant to. The shot made me aware of a new obligation. I couldn't deny it and say of course you are attracted because she is beautiful or because you are in a desert. I did not feel trapped, but knew where my orders were."

Staying open to the live symbol around which our instinctive animal energy clusters, breeds in us compassion for what is left out of our ego organization. Those left out parts push us to include them, like the rabbi woken up to indulge in midnight eating, or the woman ever beckoned by a new animus projection, or the psychiatrist compelled to eat milk food in the pre-dawn hours, or the woman devoted to spiritual realization being seized by anal itching, or the efficient woman compulsively losing things. From an ego point of view those persistent patterns in ourselves or our analysands amount to repetition compulsions; from the perspective of the whole psyche those patterns are the Self pushing in. From the ego point of view these are problems that persist despite all our efforts to upend them. Synchronistic consciousness recognizes them as the unknown, the disturber, the "alien 'other' in oneself," "this barely understandable thing" which Jung says, "the alchemists, with astonishing accuracy, called . . . Mercurius" who is "God, daemon, person, thing, and the innermost secret in [us]. . . . the source of all opposites . . . duplex . . . capable of both" (ibid., 481).

Fear of this mysterious thing, fear of this kind of simultaneous consciousness, makes us make deals to cut off parts of ourselves or of our neighbors or of our world. Deadness results. We need to seek out what patterns our inner ego-Self conversation takes. We can look at problems in our relationships as outer manifestations of inner blocks to coming alive within ourselves.

For example, a woman's grief at her husband leaving her, even though she knows that he refused to work with what was good in their relationship to secure their future in a thriving way, and even though her dreams tell her the same, and even though she is an exceptionally intelligent, efficient CEO, discovers two things. She did really love this man, always a gift that enriches us even if painful, and she holds onto the loss in order to avoid arriving at a deeper fear that has dogged her whole life. She fears living alone, getting old, dying alone. The accent then falls on the wrong syllable—the grief is inflated in order to dodge the primal fear of living and dying her own singular self.

Jung talks about this problem in terms of can we hold both opposites in consciousness simultaneously. In this example that would mean: How do my CEO strengths talk to this abysmal fear of being alone in life and death? The strengths and the way they are managed through the ego live far apart from her fear of sinking, drifting.

✓   Listening to the Self means admitting a different order, not the logic of either-or but always the inclusion of both-and. At the same time I am getting clear about my own goals, I am interrupted by something coming from my unconscious disrupting them, leading them down another path, mixing with your goals and path, and your path being disrupted by something in your unconscious. So right away it is not me versus you, my goals versus yours, but both of us suffering the intrusion from our own unconscious mixing with our own consciousness, as well as the two of us mixing with each other. The plot thickens, gets complex, and our complexes stir this pot, seeking to cook us down to our own personal way that shows itself to us if we risk creating it as we go along.

For example, the middle-aged woman whose husband fell gravely ill felt all the spokes of her wheel going out from under her into opposite directions. She skipped over the confusion and panic she felt, with the summary statement (which was really an attack leveled at herself), "I don't know how to live!" She would fall into fragments, this bit dissociated from that bit, anger vying with love for her husband, panic battling need to control the situation of his care. Instead of feeling all the pressing tension of these opposites, she felt numb, humiliated, and a failure, repeating the mantra, I do not know how to live.

She let go of a prior image that both grounded her and fed her energy. She had called it her link to the earth, a humility in the sense of being held securely down to the ground, not inflated or deflated and then ashamed. She called this her "humus connection" as in that black spongy matter that is the product of a compost pile—both light in weight and richly nutritious for the soil. She happened upon that symbol of the humus connection out of a previous fragmentation, this time around a success. She had made a concise, interesting presentation at work, keeping many details in focus and organizing the whole around central questions she wanted others to address. She was pleased with how it had gone.

Out of her excitement, she asked the supervisor his opinion. When he said, well, it was a bit abstract, she felt shame. What surprised her was the shame was not for his implied criticism, which she felt was off the mark. Her shame was for not being able to hold her excitement, but parceling it out to her supervisor to hold, under the guise of seeking his approval. She let go the vibrant energy of the humus connection and thought about her supervisor's opinion instead. A dream that night confirmed her view and showed how dangerous it is not just for ourselves but to others as well to mislay that energy connection when it comes to us.

In the dream, she gives the driver's seat over to her husband who represents in her a rigidity and a refusal to ask questions. When he is driving she notices a suspicious van darting off the highway into the woods. At the same time she sees approaching in the sky three military jets. It feels ominous. She tells her husband, quick, get off the highway, turn around, regardless of traffic and honking. He remains oblivious. She pleads and persists, and he finally does, but not before she sees the third jet as if intentionally dropping altitude despite the other two trying to prevent it. She and her husband barely escape as that third jet crashes into the highway to wreak havoc and destruction, an attack by a terrorist. Many cars on the road are destroyed, people hurt, killed. This example illustrates the merging for many New Yorkers of collective and individual trauma since 9/11.

When she loses hold of the terrific energy that flows through her from her success with the presentation, it is as if the energy crashes on the highway and hurts others as well. Without her containing and following its flowing into her life, getting it domesticated so to speak, it is as if the energy is as big as a jet-fueled plane that endangers everyone as it crashes. When she loses hold of all her reactions to the stress of her husband's illness and numbs out, the energy again goes wild, not controlled through her but buffeting her, threatening to defeat her entirely, making her feel incompetent to live, even flirting with suicide. What we do, or do not do, affects others, too. The dream showed her that. We do not have personal problems in isolation from communities in which we live. Our personal problems reflect our culture's problems and our collective conflicts reflect our personal struggles. This perspective locates our personal problems in a shared container and we can see how working on our complexes contributes to the world's healing. Insofar as this woman can live her connection to energy and channel it, it does not dive out of the sky to hurt others.

Jung makes much of the psyche speaking to us in image, affect, instinctual energy which we must house. The symbol is alive, not a piece of information which we can take or leave. It requires a wholehearted response from us with imagination and feeling. We invest feeling in paying attention to images that spring up from the unconscious. Some images grow into symbols which offer us the best lead, the most appropriate point on which to meditate. Through the space of conversation between our ego consciousness receiving, responding, fashioning, and being fashioned by such symbols, something shifts, a way opens. The symbol transforms into a guiding presence.

This shift has to do with the Self functioning as a bridge to what lies beyond the psyche. No symbolic form can capture the infinite yet our symbols bear the infinite toward us, and we depend on them to engage in conversation with the infinite; yet the symbols contain their own destruction because they are merely finite human constructions. Way before it was fashionable, Jung located our aliveness in this space between relativism and absolute knowledge that postmodernism tries to articulate.

In analytical work, the symbols that coin our discourse cannot be exchanged because they convey in specific incarnate forms the reality to which they point. The symbols that emerge in analysis bring together elements of being. Symbols will not work in treatment if we do not connect to the being the symbols configure. The analyst's own bridge to the infinite, our belief in the work of analysis, confirms the reality the symbols point to, and enables the analysand to see it in his particular way, and both analyst and analysand to recover the analytical moment as itself a symbol.

Together they create a field, a third under the shadow of the fourth (see chapter 7) out of which the new appears. Reality holds both persons, for our life as analysts is happening as is the patient's. Together they are held in this field, but if they do not see the reality generating the field, it does not get into the specific ego situation of each person living it in their unique ways. As von Franz says, "every person has in the depth of his psyche that which he needs, that is, his own access to the ultimate primordial ground of his being. . . . He has an opening at the deepest level of his psyche where something eternal can flow in" (von Franz 1997, 372).

The analyst hovers near what Marion Milner calls a "primary state of madness" where dream and outer perception are not separated, and we live from there again after having achieved separateness. Only thus do we reach the vital illusions from which we live and love what is worth living for (Milner 1957/1979, 29-30).

Deadness

Deadness kills the space and feels like the opposite of conversation where currents of energy flow through us from beyond us and out to others and from them to us and back to beyond us. Deadness feels sterile, nothing growing. It feels useless, no point, no pep. It feels as if some parts of us (or of others, or of our relationships to them, or to God) have gone into exile. Like the Russian Gulag Archipelago, we do not know where those parts are now located, probably somewhere frozen; we do not know if we will ever hear from them again. At best we can stand in line with the poet Akhmatova outside the prison, like the woman behind her with lips blue from the cold, waiting hours to hear if anything will be told about their missing sons, brothers, fathers, husbands. "Then a woman with bluish lips . . . woke up from the stupor to which everyone had succumbed and whispered in my ear (everyone spoke in whispers there): Can you describe this? And I answered, 'Yes, I can.' Then something that looked like a smile passed over what had once been her face" (April 1,

1957, Leningrad, Akhmatova 1992, 384). She thus made something keenly alive about a deadly experience in her poem "Requiem." Deadness feels like goneness, no moreness, lostness. It comes from cutting off parts of ourselves in order to save the rest of us.

When we make an unconscious deal, we swap aliveness for restriction in order to feel safer, avoid pain, survive some blow that seems to us unbearable, that would destroy us. We fear we are empty inside so we cover it up with manufactured control, or made-up excitement, or self-promotion. The emptiness can never change if we refuse to experience it, and in the company of an other. We need an other to depend on when we turn our face to see the deadness. Whatever we are afraid of, it requires our attention; we must go down into it, look around, not knowing if and how we will come out. Fear of doing that makes us make trade-offs with ourselves.

For example, we may deny our absence of genuine response of spontaneous thought by a fog of erotization that appears animated, but in fact just conceals blankness. Clinical work is endangered by this unlived life. The analyst may fall into collusion with this cloudy sexuality, fail to perceive it as just so much smoke. Nothing erotic is going on; it is avoidance dressed up to look thrilling, but in fact is false, a disguise. The analyst may fall blank, caught in the haze, confused about the mismatched erotic tonalities that bespeak aliveness but cover up having fallen into vacancy.

Another type of bargain that makes us go dead amounts to pushing the feared effect into our body, and it, poor body, like a faithful beast, has to shoulder our burden for us. We may suffer a sore throat, as one woman did, for two decades that somatizes but does not communicate the fear of speaking our own words, finding our own voice.

Sometimes the unconscious exchange gets fixed in place and repeats over and over again in repetition compulsion. This often happens as result of trauma—a harsh blow dealt by terrorist attacks, or the violence of war where one suddenly is treated like an object to be put in a rape camp, shot, dismissed into hunger or homelessness. Attack on our body or emotions or psyche by another person we depend on and have no escape from makes it feel urgent to cut a deal with ourselves to reduce our suffering. If we survive, and often in order to survive, we must blot out this abuse so we can grow around it and not be literally cut off and made dead. We put parts of ourselves into cold storage, or bury them in the not knowing of unconsciousness; it is too awful to remember what dismembered us.

Cumulative trauma, that is, increments of neglect or harm over years, can also make us go dead, split off parts of ourselves, like capacities for hope or insight or anger. We can repress parts of ourselves like our sexuality as a protective mechanism. This deal we make is to keep alive, and we can only be impressed with the ingenuity of the human psyche to develop defenses in reaction to such shocking injury.

These reactive defenses protect us but remain rigid, strict, unyielding, unable to be given up when no longer needed. Defenses we grow in response to our own impulses prove more supple, capable of adapting to new circumstances because they respond to our impulses, find channels of expression and protection for them rather than repudiating them as if they are not-me.

A particular deal all of us make to some degree, in my experience, arises out of fear of our own power to destroy, to be destructive toward others, particularly those we love and depend on. We mute our access to our own aggression lest it prove destructive to someone we love. We arrest growth of our aggression that then stays primitive, crude, sort of an eye for an eye. In adolescence, when your son wants to argue about saying good morning, this aggressive energy slowly gets tamed. Fighting, yet still standing, still offering breakfast or conversation, tells a child that destructiveness is not going to totally destroy. No one is bleeding, relationship still goes on. This allows the child to harness this energy for living. But if we cut off the aggression, withdraw from it in order to stay safe, a big portion of our personality goes into limbo, becomes entombed, annulled because we cannot process it. For example, a young woman enmeshed in her family of origin could only contact her aggressive energy by fleeing to the other side of the country. It took hard work not to blank out in the presence of family when she returned, and not to succumb to self-attack for "not living *my* life." The task was to relate to and use her aggression in her living.

Bion talks about beta elements that are things we lived through but did not process into image or thought or feeling. These events just circulate through our psyche like so much space junk orbiting around our ego. These unintegrated elements in our psyche can cause us to have accidents or sexual break-out episodes or eruptions of rage. Going dead brings serious consequences to others as well as ourselves.

Repetition compulsion, where we repeat in the present the kind of relationships we have had in the past, also shows a positive element. Trapped in the same ending again and again, even though the beginnings with each partner or each job or each analysis may differ, lies in the persistence of the psyche to speak out our pain, even if in unintelligible form. It is unintelligible because pain compels behavior that bypasses our consciousness. We are trying to get the message, get it right, master the problem. But the negative import is that the ego is not listening, so the story can only be told in behavior that fascinates and humiliates us at once, in action that circumvents our ego to reach its predetermined outcome. The space of conversation between ego and Self collapses and symbols that might mediate the unknown to consciousness go dead instead. In religious ritual, for example, we may go through the service by rote, never quickened in spirit or fed in the soul. Or we unchangingly imitate, for example, a passionate sexual encounter, but remain untouched. Or pretending interest in an idea, a person, a political cause masks a deadly indifference, an unreachableness we experience but do not understand. The repetition repeats itself to go on trying to reach us, to tell the story where we are caught, symbolically to enact the pieces missing from our ego net, trying to restage the original trauma to find a way through it (Ulanov 1992/1996, chapter 3).

For example, a woman caught in reacting to others at the expense of her own voice felt depleted to point of exhaustion from trying to fit into others' points of view, a hold-over from a childhood seeking of her mother's love. If she did not comply with her mother's views, she felt cut off, rejected, argued against in a way that shut her out from nurturing love. The mother would give her the silent treatment, not noticing, responding, or talking to her daughter, sometimes for two or three days at a time. The daughter would become frantic trying to find out what she had done and to remedy the broken connection. It was as if the ego-Self connection in the daughter got then rerouted to the mother-daughter connection and sabotaged there. For even when restored, the daughter was not reconnected to the source addressing and flowing through herself, but only to the mother on whom she had to keep a vigilant eye, lest she be abandoned again.

This pattern persisted into adulthood and to the woman's friendships which she felt as exhausting and from which she felt she must defend herself. At its worst, she fled to her bed, to collapse under a haze of tranquilizers and wine, an addiction that kept her despising herself as pathetic, in bed in fetal position, she said, sucking her thumb. We worked hard on this undertow, dragging it into consciousness and tossing the ball of pain back and forth. Something shifted. I did not do it. She did not invent it. From the space between us and from within her a new image generated. She spontaneously said of herself, "I felt liquid in me," flowing like water irrigating, sustaining life. Right there the repetition compulsion broke into a potential ritual space (Ulanov 1996a/2004).

The clinical task then shifts from analyzing the compulsion to comply at the expense of spontaneous response, and of addiction to oblivion achieved through pills and booze, now to address how was she to sit by the waters, to witness to the gift of liquid, to establish rituals to make possible going on housing these living waters. The ingredients of ritual are paying attention which means investing affect; taking keen interest which means giving consciousness to the unconscious; depending on an

41

other to witness this paying attention and participate in it; ruthlessly taking the new image that freely arrives and dismantles the old compulsion
to blank out which means to risk the new question of how to live next to
this water. We give up the old question of how to survive being depleted;
we submit to a feminine mode of being that gestates the new and ushers
its energy into ordinary daily living. We do not go off into some secret
place, some special corner or privileged position. We become a pipe
through which the water flows, "liquid in me." What flows in her flows
through her to the rest of us. What we do or do not do individually affects
what we can do or not do together.

Deadness Contributing to Aliveness

If we can go toward the dead parts, enter the barren places, enter the
emptiness and look around and see what is there and what is not there, we
discover the dead parts move toward aliveness. How can this be? The CEO
whose husband announced he wanted a divorce and left, had a car accident
a few months later. The accident was legitimate; she did not create it; it happened due to rain and wet leaves and had she not been driving twenty miles
an hour, the outcome would have proved fatal. She is in no way responsible
for the accident. But the psyche can make use of such things and I was struck
by its freakish nature which totaled her car and the other driver's, hence a
total smashup. It was an external version of her inner experience. She felt
her whole life had been smashed up by her husband's exit.

What made the husband's announcement so hard was that it was
only an announcement. No talking it through, no meeting to hash over
what went wrong, what had gone right, how he arrived at this conclusion,
what he felt in response to her reactions, her dissatisfaction with the marriage, their anger, remorse, regret. She had said he made a hit and run
divorce. Then here her car was hit and destroyed. (A year later she said
she did cause the accident, knowing that she did not. She got coverage
for the outer happening by investing psychic meaning into it, and

recovered some of her own agency; as Jung says, "The message is alive ✓ only if it creates new meaning" [Jung 1975, 23 September 1954, 84]).

The one injury she sustained from the car accident was to her right hand, her executive hand, and particularly its middle finger. Looking at this damage on a symbolic level encouraged her shift from suicidal ruminations expressing hurt, to giving him the finger (so to speak), expressing anger at his walking out with no discussion between them. The hand's surgery and repair required many months of physical therapy to get the fingers to bend again into a fist. It is painful and she weeps doing the exercises twice a day. She is diligent and intelligent and does what she must to regain her hand. But until we talked about it, she felt no mercy for her hand, only how hard it was, how she wanted it to be over. Her hand was stuck in an open position. Its pain opened her up to the pain she had been avoiding about living alone with her ownmost self. I heard myself say, Sing to your hand. I think I meant, love it, feel for it, be merciful to it, relate to the pain, don't just suffer it, relate to it as you suffer it.

After that a dream came: I am in Africa and odd-shaped brown seeds outline a grave. She associated to Africa a death-dealing rare kind of dysentery she contracted on a long ago trip there, so bad her husband had to wheel her onto the plane home in a wheelchair. Remarkably unempathetic, though probably from his own fear, he joked about her condition saying she was drunk. This was particularly painful because she'd had no childhood enjoying dependence because her mother was often drunk from her own disease of alcoholism that sprung, I believe, from harsh blows of fate that left her bereft and hopeless. The dreamer lost fourteen pounds on the airplane and stayed in hospital upon landing for many days, her husband not visiting her. Brown was a color she associated to her mother being alive, vital, her mother's good days, before my patient was born, when she, the mother, flew as a pilot in Alaska. Sometimes my patient wore her mother's old brown bomber jacket. The grave she associated to the death of her marriage and her fear of death, the near death from the dysentery in the past, the deadness of her drunken mother. Yet around the grave in the dream, outlining the dead place, perhaps containing it? restricting it? marking it to be known, the seeds circled it with the potential for new sprouting life, life of an alive mother which bears on the transference to me. The dream came after we had faced her suicidal ruminations over her husband leaving as avoiding the terrifying unknown of living her life and fearing her death.

Going into the dead places changes them, brings life to them and they lead to aliveness. Turning toward what feels lifeless quickens something at first indiscernible, ineffable, that communicates a stirring. This attention to what feels worn out, obsolete, exhausted, kindles, ruffles, but only if we dare the turning. Jung puts it: "If you will contemplate your lack of . . . inner aliveness . . . and impregnate it with the interest born of alarm at your inner death, then something can take shape in you, for your inner emptiness conceals just as great a fulness if only you will allow it to penetrate into you. If you prove receptive to this 'call of the wild,' the longing for fulfillment will quicken the sterile wilderness of your soul as rain quickens the dry earth" (Jung 1963b, 190).

Contemplating deadness in us, and death to come, can release us from ego striving. We can rest; we can renounce development. We can stand aside from our conflicting desires and contemplate isness. Art allows this, the still life paintings, what we all called dead nature when children when we first learned the French phrase Nature Morte for these still life paintings. We can regress to a peace before opposites emerged and just dwell in the moment, 100 percent present, a goal of Zen Buddhism. It is as if we contemplate the contemplative moment through art, not only in paintings, but also through the liveliness of dance that we behold for the performance and then, it is gone (see Stokes 1973, 121)!

In contemplating those dead areas in ourselves, those blank spaces when we sense something coming into view but do not yet see it, much as we feel an animal approaching the edge of the woods, an unconscious content makes its presence felt before it appears. We get a hunch, or a body stillness, an alertness to something about to manifest, to render itself

evident. Waiting, watching for the unknown thought to advance into our
thinking, for the epiphany of the image can take time. But it is well worth
it. The new comes in and sheds livingness all around us like light.

Sometimes the sense of aliveness coming out of deadness possesses a
spiritual quality that arises from knowing the difference between what we
can and should do, and what is beyond our powers. Concerned about our
world, whether about war or terror attacks, we can withdraw into numb
helplessness, pushing all this affect into the unconscious which means it
adds to the collective shared atmosphere. Alternatively, we can locate the
specific hinge for ourselves between the personal and collective (see chapter 6). What do I need to tend to, what shadow bits in me left untended
help build up an atmosphere of permissiveness where someone can just
shoot another, senselessly? Is it my aggression I must pay attention to? Or
my cynicism? Or my unwillingness to, in the jargon, entertain objects? So
I withdraw and shut others out so they must break in like a burglar to reach
me? I am not responsible for others' acts of violence, but I am responsible
for closing down whole chunks of energy. Then that unlived energy in me
roams the streets, so to speak, infiltrating the collective ambience that can
ignite in senseless vandalism, even arson, murder.

We can drop into the vast human shadow through a small personal
crime—a lie, a concealment, a greed, a theft. If I can find that hinge in
myself and work with it, it makes a big difference to the collective environment. Bion says we who know about the psyche share ethical responsibility to bring personal relatedness to the same level of development as
achieved in technology. Seeing the hinge of my individual shadow allows
me to see what is beyond my power to fix or help. I work on my small devil
and what is beyond me, those I let go to God, to the beyond, to the All,
to the whatever I name the transcendent (see chapter 4). I know my littler place and live that with full responsiveness to all that belongs to me.
Such responsiveness to living what is given me to live issues in responsibility. Responsibility grows from responsiveness, active alive compassionate receptiveness. That makes me reliable, answerable, credible, more

than keeping to the rules does. What is beyond me I let go to the beyond; I let go my defenses into the hands of God. This recognition of our own small place in the large scheme of things allows the limits, the terminal points, the end of life, death, to act as a booster shot to coming alive.

Whatever our religion, whatever our spiritual impulse, when we let go, we let go into the hands of a living God, not a dead one; otherwise we could not let go. A living God means creation goes on now, a *creatio continua*. The power to make something of our experience, to live creatively is supported and urged in us now, and in every now, right up to death's moment of arrival and, for all we know, into what comes after, too.

Aliveness: Regeneration

Regeneration springs up. Aliveness stirs in the mud and tiny shoots appear, so fragile, yet with a persistent ruthless energy that pushes through to live, much as the daffodil pushes through asphalt to bloom, as the luxuriant green appears in the crack on the step on a terrace high up on a skyscraper building. Amazing that life continues to create itself! The continual creation, the seeking to be lived right now today, tonight, next week, right up to death despite our losses, our injuries, what we failed to live, beckons us now undeterred by our regrets and fatigue. Invest yourselves, create with me, correspond to what I offer you seem to be addressing us. Aliveness means jumping in with all four of our feet, not just two or one, but wholeheartedness is required if we are to participate in wholeness.

This mysterious power urging us to live, to keep looking for our path is ruthless. It is energy we are afraid we lose contact with when we fall into depression, or when anxiety attacks us with panic that the animal root impulse, the root stem of us, has been cut off. This power to make something of our experience, to generate response to the new, to perceive the new coming in, to give way to excitement about having our response to our experience, to have our own original thought, or arrive at our unique pattern of feeling, our own tempo of breathing, this power enlivens us.

We live in a new space, different from the ego with its familiar round of worries, projects, plans, and plots, and different from the unconscious with its pushes and pulls of instinct, its unformulated nudges of thought, its confetti of images every night not yet gathered into a dream narrative. This space is saturated with the blessing of consciousness that allows us to look at what we experience, to consider what addresses us, to contemplate what hints we are given for what we, our little but ownmost personal self, are to be doing in this life. For if we catch that tiger's tail, we can endure suffering, persist in contributing, and feel at the last, as the prayer of Cardinal Newman voices, that when the busy world is hushed, and the fever of life is over, and our work is done, that we are brought home.

That space in between conscious and unconscious, in between self and other, belongs to every one of us even if we are ill or suffering or poor or oppressed. There we step into a livingness even if only for seconds at a time, moved by "the willingness to become transparent, to offer ourself to the Other" (Hirshfield 1998, 47). The thirteenth-century Buddhist Dōgen describes this quality of attentiveness: "Awakened, I hear the one true thing . . ." (ibid., 51). Or we see with the poet Rilke where even a stone statue of centuries ago can still convey such aliveness that its various parts that make up the whole "glisten like a wild beast's fur" (ibid., 52). We feel with Rilke in the ninth of his *Duino Elegies*, "Look, I am living!" Conscripted into consciousness of livingness, we register with him that "overwhelming Being floods my heart" (cited in Hollis 2000, 53; see also Rilke 1923/1992, 93).

Psychoanalysts are preoccupied with this space and call it transitional (Winnicott), reverie or mystical (Bion), thirdness (Green), the intersubjective third (Ogden), the transcendent position (Grottstein); it is the place we feel alive and real. We feel it urgently as the precious pearl for the sake of which we sell all we have; it is body-based and we need its embodiment.

For example, in New York City when the World Trade Towers collapsed, killing hundreds of firefighters who had gone into the buildings as everyone else was running out of them, their fellow firefighters staged a near riot when the city said it could no longer afford to handpick through the mountains of rubble in hopes of finding some remains of those dead men. It would be more economical now, weeks later, to use bulldozers to do the job of clearing the site. The firefighters insisted, and won, to be allowed to do this painful and painstaking job of recovering whatever bits of uniform, helmet, or body-part of their friends despite the time it took or the risk to their own health. This was their way of offering themselves to the other, by enlarging that deadly swift passage between life and death when the buildings fell down. It was a literal, body-based honoring of their comrades, much as our children prepare a shoe box with felt for the pet they will bury, or we plant a tree at the cemetery plot.

In Jungian terms I describe this space as the ego-Self conversation which circumscribes a cup, a circle, a container for livingness, a living substance which feels holy and belonging to the Whole of reality. It is this mysterious substance or presence hard to describe that reverses old notions. We do not become whole. The wholeness individuation leads to is not our own perfection. For often our various disturbing complexes continue, but gradually the breath is out of them. They are more boring, or we are less caught. Our wholeness is more like a completeness; we assemble all the parts of us and remain open to still more parts coming in. It is like collecting all our laundry, even the fugitive socks that seem to lead a life of adventure all their own, disappearing and reappearing at will. Our wholeness is like an ensemble, an aggregate, not a seamless excellence.

More central still, this assemblage of bits and pieces of our living through the years, even if our life is cut short by illness or accident, opens to the Whole of reality. We see where we belong. We may even advance spiritually to name to whom we belong so that the ego-Self conversation becomes more intimate. We do not become complete, but we see the completeness to which we belong. We see that each of us and all of us make up essential parts of this large unity of reality. It is whole. We are part of its totality.

More mysterious still, and stemming from our earlier question whether this power to make something of our experience dwells within us or is the transcendent beyond us, we see this alive capacity in us as characterizing the soul of reality. From our responsiveness to this presence, we increasingly feel responsibility to allow its development, its coming to fulfillment within us. The religious attitude consists in steady attentiveness, attuning to this other within, to its aliveness, which is the root of aliveness in ourselves. This is our soul task, to give wholehearted, loving respect to this living mystery for its own sake (see von Franz 1970, VII.7). Thus making something of our experience and letting it make something of us turns out to mirror another conversation between us and reality. Our responsiveness is rooted in our ability to respond to this living presence and to tend to its flower (realization).

This goal of loving this mysterious other presides over any other goals we cherish. The values we seek for ourselves and our world—peace, justice, health, mental health, a loving partner, a child, fame or money or career, even a religious value of service to others or a rocklike faith—all these are the best we aspire to but are not what results. They are wonderful by-products, but they might also be what we sell to obtain the pearl of great price.

The pearl is the livingness of the reality the ego-Self conversation is busy communicating in multiple ways. The ego is like the woman with the humus connection, strong but modest and flexible, interested and able to receive what addresses through the Self, what the unconscious communicates to us specifically and specially. The ego responds. We may object. We may put a different case to what crosses over from this other side. But we work out together in this conversation how to respond, we might say how to obey, to find how we are to be put into service of this reality that pours itself out on us, while keeping in our minds our limitations.

Double Vision

Two life projects operate here, we now come to see: our usual ego projects and what this It residing in us or conveying itself to us wants. It ushers us into a different kind of consciousness, that I think of as synchronistic or simultaneous because we become aware of different levels of reality all operating at once, all together. Our ego way of knowing by dividing things into opposites of subject and object, abstracting from experience to ponder it, adapting inner impulses to outer reality, of self to others, constructing a history, comprises one kind of mental process. The unconscious that takes us down through our personal complexes to their archetypal core images that arrange us to perceive patterns of response between ourselves and others, and within ourselves to ourselves, and that disseminate into group patterns between sections of society and between nations, forms another kind of mentation. With luck and hard work we discern the centralizing power of what Jung calls the Self archetype where order is made of all the parts, so that old enigma of three made into four makes sense (see chapter 7). The ego is one, the other is two, the unconscious field between them and within each is three, and the whole of reality is the fourth as if there all along creating a whole.

In the clinical situation these levels are a daily reality—what the patient brings, what the analyst brings, what happens between us in the transference and countertransference field, how we each get arranged by the archetypal field between us, and then the fourth, the reality that opens to us through all these levels but especially through the Self level and which has been there from the first.

We are conscious of all these levels at once, as if we are animals in the center of a clearing and things come in from all sides. We do not create the surround, and we are not passive, being done to by something else just moving through us. It is more intimate than that, like a congress, a coinciding, a complexity of many in the one, an underlying oneness in the many. We know unity in diversity—what multiculturalism at its best may be tending toward. In this field of intersecting energy between personal and impersonal, tiny and vast, human and beyond, an order emerges that includes disorder instead of being wrecked by it.

The unconscious needs the ego to focus living in space and time, and the ego needs the unconscious to interrupt order and open us up to each other and to what holds us in being. Through conscious and unconscious, the unoriginated infinite makes itself present, moving us to gratitude for its boundless abundance. This gladness is symbolized in the dance in the round after the conjunction, the meeting of love, in the Mass (Jung 1954/1958, 415, 418-19; see chapter 9).

In the clinical situation we experience this simultaneous consciousness, as things occurring to us, such as recalling a detail of this patient's past discussed several years ago that is exactly apt to the present insight; an odd body gesture, a weird image that, if dared, speaks directly to the solution being sought. These things arrive, not like the lost sheep found, but more like a new sheep that just shows up, seemingly out of the blue, but that is if we see things originating only from the ego perspective. The center is crossed and recrossed by coinciding opposites that are revealed as complexly related facets of the one thing. The center builds up to illuminate the dark by its inward intensity of presence. Such an approach lessens judgment about our problems because it sets them in a larger bowl of planes of reality, an approach both less personal but more acutely personal because it puts the question to analyst and analysand alike. Are you living all this, responding to the whole of reality and finding your part in it? This question is not academic but toughly clinical.

The person afflicted with schizophrenia, for example, is not thereby disqualified or let off from this ability to respond. That illness must be accepted and negotiated with medicine and awareness of how the illness intrudes, much as our crippled limb or degenerating joints impose on us tasks and responsibilities to care for our mind and body as we live our lives. Why are some of us felled by such illnesses and not others? I don't know, but all of us make up the whole and are faced with the task of contributing our part to the whole.

Through the ego-Self conversation we glimpse the still bigger reality of psyche-matter, subject-object, interpersonal-world, inner-outer, energy-form, time/space and eternity. Jung calls this the *unus mundus*, the whole picture, the whole thing. Everything is related, interconnected, composing one unitary field, manifesting the essential interrelatedness of all living matter (Jung 1963a, 538). When Jung uses the word *scintillae* he is referring to sparks of the whole that we momentarily glimpse. We must build up tremendous stamina to transform a glimpse into a contemplative gaze. We need religious giants, mystic geniuses to show us the whole. We compute the strain of reaching such sustained vision by the hardship of their lives—outcast, often physically ill, sometimes also mentally ill, but always in love, love unbounding, overflowing, pouring out of them as if echoing the unceasing generosity of reality pouring out on all of us. Gautama Siddhartha, the Buddha, recognized this capacity when some of those hearing him give the Dharma, the teaching, felt instantly embraced by it, the truth flooding up in them. He called them the Stream Enterers.

We experience the *unus mundus* in and through our small indispensable ego moving into and registering this unitary reality that dissolves boundaries. We experience this wholeness as that mysterious power dwelling in ourselves as primary creativity (Winnicott), as the capacity to make something of our experience (Bion's alpha function), as a life-giving choice within us (Symington), as a symbol-making function in us that bequeaths to us at once more self and more reality (Jung). Our dependence on an other to invest interest in us in order for us to come into our own creative aliveness now transposes into a vision of the interdependence of all living things, even between animate and inanimate. The ego goal in development may be autonomy, independence, but the Self goal recognizes our larger interdependence: we belong to each other in belonging to reality, and in seeing we belong together, we glimpse the wholeness of reality.

Yet we each find our own singular versions and visions of this whole. We experience it in moments of what Jung calls "absolute knowledge" where we just know something and do not know how we came to know it. It is as if all the levels of reality at that moment are accessible to us, and we know, like the bushman, a rhino is coming down this path; or like the lover who discovers he has been as if shot by an arrow of Cupid, knows this is the person he loves, this is his path; or the young academic knows this plan being voted on by her school is bad and she must get up in public and say so despite her introversion and the threat to her career. Jung talks about this experience as a revelation of what will be, sometimes descending upon us heavy as lead, sometimes making us buoyant with creative freedom to apprehend the luminosity of the world.

We are stirred to become centered around this bigger vision, becoming more and more bound to it with total engagement. We grow steady, not to be swept away again, not to flirt with other suitors, that is, other visions of reality, or indulge in the careless attitude of, oh I don't really know what I believe. We are now in the circle with all four feet, yet we know others are too with their own visions. We take care of our vision of reality, love it, house it, serve it, circle around it, let it imbue everything we do. We learn to abide by the truth confided in us, to let it plant and root us as it lives in us and changes us. This experience is what the stone marks, the fire witnesses; it is the safe harbor to which we are drawn. We are moved to unconditioned loving respect that a living mystery offers itself to us and we devote ourselves to keeping it alive, for its own sake.

References

Versions of this chapter were given to Jungian societies in the United States, to the Los Angeles C. G. Jung Institute, and to the American Association of Pastoral Counselors.

Akhmatova, A. 1992. *The Complete Poems of Anna Akhmatova*. Trans. Judith Hemschemeyer. Ed. Roberta Reeder. Boston: Zephyr Press.
Diagnostic and Statistical Manual of Mental Disorders IV. 1994. Washington, D.C.: American Psychiatric Association.

Green, A. 2000/2004. *André Green at the Squiggle Foundation*. Ed. Jan Abram. London: Karnac.

Hirshfield, J. 1998. *Nine Gates: Entering the Mind of Poetry*. New York: Harper Perennial.

Hollis, J. 2000. *The Archetypal Imagination*. College Station, Tex.: Texas A & M University Press.

Jung, C. G. 1909/1960. The psychology of Dementia Praecox. In *The Psychogenesis of Mental Disease*. Vol. 3 of *Collected Works*. Trans. R. F. C. Hull. New York: Pantheon.

———. 1954/1958. Transformation symbolism in the Mass. In *Psychology and Religion: West and East*. Vol. 11 of *Collected Works*. Trans. R. F. C. Hull. New York: Pantheon.

———. 1954/1967. The philosophical tree. In *Alchemical Studies*. Vol. 13 of *Collected Works*. Trans R. F. C. Hull. Princeton, N.J.: Princeton University Press.

———. 1963a. *Mysterium Coniunctionis*. Vol. 14 of *Collected Works*. Trans. R. F. C. Hull. New York: Pantheon.

———. 1963b. *Memories, Dreams, Reflections*. Ed. Aniela Jaffé. Trans. Richard and Clara Winston. New York: Pantheon.

———. 1973 and 1975. *Letters*. 2 vols. Ed. G. Adler and A. Jaffé. Princeton, N.J.: Princeton University Press.

———. 1976. *The Symbolic Life*. Vol. 18 of *Collected Works*. Trans. R. F. C. Hull. Princeton, N.J.: Princeton University Press.

———. 1997. *Visions: Notes of a Seminar Given 1930–1934*. 2 vols. Ed. Claire Douglas. Princeton, N.J.: Princeton University Press.

Milner, M. 1957/1979. *On Not Being Able to Paint*. New York: International Universities Press.

Rilke, R. M. 1923/1992. *Duino Elegies*. Trans. David Oswald. Einsiedeln, Switzerland: Daimon.

Stokes, A. 1973. *The Game That Must Be Lost*. London: Carcanet Press.

Ulanov, A. B. 1992/1996. The perverse and the transcendent. In *The Functioning Transcendent*, chapter 3. Wilmette, Ill.: Chiron.

————. 1996a/2004. Ritual, repetition compulsion, and psychic reality. In *Spiritual Aspects of Clinical Work*, chapter 15. Einsiedeln, Switzerland: Daimon.

————. 1996b/2004. Countertransference and the Self. In *Spiritual Aspects of Clinical Work*, chapter 14. Einsiedeln, Switzerland: Daimon.

————. 1999/2005. Between anxiety and faith: the role of the feminine in Tillich's theological thought. In *Spirit in Jung*, chapter 10. Einsiedeln, Switzerland: Daimon.

Von Franz, M.-L. 1970. *Apuleius' Golden Ass*. New York: Spring Publications.

————. 1997. *Archetypal Patterns in Psychotherapy*. Boston: Shambhala.

CHAPTER 3

CONSEQUENCES FOR CLINICAL WORK OF OUR SPIRITUAL LOCATION

Spirituality

Spirituality is a dangerous topic. Spirit itself seems to be a subject, for which we are the object. It is a living experience, "a venture which requires us to commit ourselves with our whole being" (Jung 1932/1958, 501). The New Testament tells us the Spirit searches our hearts, interceding for us "with sighs too deep for words" (Rom. 8:26, RSV) and also searches "even the depths of God" (1 Cor. 2:10, RSV). This is a living Spirit, ever renewed, pursuing its goals "in manifold and inconceivable ways throughout the history of mankind" as Jung says; "Measured against it, the names and forms which men [sic] have given it mean very little; they are only the changing leaves and blossoms on the stem of the eternal tree" (Jung 1932/1958, 538).

The impulse to individuation is the strongest urge in us; it will proceed one way or another. We are summoned to be loyal to our own being, and immediately are pulled by the opposites of freely responding to the call and feeling it is "like a law of God from which there is no escape" (Jung 1932/1954, 300). We can choose to walk to our fate, to correspond with it, or to be dragged there by a neurosis (Jung 1938/1958, 129). Yet to find that fate and transform it into destiny, and find it transformed even into providence, we must create it (see Ulanov 1995a/1996, 7, 10, 21).

Individuation means becoming all we are given to be, to engage in a living cooperation of all factors within us, where the universal

manifests within the particular and produces an individual effect. It costs
us everything, all the warring parts of ourselves within us and among us
in the world must find ways to talk with each other and grow into a community. Without such effort, such consent to include all the pieces of ourselves, even the hidden ones we fear or despise, those parts live anyway
in the atmosphere around us, poisoning our children, squelching enthu-
siasm for life, stirring up dissent with our neighbor, diminishing our joy.
Coming to be ourselves also partakes of its opposite, to become part of
others. Jung says, "Being oneself, one is like many. One cannot individuate without being with other human beings. . . . Being an individual is
always a link in a chain. . . . how little you can exist . . . without responsibilities and duties and the relation of other people to yourself . . ." (Jung
1988, vol. 1, 102). Individuation thus plants us in otherness—of other
people, and of the transcendent.

In seeking to be all that we are given to be, we must not give too
much of the Self away to the ego. Jung describes the Self as the center of
the entire psyche both conscious and unconscious, and the ego as the
center of our consciousness, what we usually identify with as me, as I, as
us. When the Self gives way too much to the ego, we try too hard to
adapt, to conform, and lose openness to the depths and heights of living
where we are surprised by what wants to live through us, speak to us, and
bring us home at the end.

All of us know someone who lives from this bigger Self. In their presence we just feel blessed. We can never figure out exactly why. They do
not speak with special wisdom or display unusual beauty. But with them
we feel more possible, able to risk, expand into all of ourselves. In earlier
centuries we might have called such a person a guru or a sage, a medicine
woman, a shaman. But in this first decade of the twenty-first century
when so much strife occurs, and need for spiritual connection presses on
us urgently and we lack common ritual or doctrine, we hear Jung say it
would be better to admit our spiritual poverty (Jung 1928/1958, 152).
Erich Neumann as long ago as 1959 said,

Because in our time the creative principle hides in an anonymity that discloses its origin by no divine sign, no visible radiance, no demonstrable legitimacy, we have entered upon spiritual poverty . . . in the guise of a beggar. . . . What is he waiting for? He is waiting for you. This means that creative redemption . . . is disguised as Everyman . . . and . . . his poverty and helplessness make him dependent on the devotion that every man accords to this Everyman. This is our situation. Wherever we find the creative principle . . . we venerate it as the hidden treasure that in humble form conceals a fragment of the godhead. (Neumann 1959, 168)

As a clinician, I look at Spirit through the lens of the psyche, recalling Jung's point that "God has never spoken to [us] except in and through the psyche, and the psyche understands it . . . [as] the eye beholds the sun" (Jung 1973, August 1932, 98). As clinicians, we ask what a person's experience is of Spirit breaking in. Does it lead to health or illness? How does the person house this visitation? As a religious person, I look at the psyche and manifestations of Spirit through such questions as, Where does this Spirit come from? Who authors such events? Who is calling?

Spirit is not a cozy presence but brings a sword, cutting through our joints, laying our heart bare. Spirit is not a thing or a content but is like the wind that comes and goes but we do not know when or where and we cannot capture or control it. We can only strive to become hollow bones, as the Sioux medicine man Fool's Crow says, or a riverbed in which Spirit's waters can flow. This warm, intense life force can upset our whole life, call us out like Abraham to a far country merely on the basis of a promise; lead us, as it did Jesus, into the desert of temptation where we entertain our ability to manipulate the most powerful symbols of our culture; it can overshadow us, as it did Mary, and make us pregnant with a life so new we must from now on begin from a different departure point. Spirit can meet us when we are fleeing like Jacob, from a crime, a betrayal, a theft, a guilt. Then it wrestles us, wounds us in the night, so that on waking we must mark this event with some conscious ritual. In

Christian tradition, the mighty energy of Spirit ushers us into the presence of the Holy, tumbling us in the conflict of opposites of inflation and humble consent. Spirit is the most intense form of life, bringing the new, yet cutting into old convictions, forcing change in how we live, with whom we live, to whom we belong.

Clinicians feel attraction and nervousness around the Spirit. We are attracted because after a century of development of our theory and technique, from all sides we see the limits of our knowledge to define what accounts for healing in the clinical setting. What makes for aliveness and its regeneration exceeds our theoretical grasp. Clinicians reach beyond their theory to something else that is present in the work. Thus we find clinicians increasingly raiding religious vocabulary while denying its referent. Bion writes of O as the ultimate, the Godhead. Bollas writes of evocative prayer, Winnicott of the sacred moment of communication, Loewald of the work of love in the transference, Grottstein of the ineffable subject in the unconscious that brings us to the transcendent position, Ogden of the inventive power in the analytic couple to create the new, Lacan of the (really) real. Only Freud and Jung, one against and one for, spoke directly of religious experience as the home of Spirit. Freud wants to throw it out altogether as fostering obsession and evasion of both reality and the unconscious. Jung recognizes the religious function of the psyche with which we must deal lest we fall ill by neglecting it, a function that seems to urge our individuation process and whose symbols point to something objective transcending the psyche that wants "to step over . . . into visible life, to take concrete shape" (Jung 1973, 10 January 1929, 59).

Spirit must become flesh, otherwise it "is a wind that is gone in no time: the wind must enter matter for it to be real. The spirit is nothing if it doesn't descend into matter, as matter is utterly dead if it is not vivified by the spirit" (Jung 1988, vol. 2, 1062). Yet Spirit can only become flesh through symbolic understanding because what it expresses transcends our comprehension. The infinite advances into the finite, presenting the intrinsically unknown and unrepresentable (Neumann 1959, 174). Thus encountering Spirit we embark on knitting together the opposites that define and assault our nature—infinite-finite, Spirit-flesh.

The individuation process is inaugurated in encounters with Spirit and urged on in successive meetings with it throughout our lives. For example, a patient seeks analysis with me as a Jungian, after earlier work with an analyst of another school, precisely because, she says, she seeks Spirit and to grasp spirituality. This sounds very grand, but the treatment begins in a big mess which I make and only later see was arranged to make by an unseen something constellating an encounter. Mix-up of scheduling our appointments needs to be straightened out. She immediately questions who I am. I hear myself answer, I am the one who makes a mess. This spontaneous answer turns out to be pivotal in the unfolding treatment, for she is prepared unconsciously to ascribe all order, knowledge, and power to the other, reflecting her early relation to her mother with whom she felt she had to comply to be loved. Such pressure for perfect control also afflicted her inner life. A recurring nightmare from the age of five pictured her at the controls of a giant spaceship "that was fun but if I mess up a big explosion is going to happen. I must keep it going. I am responsible for everything. I'll be up there getting all that love and attention and if I do not stay up, I'll crash." She felt fear she would destroy both self and other. She said of her adult life, "I make others feel good and under it is pure self-hatred for currying favor." Overwhelmed by both constriction to adapt and need to control lest destruction ensue, she would take to her bed with wine and Valium that brought her blessed oblivion, a kind of liberation from pressure. "Pills are spirituality," she said. The opposites of addiction and spirituality framed this analysis, and the opposites initiated our relationship. My making the mess challenged her transference of control to the other.

This woman felt deep suspicion of religion, and we can imagine it loomed as an entrapping institution to which she must conform. Other analysands abhor religion as dried-up systems that bully us with shoulds and should-nots, or power plays dressed up as compassion. Clinicians interested in spirituality also often disavow religion, either having bad experience with it themselves, or no experience that it offers a path. Religion is feared as full of prohibitions and prescriptions, with a score-keeper God inducing in us such magic thinking that if we sacrifice this sheep we will not be struck by disaster.

Spirit is the giver and taker of life, a brute fact of nature, that great paradox which we cannot express—hot and cold, above and below, light and its overcoming, our animal root-impulse and our highest flung intuition of unitary reality (Ulanov 2002, ix). Spirit brings the hammer and the anvil between which we are pounded into new shape (Jung 1988, vol. 2, 1134).

For us in this new century, Spirit is no longer conjugated in metaphysical abstractions above the tumult of instincts, political strife, and social congress. For us, Spirit is down in the midst of life, into matter and what matters to our concrete ordinary selves. How do we love the center when it shows itself in so many different forms? What ways do we meditate steadfastly on the center while paying taxes, getting our children through school, doing the laundry, keeping a job? How do we love the ultimate when our bodies hurt with pain and age toward death? How do we make sense of divine providence in the face of abysmal poverty in Latin American communities and in North America's Appalachia? What do we make of the sightings of the Virgin Mary just prior to the outbreak in the former Yugoslavia of savage civil war, complete with rape camps and genocide? How do we go on loving when death takes the object of our love? What comfort blesses our mourning?

Spirit in our time is down in the flesh of our own small selves, in relationships with other people, with the unconscious, and very much in the specific cultural communities across our world. Cultural influences on our perceptions of healing and of illness show the inextricable link between spirit, psyche, body, and society. For example, trance states in non-Western cultures do not bespeak primitive dissociation but a different non-dualistic way of experiencing reality (Kleinman 1988). Our postmodern globalization bombards us with information and makes not just for a world community but also for fragmentation and "promiscuous arousal created by constant change and no real live engagement with the local living in definite form of body, culture, space and time" (Kleinman 1997).

Religion is concrete engagement with Spirit in definite form of ritual, doctrine, worship, spiritual practice. Religious traditions manifest in time, space, and community the address of the Spirit which we attempt to incarnate. At Sinai when God offered the Torah through Moses, the Israelites first said, We will do, before they asked to know, to understand what Torah was (Levinas 1990, 33). That wholehearted response to God with all the soul, mind, and strength (Deut. 6:5) so plants us in the transcendent that it was carried over into Jesus' words as the first great commandment (Matt. 22:37-38). Responding to otherness preceding self-reflexive knowing is our whole-making response to wholeness coming into time and space. In Christian tradition, such wholeheartedness is seen in Jesus who gives all to Christ, even into death, to the Christ who lives in unbroken linking with the unimaginable, unoriginated source called God, that free presence that precedes any law, any spiritual practice, any ritual.

Religion tries to give a name to this origin point and to locate the residence of this God in our human family and day to day living. When religions remember that no image they hold can be equated with this unfathomable God, religions create a narrative, a creative repetition instead of a repetition compulsion, always pointing beyond to the center that is. That isness pours out on us generously, inexhaustibly. Theologies are nicknames for what remains outside our visions, exceeds our social and personal constructions of reality. Theologies, at their best, mark the absence of the Holy because it cannot be captured in any of our systems, yet theologies also mark traces of its presence.

Religion at its best employs radical deconstructionism long before its fashionable postmodern appearance. Deconstructionism spies the gap between religious symbols and language and what they point to, indeed the gap between all our systems of human apprehension and the reality they symbolize. Deconstructionism offers radical critique of the ground of knowledge of the Holy, but is not an affirmation of groundlessness. It cannot destroy the implication of presence. In this sense deconstructionism displays a *via negativa*, a negative theology, saying what the ultimate is not, a time honored obeisance to the divine.

When religions fall prey to the inevitable human habit of reification, fixating on an object that symbolizes the Holy and equating it with the Holy, then religions dry up because nothing finite can contain the infinite. What those of us gripped by Spirit need to remember is the seeming desire from the Spirit's side to come into our daily life, to be lived and loved, not as precious relics but as living breath on the cheek of our neighbor, as the adamant foot on our stiff neck, as the blessing bountifully bestowed on us in the still small voice. We need to make an earthly residence, an ark, a tabernacle, an abode for the divine, to offer it hospitality. How to house this flame?

When aware of such spiritual questions, the clinical task changes and that is the principal consequence of spiritual location for clinical work. Our focus shifts from how to survive this problem, how to recover from this trauma, how to understand this compelling complex to one fundamental issue: How much lightning can we stand?

Analysis

Religion and depth psychology used to be one big river called the care of souls. In the twentieth century this big river became two. Freud said outright he wanted to establish a "profession of secular ministers of soul, who do not have to be physicians and must not be priests" (Bettelheim 1982, 35). Jung said the soul was *naturaliter religiosa*, and that our religious instinct that shows itself in the drive to individuation is a "vital link with psychic processes independent of and beyond consciousness, in the dark hinterland of the psyche" (Jung 1940/1959, 261). Depth psychology has acted as a new hermeneutic for religious life, interpreting unconscious affects, their dynamic interaction, and how they influence our relationships to each other. The flesh the Spirit inhabits is also the psyche.

At the turn into this new twenty-first century the two rivers, now called psychoanalysis and spirituality, come toward each other again as two parts of a greater whole. Clinicians ask what this mysterious something is that makes an analysis work, and raise what are, in effect, spiritual questions. What is the source of Self, in Jung's vocabulary, that does the doing of analysis? What is this mysterious presence in the work of therapy that allows the analytical couple to behold something new that releases healing? What is it that makes for aliveness?

Religion says we must name this presence if we want to go on relating to it. This does not mean proselytizing in the consulting room, nor in any way forcing on our patients our own spiritual experience or religious convictions, any more than we would force on them sexual practices or how to manage their money. But it does mean we must be alert to this aspect of our countertransference, to what we bring into the room, what we contribute to the countertransference-transference field from our spiritual location. We probably never mention this explicitly, but it is there, just as is our sexual presence, our moral quality. I have even heard it suggested that analysts in training learn meditative practice as it enhances empathy and evenly hovering attention so necessary for the work of listening to the analysand (Kakar 2002).

We need to be aware as clinicians what we believe and do not believe about the reality the symbols we employ in analysis indicate. Analytical work is itself a symbol that points to the reality that we are living in our offices hour after hour, day after day, year after year. We are not outside it, appreciating the experience aesthetically but not really believing it. The reality communicating through archetype and symbol and through the analytical couple is what galvanizes healing (Ulanov 1995b/1996, 154). But to accomplish this end, we must acknowledge this reality and live in it with all the necessary disciplines belief in it brings.

Religion goes even further when pointing to the source, the origin point, by declaring it is interested in us, may even have intentions toward us, what we would feel as desire for relation to us. To explore this possibility we need spiritual practice, to test the waters, not to drown in them, nor to dry up parched too far away from them. We need consciousness of what pictures we hold of wholeness, of reality, and what symbols bring it near. We need consciousness, in Jung's terms, of our experiences of the Self and what it links us to. How do we sit in reality? What meaning do we imagine? What belief do we live in the work we are doing? How we see it influences what we see; it is our postmodern construction of what is there to be found.

For example, what looks destructive in a patient destroying the previous good session's work in an explosion of anger may, if looked into instead of just at, reveal itself as an effort on the part of the analysand to communicate through anger the fact of gaps, of intolerable nonconnection. The anger is hurling a rope bridge over the chasm the patient feels between us to resume contact, and it is now possible to hurl the bridge because of the last session's good work. Moreover, the anger may not be entirely personal. Though it stems in part from early object relations marred by the analysand feeling cut off repeatedly by her parents so that her childself was wounded, the anger may also announce the advent not of her wounded child into the analysis, but of *the* child in the psyche, both hers and mine. In the archetypal child motif lurks the eternally new, always born as a child in poverty, in danger, or here, in anger. This child presence overcomes the gaps to make for unity. Precisely because we had a good session, her anger heralds this new possible joining breaking into the analysis.

Analysis is the place of lightning. We never know what is in store for this particular analysand, nor how this person will change ourselves. Analysis means risk, not knowing, beholding the infinite in this finite person, and how he or she is held in the infinite. Analysis dares encounter with the unknown. What are the consequences for clinical practice of our spiritual location? How does it influence how we see the analysand and the process of individuation?

Madness and Hatred of the Spiritual

Madness, from a psychodynamic perspective, threatens when no symbolization occurs. Then we are given over to emotional and intellectual rigidity, to a literalistic attitude, to collapsing symbol into sign, so we really believe our projection conveys true perception of the other, our delusion detects the hidden character of the analyst, that our obsession can ward off danger. Madness, from a spiritual point of view, is not being able to link up to the source. Then we cannot construct a fitting lifespace (Deri 1984, 323-24) but get stuck in the trauma repeated in dreams and reenacted in relationships. This is illness from too much rigidity. Like my analysand who as a child dreamed again and again she must fly this huge spaceship that was going out of control, we get swung between opposites of omnipotence and impotence. A psychotic part of us attacks our inner freedom to make deep realizations because we fear that more self-knowledge where we make our own judgments, our own insights, our own free act of responsiveness, will bring more burdens. We fear this inner anointing to greater responsibility. For when an unconscious content crosses over into consciousness, as Jung says, it imposes on us an ethical demand. We must find ways to live it, be changed by it. Our fear is troubled by presence of possibility. We may hate the Spirit that would liberate us.

To refind our ability to symbolize means we must let our wounds remain open, not close them up by premature interpretations, but sit in the ashes, suffer in the prison, go naked and ashamed until right there in the suffering a healing spark strikes. In the resurrection stories of Christianity, Christ arises in a wounded body. We must give up the rigid identification with our theory, for example, as protecting us from being wounded. An analysand allowed herself to experience fully the pain she felt in the past as a child in relation to her mother and, in another session, to feel the pain she felt in the present in relation to her husband who had suddenly announced he wanted a divorce. In both sessions, the open wound registered in her body. She could smell the sweet/sour alcohol on her mother's breath. In the session about her husband she felt first a consuming hunger: "I'm starving for a bagel and cream cheese right now," she said (food she not often indulged in); "I'm starving for conversation!" (which he lacked). She recalled his competitive taunt when she announced early on in their marriage that she was pregnant: Does this mean I can now beat you in squash? Immediately a prodromal syndrome started with the slashing pain of a migraine attack. Our body often carries our wounds.

Analysands illustrate how we seize on half measures to avoid the inner freedom from which the capacity to symbolize arises. One man misses sessions; another lights bonfires out of substitute issues so the hour is up before we get to the real point; a woman attacks as stupid her intense missing of sexual happiness with her husband who suddenly died in an operation; a man denounces himself for not knowing all sorts of things he could not know, as if he could be omnipotently and narcissistically in charge; another man goes after what he calls skirts on the street instead of sticking to the task of creating his poems which plant him in reality. We fasten on something that comes to act like a God-image that we hold onto fiercely, insisting in a mad way to ourselves that this god—of the market, of money, of prescription drugs, of a sexual pattern, of a specific religious ritual—is the God, the infinite. This rigidity is doomed. As the poet Rilke writes, "Wait, from the distance hardness is menaced by something still harder. Alas—a remote hammer is poised to strike" (Rilke 1906–1926, 571; cited in Neumann 1959, 197).

Our resistance to the call to inner freedom, to our ownmost being, to the work of symbol-making springs from fear. We feel pulled from fixed delusions or rigid routines or insistent transference dramas toward formlessness. Whatever instigates our individuation process exceeds our intellectual grasp; it pulls us toward itself which lies beyond the forms of our finite understanding or vision, away from familiarity and family custom. Behind the primitive agonies that Winnicott describes as falling forever or going to pieces or feeling unreal in the world (Winnicott 1962, 58) is this infinite freedom, the freedom of the infinite, or the freedom that is the infinite's and not our own, yet it summons us.

We protest we cannot, dare not, and stick to our old madness. But the psyche may tell us otherwise. One woman dreamed of what she called an animal-man, a man she knew as a dancer in real life and respected. She said to him, I cannot dance. But he replied, No, it is that you will not dance. You can if you will. The dream-man takes her back before the trauma that ruptured her relation to the Self, symbolized in the dream by his suddenly backing up the car down the road of her childhood home, like a swift regression. What will she do with this new realization that the rupture can be healed, that she can dance? She is now troubled by presence of a turning point (see Ulanov 1998/2004, 298-302). Jesus in the Gospels warns us not to miss this possibility, not to be like those children who call out, "We piped to you, and you did not dance; we wailed, and you did not weep" (Luke 7:32, RSV).

We may object here and say but this line of approach could result in blaming the patient for not being willing; it could degenerate into urging willpower. That danger is real as a shadow side of any spiritual practice, as a theological sadism that bullies the ego and forgets the mysterious urgings of the Self. That is one of the worst consequences of spiritual practice for clinical work. It contracts upward into ego alone and makes wholehearted willingness subtract into willpower. But not if we feel the form coming into matter between the opposite madnesses of rigidity or chaos. Then we feel live, open-ended questions circulate in the consulting room: How to make a form here and now in this limited life, in this country, in this town, in this economic bracket, with this education or family, or their lack? Something addresses us; we must respond. Will we say, We will do before we fully understand it? Will we refuse out of dread and abysmal fear? For the Self, in Jung's terms, interrupts, disrupts, commands, recedes, will not be harnessed. How can we tame this horse? Will this horse run away with us? We want to capture this freedom, this other and make it behave. Thus we may hate this spiritual background, this Spirit in the background of our analytical work because we cannot domesticate it.

For example, a highly educated and psychologically developed professional who also was a devout Jew harbored intense dread of the impersonal Self trampling her personal ego, as if she would be cast into outer darkness, a no-thing place, like a speck of dust. "Can I trust that something beyond my ego does not just ignore me or inundate me?" she would ask. She projected this fear onto her literal death, but felt it as a present danger, too: "the numinous could crush you. I feel awe to what is beyond, but I do not feel held by it. I feel terror this big impersonal numinous could come in and squash you." This primordial fear translated into having to "get it right" with her clients, fearing not-knowing states; panic when her husband did not keep to the budget plan; how to keep her household duties, her religious life going. She said, I have blinders on; I don't want to see anything; I am oppressed by one more thing to do; I don't want it. Yet her vigilance felt deadening to her alive, unconventional self. She descended from this vigilant ego attitude to a free, vital self through a new image appearing early on in analysis. A big gobbling mouth emerged: I want to gobble, eat, I want sex; instinctual depths loomed up from below.

Her spiritual connection to the resources of Judaism was long lived, genuine, and deeply moving, yet she felt terror of not existing, and intense desire to be "living all my life and tolerating non-knowing." She yearned to be free from the construction that infiltrated her life with her husband, her professional work, her finding her own creative voice. She wanted to trust "that something bigger than the ego will provide, that I don't have to be perfect, or afraid of gobbling, that I don't have to figure out what is right." In her case building up the ego's response to Self brought release. She said she "got off the train to the concentration

camp." By that she meant that she saw that this death trip was the structure in her that was becoming obsolete—the structure of her fear
matched by a constraining vigilance to do it right. She said I do not need
this structure anymore where I do not let myself fill up with joy and
gladness of a life I have.

She needed to get to the Self through her ego, to harness her aggression, to follow the waters of feeling that softened the rules of her many
accomplishments, including how I as a mental health professional should
conduct myself in the analysis, for I often failed her expectations of the
correct analyst, by allowing my own personality to show through my
responses to her material. I met with disapproval which on an ego level
was correct; on a Self level I found myself positioned by the transference-
countertransference field between us to expand the boundaries of analyst
and analysand to being two citizens of the universe, two women fully in
life. I was unwilling for her to push the god of analysis into me. When I
displayed my own idiosyncrasies, she was required to sift out her idea of
what an analyst should be, to create her own analysis. She "braided" a
fuller connection to the Self by "filling up with what is, living all my life."
Though fallible, and often corrected, she said of me, "I need this deep
connection with you to sustain the root growing down."

This example touches on another way we may hate the spiritual back-
drop of analysis. If we are afraid to give up rigid identification with some
theory or some person or some mode of conduct as the god, the truth, lest
we dissolve into chaos, we are equally fearful of leaving chaos to come into
definite form anchored in living. Such refusal is not from unwillingness but
from feeling one's spirit has been shattered. One analysand dreamed of the
murder of her soul, pictured in the dream as an animal whose species was
made extinct. The dream staged the murder by her father in a little outdoor
theater, and followed it by a drama of suicide contemplated by the dream-
ego. We could rightly say that to dream this dread-filled catastrophe offered
the dreamer a place to stand, to gain a foothold to look at this awful soul-
murder. For Jung, bundling terrifying affects into images offers us a chance

71

to relate to what happens to us and make something of it. But for this woman, the trauma lived on in her in the form of renouncing her talents and opportunities in life to thwart her father's ambitions for her and his pleasure in her talents which blossomed early in her childhood. She lived to defeat him. When I discovered that the extinct dream-animal in fact still lived "down under" in Australia, an apt image for the unconscious for someone living in North America, and in a symbolic way meant that her soul was still alive, she defeated me with no response. The need to come into life in definite form did not happen. She died young, before her father, to his endless sorrow, and to my sorrow as well.

Love is at issue here, refusal to love something that has ignited us which would mean bringing it into form in living here and now, and also mean renouncing activities that distract us from it. For some of us the specific form we attack and want to get rid of lies in our shadow. But that is the balm in Gilead, the savior born in the lowly Nazareth. Rejection of this despised part keeps us from being able to make deep realizations within ourselves and with others (see Symington 2001, 25-27, 45). If we do not have all our feet under us, all the parts included, meaning our shame, our fear, our petty meanness, our corrupt behavior, where we cheat or lie, where we refuse to respond to others, we cannot create. Spiritually, we refuse to see that the shadow belongs to something bigger, and can sometimes be the agent of our transformation. We want to isolate our envy, for example, cut it off from every other part of us, instead of finding in envy a sighting of the good. Kierkegaard says envy is admiration gone sour. Where envy exists in us, so does lavish recognition of the good (Ulanov and Ulanov 1983/1998). Loving someone, loving God, loving the process of individuation, loving the good, means loving all out, heart, mind, soul, body, all the parts. Where the good exists, others thrive.

I remember a fourth grade teacher of our son. His father and I would go to parent-teacher conference sitting in those tiny chairs at little desks. The teacher was shy, hardly looked me in the eye, did not give any direct answers to my maternal concerns. Yet with this teacher I had seen my son bloom, as if a red geranium blossomed out of his head. How did this happen with this wary person? He loved his teaching and the children flowered. What is this mysterious power to make connections, to make something alive, to inspire and to steady, to chasten and excite?

It is a tremendous power that inheres in all of us. When psychologically we take the route of madness, and when spiritually we hate the spiritual, we want to push this creating power into other people, make them carry it, make the religious system carry it. We flee this freedom; we fear it. We want to get rid of it by making a god out of someone else, something else (Symington 2001, 30, 161-62). This is where religion turns fanatic, indeed demonic, and acts as a portal for gross inhumanity to each other.

Even in the privacy of the two-person relationship of analysis, both analyst and analysand face the task of embodying this power. The philosopher-theologian Jean-Luc Marion sums up this ethical and community dimension in his meditation on the human face. The face of the other in our consulting room is "the place from which we are seen. . . . In the face of the other, we experience being seen. . . . We experience another world. We are not alone in that world; there is another external player out in the world, as I am." This reception of the other breeds ethical connection: "The unviewable face of the other's gaze only appears once I understand, by surrendering to it, that I must not kill it. Certainly I can always kill the other, but then it will disappear as a face; it will freeze as an object, and I will know that I am a murderer." And I will lose being seen. Thus the other's face "must not appear as object but as call. . . . It is invisible because it is a place where I see that I am seen" (Marion 1999).

The Consequences of Our Spiritual Location for Clinical Work

Where clinical work and spiritual practice meet is in recognition that we have in us the power to make something of our experience and to register that our experience makes something of us. In Jung's terms, the ego must create and construct its path in order to find the Self that objectively exists as a way for each of us. Even if we describe that path as no-path, no-self, an objective path exists, opening before us. We do not find it if we do not create it; yet creating it, we find its thereness, opaque as lead, obdurate, yet light as light itself.

We can look at this power in the psyche of each of us from bottom up or from consciousness down. Ego, our conscious sense of I-ness in relation to others, meets and mingles with the archetypal level of the objective psyche, whose influencing images can act on us unconsciously or appear as powerful transformative images that guide our adult lives. In addition, reality manifests through these conscious and unconscious psychic layers. Or we can begin with reality, patterning itself in archetypal motifs, stirring up affects we grasp through images which then we can translate into vocabularies of consciousness. Reality speaks to and patterns all of us and each of us, with each other as well as through our dreams, in our social forms of art, in economic and political symbols. When reality meets us we experience it as numinous, as a spiritual event, a religious experience. The religious experience lasts because it does not remain a discrete event but becomes a capacity to live connected to the source. We experience the creation of creating.

Spiritual practices are ways we devise to keep going on exercising this capacity, to continue participating in the ongoing process of creation. We know moments of inner realization, acts of freedom, of deep understanding and emotional initiative where we come into possession, if even for a moment, of all parts of us, and a sense of communion with our neighbor. Through this creative act we make all these parts into a unity. This zero point makes a space where, for a moment, conscious and unconscious marry (conjoin). Inner and outer, I and you, us and them, all the opposites wed in a creative unity. From this unity a third term arises. A part of the one reality to which we all belong "lingers in the beauty of the moment" (Neumann 1959, 203).

74

An example of this third term is the following symbol a woman
dreamed or received as a gift from her dream, a symbol which bodied forth
the culmination of a long period of analytical work, making audible the
unity achieved. She dreamed, "The Grail cup sings!" Another example
comes from the woman who came into analysis addicted and looking for
spirituality. She surprised herself. A new symbol appeared near the end of
her analysis through which the gusto and beauty of reality spoke. Located
in her body in the perineum, that the dictionary describes as "the diamond-
shaped area corresponding to the outlet of the pelvis," pulsing with free
energy, "on a strong, fat stem" bloomed "a large pink zinnia and I sit in it
as a bee." She alluded to still another symbol which made her feel connected up to the source, but she did not confide it, as is befitting the revelation of something numinous. It evokes modesty and a sheltering
attitude in us, born of reverence.

Such a free act of creating and finding potent new symbols is possible even if we are poor, ill, on the brink of dying, in sorrow. We can still
feel the breath of the infinite on our face, the regenerative word spoken
into our ear. The woman who had the bodily experience in session of her
open wounds from mother and husband, heard her inner attacker, imaged
as a harpy, say, You will be all right; you will not go hungry, and then it
left her a feather! Whatever our state, we can recover deep joy in the simple happiness of being, in laughing, in truly seeing another, in welcoming
back to the whole of us the lost sheep, the split-off part from the wilderness of repression. Christ's baptism symbolizes such a moment of realization, a bestowal of blessing when the finite human receives the divine
infinite and we recognize we belong to it; it is our home country
(Symington 2001, 92).

Nelson Mandela expresses something similar to my emphasis on this
capacity in his inaugural speech: "Our worst fear is not that we are inad-
equate, our deepest fear is that we are powerful beyond measure. It is our
light, not our darkness, that most frightens us. . . . You are a child of God;
your playing small doesn't serve the world. . . . We are born to make

manifest the glory of God within us. It is not just some of us, it is everyone and as we let our own light shine we unconsciously give other people permission to do so" (1994).

To come near this capacity to make something of our experience, and not project it into someone else or install it in some religious system and make them into the god is the point on which transformation turns. Neumann refers to Rilke's twelfth sonnet in his *Sonnets to Orpheus*, saying, "in the approach to God, the soul takes fire and the blaze is the turning point as it is also a pouring forth, a spring" (Neumann 1959, 200). Our change, as Rilke says, changes others: "And Daphne, transformed, feeling herself laurel, wants you to change into wind" (Rilke 1989 II, 12, 39). All the elements of fire, water, earth, and air constellate around this turning point, when we accept this capacity in ourselves. Augustine called it the indwelling God: Looking into me I see Thee; looking into Thee, I see me (see Ulanov 2001a, 2). In Jungian terms the Self makes a bridge to a whole reality to which we each and all together belong. We feel our space there when moved by generosity and gratitude and when we make creative, personal, original response to what life gives us.

Trauma and illness, madness and pathology, soul-murder and spirit-shattering happen when we are invaded by another or by events like war, accident, or earthquake, before we are able to make something of the experience or register that the experience makes something of us. The creative process is stolen by the other, violated by natural disaster or human inhumanity. We must work our way back to the source point which is the turning point of transformation, where again creation in the no-thing space happens and we, unlike God who can create from nothing, create from the scraps left us. In that inner free action a source again pours forth in us and through us. Like a spring, love flows through us from the Godhead to the Godhead. Such creative cascade reaches beyond the individual; images springing up from the depths move many, breeding a sense of the eternal in the now so every single moment forms a turning point. Such is heaven on earth, nirvana, the freedom of no-self, the blessing of isness.

We need relationship to each other to get to this power in us, to develop this capacity to make something of our experience and to accept that experience makes something of us. We need the other in order to individuate. The Self is both our ownmost uniqueness and a crowd (see Jung 1988, vol. 1, 103). This capacity does not come into being unless it is recognized and responded to by an other, someone who looks at us with a gleam in their eye, seeing us, prizing us simply because we are, contemplating the good of us, our being. We are dependent on this other: "For you never can get to yourself without loving your neighbor . . ." (Jung 1988, vol. 2, 1019).

Psychoanalytic theories recognize this dependence and the necessity that another person meet it. They emphasize the mother's relation to the infant, as if by going further and further back into the beginnings of a person's life, the theory can capture what brings being into being in the first place. Those of us who have experienced being the gleam in our mother's eye slip effortlessly into the royal authority of children, that every child is entitled to be seen as special, unique, an original, and cherished as such. Those of us who have missed this gleam know the sorrow of not being recognized as our special self and have had to work hard to unfold. Spirituality contributes the extraordinary idea that even if we missed this wooing into being as children, it can still come to us at any point in our lives from God, from being addressed, summoned, and cared about by the center of reality. In Christianity many find this love mediated through the person of Jesus.

A colleague's example shows the need for dependency to be met and the joy when it is. She treated a little boy, nearly autistic, a patient in a psychiatric hospital. For many sessions she sat with him in the treatment room, he silent and unmoving toward any of the toys left around for him. She sat and felt his isolation and terror. Silent, they sat through whole hours. Finally, he moved toward a big beach ball, bigger than he was, and buried his face, his whole body in it, hugging it as it enveloped him. My colleague said he loved it; and felt it loved him, receiving his embrace and embracing him back.

An analysand of mine knew that the crux of her analysis depended on her accepting, instead of despising, her own dependency needs which had not been met in childhood. An intelligent and religious woman, she perceived that mysterious something in us which initiates response and creates and finds symbols for itself. She believes in it. But she also saw she could not get at it by her vigorous will or her reasoning but only by submitting to the experience of dependency in the present, on the analysis and me, the analyst. Exclaiming, "I'm not sure I can do it with you unless I am here five years" (she would be returning to her distant home within another year), marked her making her way to this surrender.

For any of us it is the same, accepting that we cannot find and create ourselves without acknowledging dependence on something beyond ourselves mediated by another person, or beloved object. In our time now, spiritual life directs us down into the creation of relationship with another person and through them to a thou, a void, an imagelessness, a beyond which creates us. We are driven to find the transcendent; it does not exist outside or beyond humans as a changeless entity. We find it in the interrelation of individuals, with kin and kindred souls. Something works in the self and the other and works them both into an expanded range of being that each feels like moreness, bigness: "It is the victory of the divine life in the turmoil of space and time" (Jung 1988, vol. 2, 979). We depend on others to offer us ways to unfold and make something of our experience and they depend on us for the same. We transform the bombardment of data into personal meaningful experience, bringing others near through projections onto them, endowing them with the lushness of our own unconscious life. Together we sort out what is whose and how to share the bounty. Interdependence counters envy and theft. There is enough goodness to go around.

Dependence means embodiment. Body means concrete bounded-ness that plants us here and now. Our spiritual intimations must take on flesh in everyday living which is the pudding in which we find the proof that it is Spirit we connect with and not our wishing and fearing. We contemplate the infinite in this particular analysand, not in general. What makes falling in love so life-changing is seeing the infinite rooted in this other and we love their blooming and want to aid it. We see the infinite in this woman or man, in this child, in this pet, in this idea, and it touches us through this other and arouses and soothes our own coming more into being. We believe in it and it uncovers all the layers in which we have been hiding. We are opened to gladness in the particular being of this other and the infinite in this particular live creature. Spirit sweeps into us through this embodied relationship. We feel plugged into an energy source, moved to creative acts which must communicate themselves in our new ability to stand up to speak against something unspeakable, to take that step to give up a destructive attitude, or a substance like heroin; to allow weeping; to enter silence folding us in and down into our very sinews, knitting us up again, but so new, we say, I was dead and now I am alive. We depend on relationship with each other to reach and live our capacity for creative acts.

The fact of the body as giving definite shape to the infinite explains the fun of being an analyst for many decades. We embark on an uncharted enterprise with each person's analysis and that imbues our work with excitement. We also see original images for the infinite as it lives in this particular finite person, and that brings the splendor of the All into immediate experience in the consulting room. Moreover, for each of us, our idiosyncratic image of the infinite includes our particular problems and gifts (Ulanov 2001b, 142ff.). The woman whose new symbol was the large, flowering pink zinnia with its sturdy, fat stem had always found a sense of a larger transcendent whole in gardening, even when she was caught in the exhausting opposition between seeking the spiritual and succumbing to the oblivion of her addiction.

Another woman who despised her thighs as too lumpy, bulky, jiggly, and fantasied cutting them down, brought at the beginning of her analysis a dream of stark imagery. She was watching a man lying on a table being ministered to by a female doctor. He had no legs, no thighs, and the doctor was pressing a pestle-like object into his pelvic cavity as if this was connected to restoring his legs. The dreamer was appalled and did not know if this was a healing or a sadistic act. To her astonishment, and mine too, much later on in the work, it was her thighs with their lumpyness which turned out to be the image of persisting to the good, to the creative freedom she sought. She said, "The doorway to the real is through the hateful, shameful thighs. The terrorist in me would get rid of the thighs." I said, the thighs had sheltered the "real you." And she concurred, "I can't get to loving relation without my thighs. My own so cruelly turning against my thighs as the place of most shame turns out to be the only authentic non-ego part of me. They escaped; the ego couldn't get them. I lost my legs and relied on my mind. Now I let the thighs be as they are and bear it and let it soften me." I said, the other side of shame is awe, and she answered, she felt little in the presence of Big; and with my thighs I feel visible, expanded, full of energy.

What wrecks our connection to this capacity to make something of our experience and see it making something of us is, basically, fear; fear of its power and that the power resides in us. We fear "the danger of pleasure" (Rosenberger 2002) that we cannot house it but will blow up; so we lodge this power in others and then attach to them like a barnacle (Symington 2002, chapter 11). We identify our image of this creative presence with the presence itself and thus head toward an explosion.

Equating our subjective symbol for God with God, or even equating our religious tradition with God, always leads to the disaster of persecuting anyone who disagrees, to outlawing other religions, to succumbing to madness where we fall into identification with this God-image, yelling on the street corner that we are the new Christ, or Moses, or Mohammad's truest servant. Or in analytic meetings with colleagues we insist our version of

Jung is the true one, banishing from our group analysts of other interpretations or schools. We use rigidity to avoid what we fear is chaos; or we do not emerge from chaos into specific form because we fear becoming trapped in a fixed system of thought, hectored by shoulds and should-nots.

We fear to take hold of this capacity to make something original of our experience lest we lose it; we fear the pain of loss. Yet creative action in the world is based on loss of the eternal. We depart from eternity to take on limitation in time and space. Death that brings loss also creates space that is only overcome by creative response in the moment (see Neumann 1959, 204). But we fear our positive creative act because then, in contrast, we will see all the negative that belongs to us, how we avoid being creatively alive and only mimic it, substitute false solutions for it, manipulate it to ego ends. We do not want responsibility for the bad we feel, so we sacrifice the good; we fear we cannot survive, so we make unconscious bargains to avoid conflict or painful emotion, but at the cost of vitality. We live, but do not thrive; we coast on the surface of our capacity.

The question here is what to do with the bad and how do our spiritual practice and clinical work locate evil? Any spiritual discipline, and any work as an analyst, must include what to do with the bad. Although in prayer we concern ourselves with suffering, our own and others', and in clinical work we address the immediate effects of abuse, violence, persecutory anxiety so great it prevents one from play, we must acknowledge the background influence of what we imagine to be the origin of destructiveness. Even if we confine ourselves to the theory of early object relations and reduce destructiveness to bad parenting, we see the parents, too, had bad parents, and all the way back to Eve and Adam. What is it that starts it all? Or is evil part of existence itself, what has been called a principle of being? Or is there a death-instinct that aims to return us to non-life, to deadness as a relief from life?

Although we focus in meditation or in therapy on the immediate experiences of the bad, their background influences how we struggle, for example, with our own impulses to inflict hurt or shame on someone who has hurt us; with whether we can admit to consciousness our thrill of energy when we see we have power to render another helpless, to win the fight between us. Can we recognize we are caught in the grip of an inflated insistence that we are right and you are wrong and you owe me and must be made to pay? Can we allow ourselves to see our split-off state, our blank denial and uncomprehension of the cruelty going on over there, in another nation, a distant people, that our nation would never do, that we cannot even imagine ourselves tempted to do? Yet our fascination with details of torture betrays a secret handshake with what we disavow. Others see it in us. None of us are innocent, which makes the Christ figure all the more astonishing. Though uncorrupt, he steps into the guilty space and says, I take the blame; I will carry what you cannot admit knowing nor endure.

If we work for years as a clinician, if we devote years to spiritual practice, we are led inexorably to the question of whence evil and what to do in the face of it. Are good and evil split, and there is no encompassing whole, but only parallel competing forces? Does evil find a place in the whole, or is it so overwhelming that we give up any idea of a whole? Whatever we conclude, even if we defend against these questions, or if we reach open-ended conclusions, it bears on how we do clinical work—what we hear, how we listen, what we make of what we receive. And it bears upon meditative practice—do we try to rise above everything we call bad as if it can be let go, or do we see it conducting us directly to the center—as Jung puts it, "If you choose to follow the way of fear, you are sure of experiencing the totality of life . . ." (Jung 1988, vol. 2, 1299); "the self—that is the precious thing which is difficult to attain; that is the hero's fight and you are alone. . . . the final fight is with yourself . . ." (ibid., 702). To see this background has ethical implications; it makes us a better neighbor: "as long as I am unconscious of the fact that a criminal or a fool is myself too, I find you the criminal and the fool. My consciousness only really integrates when I know the same in myself—when

I can say, yes, I find you an animal, and this is myself" (ibid., 837). The dark and the light of the background come into our immediate practice.

Spiritual practice and clinical perception have access to this deep blackness of reality, to its shining light, whereas at the ego level we see it only in a glimpse; "impaled by a sharp-barb of bliss" (Zagajewski 2002). Conquering evil by external means is a false dream; only living from the inner freedom, the awakening capacity to make something of our experience and see it making us, destroys evil by the power of the good, just as darkness disappears only by light, and light is destroyed by darkness.

We experience this reality that transcends our struggles between evil and good when we live connected to the source, when in Jungian language we live from the Self. But Jung says even the Self seeks to destroy itself as a symbolic form, because it is not God either (see chapter 9). It is just one of our pictures of the transcendent reality. In epiphany moments—for some in dying, for some in giving birth, in the tearing down of the Berlin Wall, in listening to Beethoven's "Ode to Joy," in the extraordinary daring of South Africa's Truth and Justice Commission, in the autistic boy hugging and letting himself be hugged by the big beach ball—in those moments we experience creative freedom in our lives and know we belong to an eternal presence.

Our perceptions of the transcendent in the finite make us live afresh, alert, filled with wonder. We feel a directing providence with its creative unpredictability of freedom. We look like the ragpicker, the beggar in the famous Oxherding pictures, but when he passes by, the cherry tree bursts into bloom. We are the ass on which Christ sits as he rides into Jerusalem. We are not the object nor the subject. We live in the whole. And there is no end to this whole.

We arrive at the turning point which becomes the linking point to the source we contemplate. We see it in the analysand who accepts her despised thighs, discovering the rejected stone is in fact the corner stone of the new structure she builds and finds building within herself. We see the origin point in the analysand who breaks through to more elbow room, more freedom to create her life instead of obliterate it in Valium, and who gets her own custom-made pictures of the whole, symbols of transcendence like the flowering zinnia. We touch this taproot when we find we can say the confronting word in a session, or risk loving, or keep our mouth shut, let a grudge go; we can hear it in the silence of a flower blooming.

We are in the absolute and the infinite and it is in everything and has many forms. We cannot grasp it or get separated from its presentation in concrete shapes in our daily life. Spiritual practice means being alert to this fact (hence death is so awful and mourning so hard because we have lost the embodied form of the other and must work to find their new form in the infinite). We work to sustain a quality of consciousness attuned to the transcendent in the ordinary. This alertness lends zest to living, a contagious joy.

Our symbols for this whole reality need us in order to evolve and grow beyond us. Our symbols reflect a more complete reality than we can consciously grasp, but which opens us to each day as new. Spiritual work and individuation mean deepening, broadening, clarifying the vessel of our awareness to give adequate expression to what pours itself out on us inexhaustibly. Attuned to this generosity of being, we experience the archetypal and conscious worlds no longer in polar tension. Consciousness turns toward the unconscious and becomes more pliant, more supple, more permeable. Then we can speak in analysis from ourselves more than about ourselves. We can find our depth by being found in the depths. The clinical question links with the spiritual one: How much lightning can we stand?

References

This chapter was originally given as a presentation at a conference on Depth Psychology and Spiritual Practice, sponsored by the C. G. Jung Institute of San Francisco and Deep Streams Zen Institute; and also to the C. G. Jung Institute in Seoul, Korea.

Bettelheim, B. 1982. *Freud and Man's Soul*. New York: Knopf.

Deri, S. K. 1984. *Symbolization and Creativity*. New York: International Universities Press.

Jung, C. G. 1928/1964. The spiritual problem of modern man. In *Civilization in Transition*. Vol. 10 of *Collected Works*. Trans. R. F. C. Hull. New York: Pantheon.

———. 1932/1954. The development of personality. In *The Development of Personality*. Vol. 17 of *Collected Works*. Trans. R. F. C. Hull. New York: Pantheon.

———. 1932/1958. Psychotherapists or the clergy. In *Psychology and Religion: West and East*. Vol. 11 of *Collected Works*. Trans. R. F. C. Hull. New York: Pantheon.

———. 1938/1958. Psychology and religion. In *Psychology and Religion: West and East*. Vol. 11 of *Collected Works*. Trans. R. F. C. Hull. New York: Pantheon.

———. 1940/1959. The psychology of the child archetype. In *The Archetypes and the Collective Unconscious*. Vol. 9.1 of *Collected Works*. Trans. R. F. C. Hull. New York: Pantheon.

———. 1953. *Two Essays on Analytical Psychology*. Vol. 7 of *Collected Works*. Trans. R. F. C. Hull. New York: Pantheon.

———. 1973 and 1975. *Letters*. 2 vols. Eds. Gerhard Adler and Aniela Jaffé. Trans. R. F. C. Hull. Princeton, N.J.: Princeton University Press.

———. 1988. *Nietzsche's Zarathustra*. 2 vols. Ed. James L. Jarrett. Princeton, N.J.: Princeton University Press.

Kakar, S. 2002. Psychoanalysis and Eastern spiritual healing traditions. Lecture, Association for Psychoanalytic Medicine, New York City, April 2.

Kleinman, A. 1988. *Rethinking Psychiatry from Cultural Category to Personal Experience*. New York: Free Press.

———. 1997. Everything that really matters. *Harvard Divinity Bulletin* 26(4).

Levinas, E. 1990. *Nine Talmudic Readings*. Trans. Annette Aronowicz. Indiana: Indiana University Press. I am indebted to Adina Oskowitz whose class paper discusses the Israelites' reception of the Torah, in Psychiatry and Religion 431 Seminar: Jung. New York: Union Theological Seminary, Spring 2002.

Mandela, N. 1994. Inauguration speech. South Africa.

Marion, J-L. 1999. The face: an endless hermeneutics. *Harvard Divinity School Bulletin* 28 (2/3): 9-10.

Neumann, E. 1959. *Art and the Creative Unconscious*. Trans. Ralph Manheim. New York: Pantheon.

Rilke, R. M. 1989. *The Sonnets to Orpheus*. Trans. Leslie Norris and Alan Keele. Columbia, S.C.: Camden House.

Rosenberger, J. W. 2002. Personal communication.

Symington, N. 2001. *The Spirit of Sanity*. London: Karnac.

————. 2002. A *Pattern of Madness*. London: Karnac.

Ulanov, A., and B. Ulanov. 1983/1998. *Cinderella and Her Sisters: The Envied and the Envying*. Einsiedeln, Switzerland: Daimon.

Ulanov, A. B. 1995a/1996. *Spiritual Aspects of Clinical Work*. In *The Functioning Transcendent*, chapter 1. Wilmette, Ill.: Chiron.

————. 1995b/1996. Self-service. In *The Functioning Transcendent*, chapter 8. Wilmette, Ill.: Chiron.

————. 1998/2004. Dreams: passages to a new spirituality. In *Spiritual Aspects of Clinical Work*, chapter 11. Einsiedeln, Switzerland: Daimon.

————. 2001a. *Finding Space: Winnicott, God, and Psychic Reality*. Louisville, Ky.: Westminster John Knox Press.

————. 2001b. *Attacked by Poison Ivy: A Psychological Understanding*. York Beach, Maine: Nicolas-Hays.

————. 2001/2004. After analysis what? In *Spiritual Aspects of Clinical Work*, chapter 17. Einsiedeln, Switzerland: Daimon.

————. 2002. Introduction to *Animal Life in Nature, Myth, and Dreams*, by Elizabeth Caspari. Wilmette, Ill.: Chiron.

Winnicott, D. W. 1962/1965. Ego integration in child development. In *The Maturational Processes and the Facilitating Environment*. New York: International Universities Press.

Zagajewski, A. 2002. *Without End: New and Selected Poems*. Trans. Clare Cavanaugh, Renata Gorczynski, Benjamin Ivry, and C. K. Williams. New York: Farrar, Straus and Giroux.

CHAPTER 4

THE UNSHUTTERED HEART

When planes smash into our city leaving thousands dead, and others orphaned, widowed, or dragooned by grief into the nether zones of mourning, then we are pushed to things eternal. What do we believe, what beliefs have crashed under the weight of catastrophe, what is our vision of life and reality? More particularly, drawing on our life as women, what do we discover about our own resources, our own possible contributions to others in this time of dire need? Collective trauma has taken us down into archaic energy that dismantles life as we knew it.

The philosopher Louis Lavelle tells us in his meditations that when we are hated, and any of us who have traveled abroad recently feel the animosity directed at America, we grab onto what we really believe, as if we had talons curled around the only essential thing left to us that sustains us in the face of adamant hostility (Lavelle 1973, 125).

Any discussion about spiritual life is affected by this collective trauma of 9/11. I emphasize collective because in addition to personal shock, grief, outrage, fear, especially for those of us who were near or in those buildings crashing to the ground, and for those of us who lost someone dear to us, someone irreplaceable and unique, there is the shared witness on television, radio, newspaper, of this attack. Its reverberations still echo through us as a local neighborhood, as a city, as a world. Our personal experience is set within the larger bowl of a shared common experience. Hence any response we make must include a collective as well as a personal dimension.

This terror brings us as citizens on the east coast of the United States right into terrors people suffer in Bosnia, Jerusalem, Ramallah, Baghdad, Tokyo, Belfast, Rwanda, Gujarat. We know not only in imagination, as before, but now through our own body senses what it is to live in terror— the stench of the air, the smarting of the eyes, the skin rash from the smoke, the sound of bodies banging into the ground, the mental confusion of what to do, to run, to stay, how to help. Archaic energies tear up our certainties, dismember our clarity. Even now with order restored on the surface of life, the anticipation of more terror haunts our dreams, or produces symptoms in behavior—like the ten-year-old boy, a macho ice-hockey athlete whose father was killed on 9/11, now is also a frightened boy if home alone or in bed alone, who appears at his mother's bedside in the middle of the night wanting to climb into safety because "I heard a noise." Another boy of ten wails with prescience beyond his years, why does this have to come into our lives! It is true; this generation of children is marked in a way none of the rest of us are by this collective event of terror.

From spiritual practice, we also know that prayer thins our defenses, and dissolves our divisions from one another. We see on our neighbor's face, she who holds views as passionately as we do yet on the exact opposite side, the same emotions we feel, of compassion, confusion, fear, determination so like our own. She whose views we opposed is also now our sister. How can we hold the sameness and difference between us? Praying annuls our ability to numb out the terrors of the world. That hungry child in Somalia looks at us with our own child's face; that woman abandoned to the rape camp has the face of our niece, or daughter. Prayer is dangerous: it opens the shutters of the heart; it leads us gently but inexorably to live here and now in this new century with all its shiftings of power, with an unshuttered heart.

What is that like, to live with an unshuttered heart? And what is it like particularly for women? Do we as one half of the human race know things that we do not know consciously, feel things at the depth of our being that we want to bring to the surface of consciousness to contribute to the conversation of all the differing views among us in this pivotal time? The mother of the hockey player, whose husband was killed the second day on his new job, sought out seeing an analyst in order, she said, not to skip over something essential in her shock after the 9/11 experience. A competent woman, she knew somewhere in herself she was surviving for their two children, but that she could not be close to anyone else's grief for her husband. She could not join with his parents in their loss, or with any of his good friends. It was too much, she said, to add their grief to hers. Only two years later does it come up. Her surviving, competent heart slowly thaws its frozen state, slowly opens toward becoming unshuttered.

To reach this depth level where things come up from below, where light is glimpsed in the deepest dark into which we get plunged, we need to look at the psyche and at religion. For there we come upon emotional facts or primordial images or instinctive responses that we do not invent, or force on ourselves as something we should do or be or think. Psychologically, our ego comes upon what transcends it. Religiously, we speak of an autonomous presence meeting us. Independent of our conscious viewpoint, It is there, objective, making us, who usually assume we are the subjects looking out on the objects of our attention, see that truly we are the objects of this bigger presence. It is the subject.

Religion and Psychology

Religions over the ages have named this presence—Elohim, Yahweh, Suchness, Thatness, It, Allah, God. We speak of it as infinite, unoriginated immensity, as the Holy. Psychoanalysts speak of the objective psyche, the unconscious, the core self, the true self, the mysterious power in us to create or defeat relationship to life. From a religious point of view, we can understand this psyche that addresses us from beyond our control in our dreams at night and in our symptoms that interrupt our day, as another kind of flesh through which God touches us. There is no dimension of human existence that can close itself off from the Holy. God can speak to us through our psyche just as surely as through our social movements, politics, historical events, our friends, our corporate worship, scripture, our theological doctrines and symbols. From a psychoanalytic point of view, we can understand religious tradition as the impulse to name and converse with this transcendent dimension of existence and to keep inquiring into it and telling each other what it is.

This depth that transcends our consciousness is there for all of us and connects our individually different lives. In addition, as women, whether we are single, married, celibate, sexually active, mothers or free of children, aunts, grandmothers, great-grandmothers, lesbian, straight, orphaned, widowed, partnered or solitary, old or young, we ask, is there something we share in common as women that we learn from these depths that precedes and transcends our differences? Is it possible to speak of a feminine mode of being?

Traditionally, the answer was yes. Jaroslav Pelikan writes of Beatrice as "the lady leading me to God," "pointing beyond herself to the Highest Wisdom . . . the Primal Love . . . the High Artificer who fashioned this suffering city" (1990, 2). For Boethius, the feminine "Philosophia," who came to console him as nurse and teacher, says to him, discover your wound if you would be healed (ibid., 39), a truth that underlies all schools of psychoanalysis. The Church is described in Dante as Bride of Christ, and also as "sweet lyre, bark of Peter, the good plant, the beautiful garden" (ibid., 80). Mary is imaged as Queen of Heaven, the new mother of all living who opens the wound and pierces it; she turns the key and becomes the dwelling place for the Divine (ibid., 102, 104, 111). Sophia is personified divine wisdom.

The Indian spirituality of Sri Aurobindo emphasizes Shakti as the force of the divine mother who brings the spirit of intellect down into practical living, joining mythopoetic thinking and scientific reasoning, recognizing both as essential to full living, again another truth that underlies psychoanalysis. Knowing our finiteness puts us in a place to experience the infinite whose spirit transcends our religious differences.

In Kabbalistic mysticism of Judaism when the vessels God made to hold the light shattered, the feminine Shekinah went into exile. Spiritual practice turns on the return and remarrying of the feminine Shekinah with the ten Sefiroth of the Tree of Life that reveal the transformations and movements within God that affect us in our world. We participate in the Tikun, the recovery of the feminine to the divine, for in the Zohar the Torah is the feminine consort of Yahweh. The Shekinah must make love with the masculine part of God to heal the broken Tree of Life and unify God. The opening of the Sabbath is the welcoming of Shekinah into our house.

In Sufi mysticism of Islam, "it is in the Image of the Creative Feminine that contemplation can apprehend the highest manifestation of God, namely creative divinity. . . . the spirituality of Islamic mystics is led . . . to the apparition of the Eternal Womanly as an Image of the Godhead, because in her he contemplates the secret of the compassionate God, whose creative act is the liberation of beings" (Corbin 1969/1997, 159).

Primordial images of the feminine abound in religious traditions, in myths all over the world, including the destroying power of this feminine mode of being—as witch, furies, siren, hag, whore of Babylon, devouring mother, Kali (see Neumann 1955, 147-208). We see in the use of these human images for the divine not an inferior spirituality but a superior one, placing the human being as the most important thing in the universe, calling each of us to responsibility for healing the universe and the divine spirit in it.

More recently, the answer was a definite No to conceiving a feminine mode of being. Those of us involved in feminist movements can well remember firm rejection of all images of the feminine because they had been fastened onto actual women and slapped them into traps, prescribing what they should be or should not be. Images of the Great Mother now applied to you and me as we gave birth to children and felt we should automatically know all about mothering in its positive meanings when in fact we were still reeling from the birth experience and the ambivalence of response to this wondrous child at our breast who stole from us not only our sleep but as if our consciousness too. One woman, newly a mother by adoption, said she lost her standpoint so ably held in running her business where she scheduled tasks and proceeded with orderly suc-cess. In the face of her newly arrived son, it was as if she slipped under-water and everything could dissolve any moment in response to his needs. She wanted to respond, loved it, but felt she was caught in a current of maternity barely keeping her head above water.

The problem is not the images or conceiving a mode of being human as feminine. Problems arise when the gap between the symbolic and con-crete levels of existence collapses. Awareness of these images as symbols for ways of being in relation to reality rescues all of us by reinstating the symbolic as a viable order of being, not allowing it to be taken literally or applied like a tourniquet to women and men. Symbols grasp reality that cannot be approached any other way. They make a bridge to ways of per-ceiving that free our imaginations from concretistic readings of the inef-fable. In the attacks of 9/11, we have lived firsthand the disastrous consequences when the symbol for God is taken literally and acted out concretely. Only by such a reading of obedience could a person believe he was doing Allah's will to kill himself and everyone on his plane as he flew it into an office building full of innocent civilians (Ulanov 2002, 198).

The Feminine Mode of Being

At the beginning of this century and millennium, we are on the crest of the new, I believe: neither to reinstate traditional images of what women should be, nor to disavow the symbols for the feminine as only entrapping; neither to return to a matriarchal universe, nor to stay stuck complaining about a patriarchal society. We have a chance to see that both feminine and masculine ways of being belong to each and to all of us, to women and men. The feminine mode of being symbolizes ways of being human, human potentialities; it is not a prescription for actual women. Indeed, in some actual men, their leading patterns of being may display this feminine mode more than the patterns associated with a masculine mode of being. Some women may display more ease with masculine patterns of doing and relating than men. Each of us improvises our own identity and what supports and defeats it, but for all of us, whenever we mix up the symbolic and the concrete, we lose both.

This returns us to the topic at hand: how to respond spiritually and psychologically as women to the trauma of 9/11. Have we fallen into the gap between symbol and concrete reality so that our God-images completely collapse as not tough enough to survive this suffering? Has the gap between symbol and concrete living caved in so that now we, too, like the hijackers, are inflated with our divine mission to destroy the enemy? What has happened to our spiritual practice? Has it fallen apart, into the gap, because God did not protect us, but deserted us? Has our spiritual practice strengthened since the attacks as our deepest perception, that from it we might bring something to help heal the suffering all around us?

Associated with feminine consciousness and spirit is the downward going road, down into the midst of things, and I believe this is the direction of Spirit in our time. No longer can we find Spirit up above the tumult of grief and anger after 9/11, in some eternal, unchanging purity of truth or reason. Ours is an age of being plunged into matter—of politics, social problems, family strife, sexual uncertainty—to find what matters, how to hold onto a truth in the midst of many people's truths, how to love God and love our neighbor in the midst of vying loyalties. The feminine mode of being is always linked with linking, knitting up, being there for one another, not at a distance guided by universal principles of justice, but rather finding justice in the midst of conflicting wounds and particular contexts.

For example, religious terms that are natural to us may offend others and suddenly we find ourselves in bristling conflict. Kingdom of God may be anathema to those living under tyranny, or under the rule of men only. It is noteworthy that the first thing the Taliban did in coming to power in Afghanistan was to subjugate the feminine as if it could be locked up. Music was banned; men must grow beards; women must be completely hidden under the burka, forbidden school, work, or even to go out of the house without a male relative. Speaking of God and the good as light and the evil as black or dark may be anathema to those of us of color and those of us for whom the dark is the saving place and the light a scorching, bleaching glare (Ulanov 1996, 211).

The feminine mode goes right into these controversies; we get nowhere by rising above them to some generalized agreement. We go down further, further down, for at the heart of our love for God, connections to each other grow among us. The feminine mode directs us into connection, linking, communion with each other, being for and with each other, accepting our body, the animal root-impulse in us, the ambiguities and mess of living, going into the wound, including all the parts, the bad ones we fear, the ones we suffer, the broken parts, not fixing but listening, knowing the new accumulates slowly out of the slime, suddenly then to be born and address us with what we could not have consciously produced by ourselves. In religious mystics, where the feminine mode of being dominates in men or women, their symbols stress continuity, not contradiction; organic growth, not fiat; conjunction of opposites, not one demoting or annihilating of the other (see Bynum 1986; see Ulanov 1988/2000, chapter 3).

Spirituality grown from this depth proves tough enough to face the archaic furies that erupt in terrorist attacks, in violence done to children, done in prisons, done to women in their own homes. This spirituality that grows from deep roots is not airy-fairy, above the rigors of life, but sturdy, potent enough to recognize God in a Russian woman's act of simple kindness when she gives a cup of water to her enemy, a German soldier, wounded in the famous battle of Stalingrad (Grossman 1985). In this profound place truth is not abstract but all mixed into events, like the blood-food of a woman's body for her baby, like her sexual body which takes the other in, and like her astonishing grasp and utterance of truth when her unshuttered heart connects with light in the depths.

Identification

Many patterns of living are associated with a feminine mode of being human—heroic, archaic, wise, enduring, vengeful, formidable. A lot of research has been done on what is associated to this feminine mode of being, its active doing and being, its patterns of relationship to others and to oneself, and to the divine (see Guntrip 1970, 257-71; Ulanov 1971, chapter 9). The force of identification in psychological and spiritual life stands out as prominent. The psychoanalyst Winnicott speaks of the feminine element as a sense of being at the core of ourselves, identified with being, before doing—or, if not, then we cannot find ourselves and feel instead maimed, as one woman in analysis expressed by saying, the part I identify with as me is unworthy, like the red blood mess to be aborted. An active feminine mode of relating revolves around being one with an other, not being separate and relating to an other, but as if dwelling in and for the other, as if one. Lacking that indwelling in the foundation of our self, we feel isolated, unhooked up, not quite in life. The feminine mode of going on being, believing in ties that bind, blood ties, sustains a growing into a tradition, into a friendship, into a creative attitude or act or, again, if not, then we fall into illness and feel the life thread of who we are has been snipped by violence, or another's refusal to see us as a subject (Winnicott 1971, chapter 5; see also Ulanov 1981/2001, chapter 4). Identification lodges us psychologically in being.

Identification plays a principal role in our spirituality, too. For we all identify with images we create of God, and feel they make a bridge between us and the divine, on a personal level as well as in our religious traditions (see Ulanov 1986/2002, 164-85). Our personal images for God are idiosyncratic, bespeaking who we are at our core and the ones with whom we have loved and identified. A child says, God is Horse; a woman analysand says, God's heaven is like a wonderful dinner party of many foods, costumes, people from all over the world engaged in interesting, vital conversations. A woman priest describes conducting the Christian Eucharist as a dance in which the celebrants have different parts and all circle around the Holy. A male priest says he imagines God like a big black momma sitting in a swivel chair tuning in all parts of the world through her many television sets. Another analysand says for her God is a strict scorekeeper, totting up when she fails and when she succeeds in living up to her values.

Our God-images are also unconscious, to be discovered, as that around which our whole psyche and life in the world revolve. It may be our love for our child, or lover; it may be our drinking problem, or our obsession with food; it may be our inferiority complex that makes us overly ambitious, or our abiding sense that God is somehow always present. Whether positive or negative, something acts as the center of our existence.

Identification as a psychological function can act positively in bringing the Vast and the All near to us in our images for God so we can pray and experience relationship on a personal level with the transcendent. Or identification can act negatively, as I believe it did in the terrorist attacks or in any place where we forget these images are symbols and instead take them as literal descriptions of the Holy. When we forget the gap between symbol pointing to an ineffable reality we cannot grasp, and concrete reality we live, then we fall into identification with our personal image of God. Jesus is how we see him. Anyone who does not identify with our image is damned. We also identify our religious tradition with our personal image for God and get inflated. We speak, then, as if for the whole religious tradition and will ostracize or persecute those who do not also identify God with our image for God.

Our spiritual practice benefits greatly from asking ourselves, what is my personal God-image? And to inquire, is there also a God-image I am not aware of that shows itself clearly as the center around which my life revolves, such as money, getting the children in the right school, living in the best neighborhood, exhausting myself in service to others, endlessly suffering an old psychological wound? What are those subjective God-images for each of us?

Our religious traditions offer us official images for God. In Judaism God is pictured as refuge and rock (Ps. 91, RSV), as fashion designer making priestly garments (Exod. 28:6-43, RSV), as wings that shelter us (Pss. 61:4; 63:7, RSV). Christian texts picture God as dinner party host, woman searching for the lost coin, as the one we visited in prison (Luke 14:12-23; 15:8-10, Matt. 25:36b, RSV). In Islam the Qur'an speaks of itself not as a fixed text but as *kitab*, expressing the responsiveness of Allah to the current situation. Of divine origin and great fluidity, *kitab* means access or insight into knowledge, wisdom, sovereignty of God. "The Qur'an lives in an eternal present, addressing itself not to a time-bound context but to the moment at hand" (Madigan 2001, 184).

Each of our traditions abounds with images for the Holy. It helps our spiritual practice to ask which traditional God-images we gravitate to, which ones repel us. But these wondrous God-images of our traditions still remain human constructs. We risk not only psychological inflation but also idolatry, blasphemy, when we fall into identification with them and identify them with God. Then we speak not only for all of our religious tradition, as if our personal God-image is what Islam or Judaism proclaims. But worse; now we fall into identification with God. All the might, power, archaic energy associated with the transcendent realm beyond our ego comes rushing through us. Like corks bobbing on a sea, like flotsam caught in a rushing river, like riders on runaway horses, we are in the grip of primordial images for God. We are swept away in our identification, acting as if we are Allah or Yahweh or Jesus. Thus Jim Jones of Jonestown directs his followers into mass suicide. In Tokyo, the sect's leader lets loose sarin gas in a public subway in the name of some religious ideal. In New York City, hijackers fly planes into the World Trade Center as if to do Allah's will.

When we forget our images are images, we lose reality. Identification is necessary for life and relationships; it is the energy linking self to other and to God; the image illuminates the sacred goal of life lived in the here and now. But identification with the image can pull us into an undertow of archetypal energy where we forget our own humanity and fall into a madness of personal or social inflation, believing we alone are the agent of social justice, religious duty, divine vengeance.

Disidentification

When the gap between symbol and the reality it points to collapses, we lose our God-images and live in the dark night of the soul. This may happen because of life's harshness, because our child dies, or our youth is used up in a refugee camp, or we are shoved on a train to a death camp, or we are hacked to death by a machete because of our religious belief. It may also happen because our God-images, both personal and traditional, have been used up. They have succeeded so well, we have exhausted them, because they are only human vessels. The ritual that always conveyed God to us fails now to do so (see Ulanov 1991/2005, 90-92). Prayers that felt meaningful, now do not. We reach the end of Jacob's ladder and a gap looms between us and the Holy we had lassoed into our prayers and rituals.

When the terrorists of 9/11 attacked this city, for many of us our God-images came crashing down. They seemed so puny, so ineffective, so unable to encompass and make sense of the horror, the untold suffering that followed the attacks. Loss of one's God-images can happen to beginners in religion and to very sophisticated practitioners. One woman, a skilled spiritual director who had finished analysis some years before, came back for some sessions. To bolster her work after 9/11 she took a trauma workshop led by a man who gave examples from the horrors people had endured in places all over the world. In response, she dreamed three dreams that were so traumatic to her she could not even write them down. She put them away but then fell into a depression that lasted the summer months. With all her skills and her deep faith, she felt overcome by powerlessness in the face of evil. She was immobilized.

Many of us can get stuck here. We disidentify from the very images that before gave us life, brought God close to us. We lose our God-images or they seem not to help us, and we plunge into the dark with no bridge to God. To deny this has happened will not make this state go away but only isolate us; to cover it up by restoring our former religious persona will only produce a brittle spirituality controlled by rules. We cannot dodge this religious crisis by reducing it to some personal neurosis. We can only face into the unknowable, consent to be taken down into the dark to see what greets us there.

This woman called for an appointment to tell me the dreams. She said, I am not afraid to die; it's that I do not know how to live in relation to this terror that afflicts all of us. I named this terror collective evil. It reminded me of what a Brazilian woman told me when I lectured there in the late summer, that the gap between rich and poor was so great and seemingly so insurmountable despite the fact that Brazil has one of the best economies in South America, that she felt oppressed by a big, impersonal, objective, economic problem that made her feel guilty, because she did not know what she could do to lessen the gap between rich and poor. She felt helpless.

The woman's three dreams were: (1) I am in a house; my father is upstairs. Someone comes in and sets wild dogs on him. I cannot do anything to stop it. He will be torn to bits. So I allowed it to happen. (2) A man is being violently beaten. I am unable to do anything. I know him but do not remember now who he is. It is a torture to hear it. (3) A male figure is lying on the ground covered with fecal material oozing out of every pore. No matter how much I wipe away his face, more and more comes out. In all three dreams she felt powerless to combat the evil that burst in.

She had few personal associations to the dreams except that her father was a person she loved and who had made her feel safe as a child. It was as if people were harming each other seemingly without personal connection to them. At this collective, impersonal level our personal defenses do not help. This is bigger, over us instead of from us. If we try to reduce this violence to our personal problem, we fall into depression as she did, a kind of reverse inflation, a deflation where we feel as if we have caused this level of violence, or Brazil's rich-poor gap. Yet if we fail to find our personal relation to this collective problem, then we live afraid, helpless.

Her personal question was, how do I relate to this? What do I do spiritually? Once she had spoken the dreams to another person, to me in our session, she felt released from their power and she could take care of herself, getting anti-depressant medication to help her over the hump and gather her energies to work on what the dreams displayed—helplessness in the face of inhumanity. It is a mistake, I believe, to treat such images only on the personal level, as if we somehow author this senseless violence. It is also a mistake to ignore the personal connection to this collective level of evil, as if we have nothing whatsoever to do with it.

The hinge between personal and collective, the decisive connecting point that allows us to participate and not be overwhelmed, is to find the one little spot where we do contribute to a collective atmosphere that allows such senseless violence to be done to people as if they are not subjects in their own right, entitled to respect and dignity (see chapter 6). This woman dreaming of senseless violence found she needed to attend to her own aggression in ways specific to her personal life. Aggression used, disciplined, aimed, and sustained, does not turn destructive. When she neglects this energy, she feels herself sliding toward depression. Examples of her doing this work of integrating her aggression with her affection are acknowledging to her cousin that they could engage in a vigorous discussion without violent rejection of each other, even though they held diametrically opposed views about Vatican II and the Latin Mass. She used aggression with her husband who often does not hear what she wants; she made connection by asserting her preferences clearly. She startled herself by blunt four-letter language to a close friend's son who was falling into alcoholism. She said, If you don't handle this drinking problem, then you f*** up your life, and got his attention more effectively than anyone else had.

More pertinent still was her examining her lust to win an argument with a close friend, to trounce him, go over the top. She searched and found she felt wounded by his disregarding her terror in the face of his giant dogs. "I feel cornered and then I want to win," she said. She saw the connection to international conflicts that go back generations, even centuries, when one party disregards the self-esteem and boundaries of safety of the other, and then the other wants revenge. That was the hinge to collective violence in herself, not to overlook the wound to narcissism but to tend it and protect it. Then we do not have to retaliate. She told her friend when they met, No dogs. In addition, she accepted an invitation to sit on a council to deal with abuse in the Catholic Church, and elected with two other spiritual directors to go on regular retreats to pray for peace in the face of world violence. She said, I let my defenses go, I let go of my defenses, to let what God wants of me to show itself.

She could not have reached this sense of contributing to the world's suffering if she had hopped over her own unused aggression. But integrating her own aggression led her to go on further, to let her defenses go into God's hands and take up action and prayer to help collective issues. She was taken down by trauma into the dark of personal depression and of collective terror; her God-images and her ego felt dismantled. Once she differentiated what was personal and what was impersonal, what piece belonged to her and required her response and what pieces were beyond her to let go into God's hands, she found herself at a deeper level than she had lived before, knit up again, her heart unshuttered, open to the world.

This woman helps us see our own tasks. What are our God-images, both personal and in our faith traditions? Which ones do we identify with? We, too, will be taken down into the dark space of losing those

God-images, disidentifying with them. Can we locate our particular piece, the hinge between personal and collective evil? To tend to that piece, to find our bearings allows us to do what is necessary for our own recovery, and is the means through which we open to the world and want to give our share to collective healing. She felt at that depth not so much that she found God, but that, once again, God found her.

Differentiating and Attending

All of us have images of God. In trauma and/or in successfully using up these images, we disidentify with them. We lose our images of the center of reality and how we matter to it. We are sometimes lost. We find in the feminine mode of being our capacity to take this downward going road to spaces both psychological and spiritual beneath the structures we have built up personally and together in religious tradition. We see vividly the gap between symbol and the reality to which it points. Here, whether Jew, Muslim, Christian, Hindu, Buddhist, atheist, we are all together refugees who cannot cross this gap from our side to God. A sense of communion can grow between us. We share this common experience in our different psyches and our different religious faiths. We consent to see different, even opposing views of God without rejecting each other as a result. We accept our not-knowing state.

In this space of dismantling of our certainties, something crosses over the gap from God's side. Something both psychological and spiritual meets us here and slowly knits us together at a level deeper than before. The psyche will respond with images, with experiences we do not invent or manufacture. We find our particular hinge between personal life and collective traumas facing humanity and that allows us to contribute to healing, in ourselves and in others. Something appears. Our job is to pay attention. That is the religious instinct—the right attitude—of responsive attentiveness to what appears psychically. We do identify with our God-images and then are forced by life experiences to disidentify with them. From the religious side, we see we do not get to God from our side. The Holy comes to us, crossing the gap in new insight into the languages and rituals of our traditions and sometimes in braiding new traditions. God gives us new God-images showing us what we can do and be, and what we can let go into God's hands. We learn, as Jung says, that "transformation leads from the depths to the heights, from the bestially archaic and infantile to the mystical *homo maximus*" (we could say *femina maxima*) (Jung 1963, 173).

We learn that transformation of our identities and of the world only occurs if all different parts are included—our God-images and God, our fears and highest aspirations, our helplessness and our awe, our sister's opposite view and our own. We learn that God comes to us from God's side but only becomes real to us through human experience, alone and with each other. The human vessel so small, so breakable, is the place the transcendent seeks to become real.

References

This chapter was originally delivered as a lecture under the auspices of Brick Presbyterian Church and Auburn Theological Seminary, New York City, February 2003. I was asked to address the question of how women specifically could respond spiritually and psychologically to the trauma of 9/11.

Aurobindo, S. 2000. *Adventure of Consciousness*. Saridabad, India: Thomson Press.

Bynum, C. W. 1986. Introduction: the complexity of symbols. In *Gender and Religion: On the Complexity of Symbols*. Eds. C. W. Bynum, S. Harrell, and P. Richman. Boston: Beacon.

Corbin, H. 1969/1997. *Alone with the Alone: Creative Imagination in the Sufism of Ibn 'Arabi*. Princeton, N.J.: Princeton University Press.

Grossman, V. 1985. *Life and Fate*. Trans. Robert Chandler. New York: Harper.

Guntrip, H. 1970. *Schizoid Phenomena, Object Relations, and the Self*. New York: International Universities Press.

Jung, C. G. 1963. *Psychology and Alchemy*. Vol. 12 of *Collected Works*. Trans. R. F. C. Hull. New York: Pantheon.

Lavelle, L. 1973. *The Dilemma of Narcissus*. Trans. William Gairdner. New York: Humanities Press.

Madigan, D. A. 2001. *The Qur'an's Self-Image*. Princeton, N.J.: Princeton University Press.

Neumann, E. 1955. *The Great Mother*. Trans. Ralph Manheim. Princeton, N.J.: Princeton University Press.

Pelikan, J. 1990. *Eternal Feminines*. New Brunswick, N.J.: Rutgers University Press.

Ulanov, A., and B. Ulanov. 1982. *Primary Speech: A Psychology of Prayer*. Louisville, Ky.: Westminster John Knox.

Ulanov, A. B. 1971. *The Feminine in Jungian Psychology and in Christian Theology*. Evanston, Ill.: Northwest\ern University Press.

———. 1981/2001. *Receiving Woman: Studies in the Psychology and Theology of the Feminine*. Einsiedeln, Switzerland: Daimon.

———. 1986/2002. *Picturing God*. Einsiedeln, Switzerland: Daimon.

———. 1988/2000. *The Wisdom of the Psyche*. Einsiedeln, Switzerland: Daimon.

———. 1991/2005. The holding Self: Jung and the desire for being. In *Spirit in Jung*, chapter 4. Einsiedeln, Switzerland: Daimon.

———. 1994/1998. *The Female Ancestors of Christ*. Einsiedeln, Switzerland: Daimon.

———. 1996. Vicissitudes of living in the Self. In *The Functioning Transcendent*, chapter 10. Wilmette, Ill.: Chiron.

———. 2002. Religion's role in the psychology of terrorism. In *Jungian Reflections on September 11*, 195-202. Eds. Luigi Zola and Donald Williams. Einsiedeln, Switzerland: Daimon.

Winnicott, D. W. 1971. *Playing and Reality*. London: Tavistock.

CHAPTER 5

SPIRITUAL OBJECTS: FROM SELF TO SOUL AND BACK AGAIN

Space

The space-in-between strikes a familiar chord in most of us, whether we speak of the space between analyst and analysand, self and other, soul and God, group and culture. This space displays a quality all its own: vibrant, pliant, actual, ample, substantial. Unless infiltrated by madness, we like this space; we thrive in it; its buoyancy supports our becoming.

What then do we become, as a gift from this space? A self, a symbolic creature, a citizen in the world with others, a contributor to reality, a soul. Most schools of depth psychology mean by "self," the totality of the personality; Jung includes cosmic and divine images in his notion of Self as the center of the whole psyche, both conscious and unconscious, in contrast to ego as our sense of I-ness as the center of consciousness. Soul, in traditional religious language, stands forth as an entity distinct from the body but embodied in the body; it is the doorway to God, or whatever name we choose for the transcendent. This door can never be locked; through it we can be laid hold of any time. The psyche, with its mental processes, enables or disables us to be a person in relation to self, to others, and to transcendent reality; the soul is our willingness to do so, to be so, and thus includes desire. For those of us following Buddhist practice, where the whole concept of self is questioned, Eckhart's words are apt: "the more deeply we are our true selves, the less self is in us" (cited in Hirshfield 1998, 140).

For us to step fully into the space-in-between enables our living straight-out, with all our hearts, minds, souls, and might; indeed, giving what God asks of Israel in Deuteronomy 6, and Jesus asks in the first commandment, so primary, it is called the great commandment. Whether religious or not, all of us want this wholehearted living, this livingness that makes us feel blessed every day and full of gratitude in response. But this space itself is empty, not as void or lack, but as fecund, fertile, engendering. Like the Negative Capability Keats recommends to poets and Bion demands of analysts, where we cease an "irritable reaching after facts" and accept the character of no self that "is everything and nothing" (Hirshfield 1998, 170), this space is nothing from which everything may emerge. Lao Tzu describes its necessity:

> We put thirty spokes together and call it a wheel;
> But it is on the space where there is nothing that the utility of the wheel depends.
> We turn clay to make a vessel;
> But it is on the space where there is nothing that the utility of the vessel depends.
> We pierce doors and windows to make a house;
> And it is on these spaces where there is nothing that the utility of the house depends.

Therefore just as we take advantage of what is, we should recognize the utility of what is not (Lao Tzu cited by Jung 1952/1960, 919; see also Geoghegan 2002, 47).

What is not in this space-in-between is set content, rules, prescribed activity. Yet the space is inhabited by lively impulse and acute alertness. Winnicott makes us see this space as beginning with infants playing with their mothers, and soon to be playing with their beloved favorite object, the one that makes transitions happen. We are familiar with these important passages from absolute to relative dependence, from private instinct-backed unconscious to a growing sense of I in relation to other, from creating a symbol to relating to the reality it symbolizes. In this in-between space illusion springs up that external reality really does match internal need and wish, hence conveying a symbol of the whole, the whole of reality holding us. This illusion allows our ego to rest from keeping inner and outer realities together, from tasks and reality testing, to let go into the adventures of play. Winnicott writes of the child displaying in play with the beloved bear, or doll or blanket, the union already known with the mothering one as the child is separating into its own self (Winnicott 1971, chapter 1).

The means or the accompaniment of these transitions is the transitional object. Winnicott investigates such objects in the lives of infants and children. Here is a lovely description by a mother of her three-year-old son at nursery school: "What do I see when I observe Christopher with his thumb in his mouth and his 'bah bah' (blanket) in his hand? He shuts out the outside. Stands firm. Regroups. Watches. Recharges. Prepares. Then he takes his thumb out of his mouth, stretches out his arm, and says, 'Here you go, Mom,' and gives me his rag. Then he runs off to join in." On another occasion, when she asks, "Do you talk to your 'bah bah?'" he replies, "No, it loves me." She wonders, Should my "bah bah" be trying to make conscious contact with God?

Adults and Transitional Objects That Become Spiritual Objects

I want to look into transitional objects in the lives of adults, both in ordinary life and in the clinical setting, and how spiritual objects grow out of them. Just as Freud said that it was his fate to discover what every nursemaid knows—the sexual lives of children—and it was Winnicott's fate to discover what every parent knows—that their children create a unique favorite object, whether blanket, bear, or doll as their soul's companion—so it was astounding to me to see in my far-flung travels this past year, that transitional objects belong to every size and age of person—teenagers, grown-up men and women. The airports are full of them! And often disguised as belonging to their children. One father I suspected of trying to pawn off the stuffed animal he clutched as really the possession of his young son, but the way he held the bear revealed his own special relation to it. Standing in line for hours on entering Cuba, a middle-aged woman three people behind me held a big blue rabbit. Because of the long wait, we all got talking to each other. "Nice bunny," I said. She smiled and rubbed her nose on its fur. My son, recently back from Buenos Aires, said on his plane a woman arrived with a bear in its own Louis Vuitton bag; the bear spent the ten-hour trip on her lap.

The *New York Times* presents a love letter by the famous athlete Michael Jordan, addressed to "Dear Basketball." It begins:

> It's been almost 28 years since the first day we met. 28 years since I saw you in the back of our garage. . . . Then I started seeing you around the neighborhood and watching you on television . . . I started to wonder . . . We hung out a few times. The more I got to know you, the more I liked you. And as life would have it, when I finally got really interested in you . . . you left me off the varsity. You told me I wasn't good enough. I was crushed. I was hurt. I think I even cried. Then I wanted you more than ever. So I practiced. I hustled . . . Coach Smith was teaching me how to love you. . . . In some respects, you've become my life. My passion. My motivation. My inspiration. You're my biggest fan and my harshest critic. You're my dearest friend and my strongest ally. . . . Let me say it for the world to hear. Thank you. Thank you, Basketball . . . for everything. . . . I know I'm not the only one who loves you. . . . But I also know what we had was unique . . . special. I love you, Basketball. . . . Much love and respect, Michael Jordan. (*New York Times*, Sunday, April 20, 2003)

We can hear in this love song that this transitional object has grown into much more, what I would call a spiritual object. It reveals to its composer what life is all about, what he loves, to whom he belongs. All adult transitional objects bear this spiritual potential, I suggest.

I have seen adults manage the chasm of grief through an object that can be called transitional. Sometimes the object is one that was already shared with the lost loved one. One widow, whose husband died unexpectedly after a "successful" surgery, attributed to her husband the capacity to play, to take Saturdays as unplanned, to go out for lunch, have a martini, take a nap, go to a movie, or into galleries. With him, she shared a bear called George, whose permanently five-year-old personality was robust, assertive, pugnacious, thinking he knows everything. George loves cannons, cymbals, bells, she said; he should play them all and conduct the *1812 Overture!* She describes how George's vivid presence invites others to join in the play. When she and her late husband were traveling in Asia, his secretary faxed that George had moved into his desk and his business of advising about stocks. George is yelling, Buy! Sell! Hold! the fax read; George is buying Havana cigars with her husband's credit card! Recalling George's exploits in the analytical session invited her into playing around with her grief, so colossal that she had just blocked it out for two years. When she then came for treatment, the grief was as fresh as the morning the hospital called to say her husband had died. Aspects of her husband, and herself, and their relationship were conveyed in George. Now she played with him anew, saying he "needed lots of encouragement because he is one of those endearing but bossy, frequently in error but never in doubt types, so he gets himself into lots of jams." She hugged George a lot, needing affection, and was then able to yield to the huge grief for lost lovemaking that always followed the preamble of affection.

Another widow found and created a new object from a Christmas gift from one of her children, as her husband, much beloved, was entering a long day's dying. The son said, you take care of Pop and everyone; here is this bear to take care of you. The son was a grown young man but nonetheless inaugurated the sense of fun when he exclaimed, this bear jumped off the shelf in F. A. O. Schwarz toy store when I went looking for your present. He just leaped right into my arms! Her husband entered into the game by volunteering the name Pythagoras in response to her musings about the personality of this bear as a mathematician, meditating on things eternal, the structures of the universe, the numinosity of numbers. After her husband's death, the bear then entered the space of her loss, not to deny it, nor to substitute for the husband, but to companion her in this emptiness. The woman reported that the bear kept her sane, able to weep and yell and rage, and go about her daily life. The bear, she said, kept her connected to creative spirit. Making a pun, she said, in the face of the unbearable she could bear it; in the face of nothingness, she could live willingly in the land of the living. The bear carried her capacity to love.

The woman with George also illustrates how a transitional object comes into being in relation to transference to the analytic process. Some months after the play with George renewed, which allowed her a way to enter her grief and not be drowned, to talk about play with her much loved husband and not dissociate in order to survive his loss, she bought a new stuffed animal, "a large very soft rabbit with floppy ears, very cuddly; I feel at home with the face." She named him Basil. In contrast to George, she said, who is definitely his own person and in charge of the bedroom, the Boss, Basil is an intellectual, sensitive sort of name, slightly effete, and works well with my emotions with which George is acutely uncomfortable. Basil, she said, is the be-ing part of life, a broad side of emotions that tempers intellect. Basil gives advice: just to let the feelings wash over me and without being critical and demanding of explanations. Basil helps with her sexual loss. "Basil is particularly soft and comforting. I lie flat on my back with B on top of me. He has floppy arms that almost look like penises which invariably fall on my breasts and it feels wonderful. I think of anything I can with [my husband] to help me get through it. Part of me doesn't want to get through it. I want it to continue to see if concentration can make it real in my imagination."

Here she is using Basil, I believe, not just to survive the loss, but also to preserve the state of grief in which something can be created that restores her love with her husband in a new symbol. She likened waking with Basil face to face, with the past awakenings with her husband who clearly was also her lover; they would awaken with arms and legs entwined. "With your head on the pillow," she said, "you only see one eye of the other person which is funny and we'd laugh. Basil with his one eye, I swear, looks like my husband. It was fun and very comforting. I like sleeping with Basil. I don't think George minds as long as he can order Basil about." This relaxation was connected to our work: she said, "I exported a sense of permission from our session yesterday . . . it is okay to have these feelings—whatever they are—and it doesn't matter what they are. Never felt that way before. Never felt that any of my emotions that are remotely pleasurable are okay. It's very liberating. Felt like a monumental weight was taken off me . . . amazing . . . like the birth of an infant."

A cluster of characteristics stands out about these transitional objects: they play a pivotal role in the space of waiting (in line in Cuba), the space of growing skills (the dear basketball), of recharging (the three-year-old at nursery school), of negotiating loss (the widows). These objects are actual, a definite entity that interfaces with the material world. These objects are not-me, but located in the world. We possess them, they mirror us as subjective objects (that is, they reflect us back to us), and they exist objectively. We experience dependence on these objects and they accept it; we invest them with our deepest needs that find shelter there. We are absolutely committed to the personalities of our objects; they are not exchangeable.

These objects help us process our inner life. In Bion's terms we put into the objects raw beta elements—the undigested bits of experience that initially can only be dealt with by expulsion; and our experience of the object—the bah bah, George, the bunny—helps convert the bits into alpha elements, that is, owned feelings, thoughts, images, that Hanna

Segal tells us then "lend themselves to storage in memory, understanding, symbolization, and further development" (Segal 1991, 51).

The T.O. (transitional object) becomes our first symbol if we are little and an enduring symbol if we are big. As symbols, these objects become alive with meaning that is both discovered and created. We name these objects—George, Basil, bah bah, Pythagoras. I did not ask the blue rabbit's name. I felt that was too intrusive a question, thus reflecting the biblical notion that to know a name is to enter into that personality's being, with all the intimacies of sexual congress associated with the biblical idea of to know. As symbols, these T.O.s display the paradox inherent in all alive symbols. They convey the real objectively there, external to us, the world, others, a real objective meaning and power of being; and they embody the real subjectively here, a subjectively endowed meaning and power of being. Found and invented, these symbolic objects invite us into the space of illusion where simultaneously we know and do not know that this object is just a stuffed bear from the store and also the purveyor of creative spirit itself. These separate, disparate opposites we feel really do match up into one imaginative whole.

These objects also exert a fascinating effect on other people: they enter into the game, join in the play, and refer to George or the bah bah. We all show respect for this illusory space, never violating it with snide reductionism, saying, oh this Basil was purchased in a store; you made all this up. Of course, the woman did, and yet Basil bodies forth a be-ing that abides in the face of death; it nourishes her. These objects evoke play in us, the observers, an answering attitude of respect, reverence, and fun.

Spiritual Objects

Winnicott explores the first transitional space between mother and child and its replication in treating people in analysis. I am exploring the space-in-between as it opens between us and reality, the transitions we make to what we believe in, or say we do not believe in. Transitional objects merge in with what I am calling spiritual objects. They share in common all the characteristics of the T.O. and the fact that they are not exchangeable objects, but unique, radiating a presence that both shelters us and sponsors our thriving. All spiritual objects emerge from being T.O.s, but all T.O.s are not necessarily spiritual objects, except in their beginning phases.

Just as the T.O. facilitates in the baby's mind the transition from merger with the mothering one to emerging "as an object to be perceived rather than conceived of" (Winnicott 1971, 96), the spiritual object shifts our attention to what it symbolizes, that there is a reality objectively existing outside us brought near by this object. We inhabit the illusion that this reality knows us, lives in relation to us. Yet, simultaneously, reality is not an object, but more like the air we breathe, the energy of living that courses through us. But we need an object small and potent enough to make reality graspable, relatable. The object shrinks the hugeness of the All and the Vast to manageable size so we can touch it.

Another example is of a ninety-five-year-old woman facing death. Although enjoying remarkable health and independence until this last year, now she was in hospital and bodily systems were breaking down. A sophisticated and intelligent professional, she now felt alone, frightened, and spoke of wondering about the next life, religious beliefs, which she did not have but showed keen interest in. Receiving a small bear as a gift, she named it after a beloved bear belonging to the giver, calling it Cyril II. Whenever the two friends visited, their talk always included what had been happening with Cyril II, her companion, she said, in her spiritual wonderings. She said in the night, she felt less alone with Cyril II who made the coming death and what came after talkable about, a size that could be carried in thought and musings. Her caretaker joined in the play, bringing her a smaller and feminine bear to accompany Cyril. The woman called this new bear the Companion and kept it close to Cyril II.

The spiritual object possesses the potency of a true symbol, acting like a two-way bridge between our small consciousness and the magnitude of the All. Jung says, "To be effective, a symbol must be by its very nature unassailable. It must be the best possible expression of the prevailing worldview, an unsurpassed container of meaning; it must also be sufficiently remote from comprehension to resist all attempts of the critical intellect to break it down; and finally its aesthetic form must appeal so convincingly to our feelings that no argument can be raised against it on that score" (Jung 1971, 401).

Our spiritual objects perform an eliciting function, beckoning the soul into conscious experience. We get a sense of an other deep inside us who knows about things eternal, about what really matters. At the same time the reality the soul connects to outside ourselves comes into view, bringing us glimpses, intimations. Just as the transitional object builds up the sense of self and symbol, so the spiritual object builds up the sense of soul and the reality to which it belongs.

The soul occupies an intermediate position between our conscious sense of I and the inaccessible depths not only of our own unconscious, but also the reality that reaches us just as much through our unconscious as it does through events and people external to us. The reality that speaks through all these points of access is what has been called God, operating from these depths, both internal and external to us, and the soul functions as receiver and mirrorer.

What the soul perceives are symbols, patterns of energy full of affective charge and spiritual value (Jung 1971, 425). The soul itself is only an image and it traffics in images, connecting those of consciousness to the unconscious and those of the unconscious to consciousness. When a beloved T.O. also carries spiritual valence, our experience of our own soul and the ineffable reality it conveys via images (or sounds, textures, tastes, smells) emerges. The spiritual object brings to us palpable and imaginative experience of the spirit by which we live, our animating connection to being itself. God is not an object to be known, but a subject to be loved. Hence our T.O. and spiritual object evoke in us crossings and connections from self to soul to transcendent reality and back again.

The object of George or Cyril helps us relate to what otherwise would drown us. The loss of love, or of a true mate, comprises one of life's disasters and great sorrows. We can easily go under the waves. The abiding being of a Basil while one is gripped by despair—for what the loved one suffered, for the life lost, for the fear of living without loving, for the hole in one's heart, as one man put it, that always is there and he can never fill it but only grow around it—enables one to submit to storms of grief and come through them. Basil conveys that the source of reality knows and accompanies our suffering. We know, if only in moments, that we are known.

The power of the spiritual object lies in conducting libido from what is symbolized, the All of reality itself, into us, the subject. We find ourselves then between inner and outer reality with a margin of free choice. If all the libido rests with the object, we live in thrall to it as if the object has absolute value, and we gain no subjective freedom. In the symbolic space between self and the reality symbolized, we unfold our stored possibility to play, invent, discover, originate, be found.

The spiritual object permits space to emerge where our dependence shifts from the mothering one or from the analyst to reality itself and onto the forms with which we symbolize it. Like Cassirer's spiritual organs of the universe, we build up the forms that conduct the invisible into visibility (Cassirer 1946, 8). Will our symbolic form be one of the arts, or religion, science, sports, the sound of Count Basie? Mozart said of this space:

> When I am . . . completely myself . . . say, . . . walking after a good meal, or during the night when I cannot sleep; it is on such occasions that my ideas flow best and most abundantly. *Whence* and *how* they come, I know not, nor can I force them. . . . But why my productions take from my hand that particular form and style that makes them *Mozartish*, and different from the works of other composers, is probably owing to the same cause which renders my nose so large or aquiline. . . . I really do not study or aim at originality. (cited in Hirshfield 1998, 36)

Spiritual objects not only introduce us to invisible reality made visible, but inject a sense of the ridiculous, the fun of it. We know this is a bear or a rabbit (or a religious relic or scientific experiment), not the ineffable spirit of life, and yet it is. It is both at the same time. We gain the intimation of spirit because we are not identified with the object. Our soul's horizon stretches out; we gain space, spiritual latitude to chart our journey. Jung writes, "Even the enlightened person remains what he is, and is never more than his own limited ego before the One who dwells within him on all sides, fathomless as the abysms of the earth and vast as the sky" (cited by Lambert 1987, 64). How can we help but laugh, join in the fun, to find in the big blue rabbit the gift of inexhaustible energy watching over us as we stand for hours in an airport line inspected by the officers of a totalitarian country. The rabbit brings the creative spirit into view.

Spiritual objects, then, partake of a particular kind of paradox. They are at once immanent and transcendent objects, and they reveal a reality beyond the human that yet lives in it. If we speak in religious language, we want to say that spiritual objects reveal a God who is transcendent and immanent both. What the spiritual object symbolizes is God Almighty, or whatever we put in the place of the divine. Our spiritual object may stay inhering in the transitional object of the Blue Rabbit or George; or it may differentiate out from the stuffed species into a saintly relic, a cross, a sacred rock.

Dependence extends now two ways. We depend on the spiritual object to make the Holy near, reachable. And it is as if the Holy also depends on the spiritual object to declare itself in terms we can grasp. We are able to converse with the ultimate, to enjoy congress with it through our spiritual objects. The Holy, the invariable reality, utters itself through our spiritual objects. A real divine presence uses the spiritual object to display its own objective reality as a subject independent of our projections. The spiritual object is evidence of the presence of something real.

The paradox of the spiritual object matches the paradox it woos us into experiencing. On the one hand, we feel increasing dependence on our spiritual objects, as if we were the child and the spiritual object puts us in touch with God as the parent. On the other hand, we enjoy a good measure of autonomy characteristic of an adult. Lambert points out that this paradoxical state defines mystics who rest in quietness with their God and who also show tremendous vigor and activity in their external lives serving that God (Lambert 1987, 51). We only have to remember how Teresa of Avila founded new convents all over Spain when she was advanced in years, not in good health, with no financial backing, and no roads, only muddy ruts and frightful weather. Complaining to God when once again her wagon lurched and tossed her into the mud, God answers, I do this to all my friends; to which Teresa retorts, No wonder you have so few!

Spiritual objects put us in touch with something there; we contribute to it with our imaginations and investments of libido and we find it other than our designs, a presence we did not originate, nor invent out of consciousness. With our spiritual objects we play around with the union of two spheres of being—our limited finite humanness and the infinite ultimate meaning and power of being. We do not translate one into the other, nor take one to substitute for the other. Spiritual objects reveal to us the divine-human nature of living. By creating and finding our spiritual objects, we do the projecting and the containing, instead of the parent doing it; we do the expressing and converting of painful bits, the making something of our experience. A little girl of three was putting her larger duck separate from her littler duck. Her grandmother said to her, why not put them together. She replied, No. Mommy has to go to work. She was working out loss and union which has to do with transitional objects, and she was also working out her place in the universe, what there is to depend on besides Mommy, through Mommy, which Mommy herself may depend upon. She is searching for what is there that is not the sum of her projections, but exists in its own right.

Madness and Spiritual Objects

With transitional objects, we are familiar with the role of destructiveness in the infant as establishing the externality of the object (Winnicott 1971, chapter 6; 1989, chapter 34). Destructiveness in the beginning of life is a part of primitive loving, love with teeth, so to speak. Aggression as aliveness that has nothing to do with anger or intent to hurt. Going at the mother with all the force of gobbling, ruthlessly, without thought of consequence to self or mother of one's instinctive attack out of hunger or lusty loving, discovering that mother survives out of herself, and is a subject in her own right, allows the infant to knit up this exciting mother with the quiet mother who holds and handles the baby and presents objects of the world to the baby in manageable bites (Winnicott 1963/1965, 74-77). All to the good.

But what of the adult intent to hurt, the intent to attack and harm or dominate or obliterate? What of the intent to select and stalk one's victim, knowingly to take advantage of them in molestation or sexual theft? What of the aim to defraud, knowingly robbing workers of their pensions? What then? How can that be included in one's relation to the spiritual object? How does the soul survive its link with the objective spirit when we want to destroy that spirit, wreck it, dismantle the good (Ulanov and Ulanov 1983/1998, 121, 135)? How do we know the spirit survives? The T.O. as a subjective-object that reflects us back to ourselves is reborn in what Winnicott calls object usage, where in a burst of instinctive aggression we go at the object without concern for consequences to self or other, and we discover the object exists in its own right, is objective because it survives our destructiveness (Winnicott 1971, chapter 6).

But a second rebirth is required of spiritual objects if they are to develop and to endure as a subject objectively there, external to us. The spiritual object conveys a reality of spirit that exists in its own right, and appears related to us as its own subject. Its subjectness surpasses that of our bear or doll; and its objectness surpasses that of the tangibility of these actual objects because the spiritual reality is imaginative, of psychic stuff, rather than fur (like a bear) or wood (like a cross). Its objectness is not impersonal, but seems to relate to us as subjects, as persons. We are dependent on this other, this objective subject, to resurrect from our destruction of it, from our intent to destroy it.

Interruption of any of these steps leads to peculiar kinds of madness associated with the soul and the spiritual life. If we stay merged with our spiritual object, what we might call the soul living in God, then we dwell in omnipotence, never separate from the object, never differentiating our will from the divine, overwhelmed by what Jung calls the divine *dynamis*, and hence capable of flying a plane full of people into an office building full of people, convinced we are doing Allah's will. The divine omnipotence becomes our omnipotence; we are mighty in our obedient act and our destructiveness is exported to murder the infidel in service to Allah. There is no spiritual object in this example because there is no space between us and the divine; we are merged. All the archetypal energy of the religious image of the divine pounds through our small ego frame, obliterating time and space, reality of others, concern for family and children, let alone the gift of our own life. We are the divine weapon and we display omnipotent control in the sacrifice of the human.

An intermediate example comes from the soul having a spiritual object that embodies the divine. This is halfway between being engulfed by the divine and feeling the divine residing in the soul which then experiences itself as vessel, as serving the divine. In this halfway place, the spiritual object carries the divine and the soul feels utterly dependent on it and at risk of annihilation if the spiritual object is lost. An example is found in the film *Cast Away*, starring Tom Hanks, who survives a horrendous plane wreck to be washed up on a small deserted island in the South Pacific. In making the film, its release was delayed, I learned, because the director could not figure out a way for a lone man to be talking about his physical and spiritual predicament abandoned from civilization on this island. To whom would he be speaking? Finally a solution emerged in what we would call a transitional object that grew into what I would call a spiritual object. From the plane wreckage packages washed up, one including a volley ball. The Tom Hanks character named the ball Wilson (from the manufacturer's label) and the problem of dialogue was solved. Wilson accompanied the man's paralysis in despair and botched effort to hang himself, his triumph in making fire, and his determination to escape off the island, risking the wide expanses of sea in hopes of being rescued back into human community. A pivotal point came in the movie when Tom Hanks falls asleep on his crude raft and the elevated flag-like positioning of Wilson pulls loose from its moorings and drifts off into the sea. Tom Hanks awakes, sees Wilson going away into the distance, panics, clutches a rope to drag the raft after him as he tries to swim to Wilson, all the time calling out his name. But the tides prove too swift and Wilson recedes further and further in the waves. The character then is faced with abandoning his raft—sure death—in an effort to swim free to catch Wilson, or letting Wilson go. He does the latter and collapses on the raft sobbing. This dramatic scene shows our devastating grief when we lose the object that has carried our connection to the living Spirit that imbues life itself for us. We are utterly dependent on a spiritual object, as if recasting the utter dependence of the infant on the parent; we the children of God rely totally on God and God's representative in our spiritual object.

The character stays in utter collapse, having lost what he completely depended upon to keep his self in being. He cannot resurrect it; he cannot resurrect himself; he cannot save himself from his own grief at loss of his beloved Wilson. Saving can only come from outside himself. The movie depicts what happens in spiritual crisis and the stark fact that if the reality of Spirit to which a spiritual object points is really real, it must tell us, show us, cross to us. We cannot originate it out of ourselves. We cannot make it happen that it comes back to us. Our utter dependence is portrayed in the film by Tom Hanks being rescued some time later by a passing freighter that discovers him. He is helpless, prostrate, semi-unconscious on his raft. We cannot effect our own salvation. If the divine Spirit comes back, it brings itself to us. It comes to us, finds us. And it brings the new, which is played out in the movie's end. The character gains a new ability to follow a hunch when he is faced with a crossroad. A sign on a package that was washed up on his deserted island, he now sees on a van, and he follows it to the house of a new relation with a new woman.

A clinical example of the same terrific threat of loss comes from a woman's dream, dreamed the night after hearing terribly upsetting news from her daughter that the daughter, feeling trapped by a situation imposed upon her, felt suicidal. The woman dreamed she was working in a foreign country and had gone to sleep wanting to awaken early to go to church. But a mob comes in and she thinks, no church, just get dressed and leave. She goes first to the bathroom, but she leaves her precious object on her bed, a stuffed cat that had functioned as a lifeline for her since the death of her husband. It connected me, she said, like a symbol of loving I relied on, was dependent on. In the dream bathroom, she remembers and rushes back to retrieve the cat. But it is too late. The mob crowds in and she cannot reach the woman who takes the cat. She protests, asks for help, but it is hopeless. The dream ends, she says, as she howls, sobs, saying she is Shattered!

Awakening, she feels broken by this dream, smashed. She says she lost her soul connection, what kept her alive, with a heart and soul and willingness. Now she wants to lie down and give up. And she feels she failed the cat, as ridiculous as this sounds, but it is true, she says. She did not protect the cat and she wails, what has become of it? Did the non-negotiability of the dream crowd, the frantic concern for her daughter's survival, rob her of her soul connection? What struck her most in trying to work on this dream in analysis was its shattering effect. She kept coming back to that—the cat was her soul, the divine, and now it was gone. This was the theft of a God-image. The collective, pictured in the dream as an impersonal crowd of foreigners, speaking another language, just made off with it.

Sometimes the examples are worse. A girl of three, reported as an adult, that sitting with her four older siblings before the fire one night they tossed her beloved stuffed duck into the flames. She did not talk for two years. We could say she lost her way, fell into despair. A girl of nine confessed to her mother that her friend ridiculed her love for her doll, saying her doll didn't really exist, it was just a toy. Her mother, my patient, said her daughter likes to believe she loved her doll into being real. Her mother told her daughter, this does not happen to everyone to have a doll like this, a remark made all the more poignant because the mother, being treated for depression, never had such an object herself. You are really lucky, she told her daughter, and that her friend does not know what is possible and why doesn't her daughter talk this over with her doll. The daughter took her doll into a long conversation and later told her mother she apologized to the doll for doubting her and abandoning her. Her mother told me she, the mother, really liked this doll of her daughter's, illustrating how our children help repair us, as the daughter allowed the mother vicariously to experience what the mother had missed in her own childhood.

The peculiar madness that strikes us in relation to our spiritual object can be summed up: we lose it and grief enters us in an irreversible way. The task is then posed to us how to go on living. Or we never found the object in the first place and got stuck in omnipotence. One little boy took his mother as his transitional object and he did not speak for years. A spiritual arrest occurs and conversation with reality through the beloved object does not happen until forced by illness, crisis.

We can disdain our dependence, mock it as too much and thus destroy the object that symbolizes how dependent we are, that we come from dust and to dust we return. One middle-aged woman, working hard on what Jungians call shadow material, all those nasty parts of us we would rather foist onto our neighbor instead of claiming as our own, dreamed of a little girl who left her beloved blanket in the dreamer's car. She dreams, I am contemptuous of her and her mother. I get what I know to be the real blanket and chide the girl for not noticing the difference. The girl whines in response and the dreamer retorts: If you are going to whine and can't say what's wrong, then go to your room. Whining is like picking your nose. It's not to be done in public. I feel quite proud of my solution. On waking the dreamer is appalled at her behavior. Heartless! Condescending! she exclaims, and we link it up to her denial of her own dependence.

An opposite problem arises when we make an idol out of our spiritual object. Then we become rigid and eventually caught in repetition compulsion at the expense of creative repetition that imagines variations on a theme, that enlarges the ineffable into resonating sound. Instead of rounds of liturgy in the temple's or church's year, repeated sacraments, or rehearsals of poetry, that build up habits of the heart, or repeated rituals of lovemaking, patterns of mirth with friends, cycles of meditative practice, session after session with analysands that bring out the meaning, the emotional truth, we get caught in dead rote, repeating words, but the fire has gone out. Slowly libido drains out of our intercourse with spiritual objects. Conversation with the reality they convey stops.

More stuck still is the spiritual object that turns into a fetish. The link between the here and the beyond calcifies into this object; our emotions around it grow dense and fixed. We cannot feel connected up (whether to our genital functioning, our security, our place in the universe) without this object. Yet we become petrified in our enthrallment to the fetish object. We cannot get to external reality, but try to control its commerce with us instead.

Spiritual madness still more serious, because it destroys others as well as ourselves, stems from falling into unconscious identification with our spiritual objects and believing, then, it is our mission to make others accept them as well. We have the tiger by the tail; indeed, we are the tiger or its major emissary. Our religious duty, our spiritual calling, demands we indoctrinate others or cast them out, utterly, as exiles. Because spiritual objects act as transmitters of energy at the core of reality, a tremendous force sweeps into and through us. Religious symbols speak of humanity's deepest longings and aspirations, reaching to the primordial source of all being. That becomes the wave on which we ride and we speak for all the saved and against all the damned. Jim Jones in Jonestown illustrates this enthrallment, ordering his own and others' suicides as fulfilling God's will. Spiritual objects may begin as fluffy bunnies, treasured bears, and precious blankets, but they emerge as carriers of reality itself, symbols of tremendous power, for good or for ill.

Spiritual Subjects and Building Up Reality

Now we must look at spiritual objects head-on and describe the world they help us create and clothe. It is more accurate to call them spiritual subjects. When I asked permission of an analysand to cite the example of George, saying I was giving a paper on spiritual objects, she, a person not in psychology but in finance, said immediately, "George is a subject." I laughed, thinking how I had arrived at this idea and she knew it all along. Right there, in the session, she began to play with the idea, saying George would want to give the lecture himself; in fact, he would come and sit on the podium and receive applause!

As true symbols, these spiritual subjects convey the reality of Spirit, or spiritual reality in which we all dwell. Something comes toward us, from its own side, so to speak. A force, a potency, elicits our participation in itself, and rearranges our inner drives, or internal objects, or archetypal patterns—whatever school of psychology we profess—and woos us into capacity to respond. Here, we are the objects of its subjectivity. It beholds us. It returns to us after destructive events nearly fell us. Without denying destructiveness, this reality offers us a way to survive it and thrive.

The story about the feminine origin of poetry (in contrast to the Orpheus myth as its masculine origin) helps here (Grossman 1992). Philomena, daughter of Pandion, king of Athens, is put among the slaves by her sister's husband, Tereus, king of Thrace. There he rapes her and cuts out her tongue so she cannot tell his atrocity. Philomena reaches her sister, Procne, through weaving, thus establishing weaving as the origin of woman's text. Through a language different from ordinary verbal discourse, Philomena overcomes the blockage of communication caused by Tereus's wicked deeds. Together they effect revenge by feeding Tereus the flesh of his own son. Discovering their deed, and the magnitude of his own, he pursues them and they are all turned into birds. Philomena becomes the grieving nightingale, which scholars find in the text of Keats's "Ode to a Nightingale."

The nightingale's song expresses the conflict between memory transcending atrocity through music, and the necessity to remember the atrocity disabled by music. Overwhelmed by the enormity of body violation that compels her to forget, Philomena sings and inspires poetry. She forgets the trauma and remembers the song as a way of defeating the trauma and creating from it, instead of the trauma living on in her and defeating her life (see Symington 2001, 107). Constantly revising the self in relation to the source that acts as our reservoir, and we as its river, ever unique and ever changing, symbol, here through poetry, shows us how destructiveness does not totally destroy. To create out of the evil done to us can be the best revenge: it did not shatter us; we rose to livingness; the trauma is a surface scar, not the marring of the center. It is not denied and it is not triumphant.

We made something of the experience that has traumatized us, that ejects us out of the universe of meaning, away from others and from nature. From this gap we make something—the book of Lamentations, Penderecki's Threnody for the Victims of Hiroshima, a mother who cooks her teenage son's favorite bacon to beckon him back to living, away from his weeping in his bedroom because the girl he first wooed with all his heart rejects him. Sometimes we are stunned, go numb, tune out. We divert the water from the source to the tributaries or it goes underground. Not until fifty years later can we return, as one man did, and make something of the death of his mother when he was still a boy.

What makes this livingness possible is the center of the universe, what we call the spirit or the sacred or the source, addressing us. It comes back to us, not destroyed by trauma, loss, death, atrocity. It comes to us and gives us power to recognize its new configuration. What we make in response inaugurates new constructions. Our egos act as the knitters, the narrative makers. It is the creator. "The human world has great stake in openness to the uncategorizable presence" (Grossman 1992, lecture 5). In response to its advance, we find and create symbols. It heralds an assembling consciousness in which we imaginatively encircle what comes to our door, what bursts it open. We do not know; we may be immersed in unknowing; we let it in without abandoning our allegiance to be willingly in the world of the living.

Relating to spiritual subjects also includes destructiveness. Any of us fumbling along in a spiritual practice will reach a point where all our images for the ultimate, the transcendent, will be smashed because they are too small to contain the infinite. As the infinite draws near through the very means of these symbols (including doctrines, texts, rituals), it overshadows the finite, darkening our symbol's capacity to mediate the ultimate to us. Our symbols themselves seek their own destruction because they are mere figures, not the thing itself. Their purpose is to usher us across their bridge, not to paint the bridge gold. Our theories that keep us able in our work by giving us a map of psychic terrain will falter, unable to capture the mystery of the living soul embodied in the person across from us in our offices. The it, itself, the Spirit as subject, will become present and the symbolic mediator will fall away. Destructiveness is built into the spiritual life, hence its aptness to help us with the destructiveness we inflict on each other. Bad as it is, it need not separate us nor defeat us. Destructiveness can find its place, just as the bird Philomena so badly hurt, treated as an object, a nonsubject, rises as a subject to sing us into savage pursuit of truth and limitless, selfless compassion.

In relation to spiritual subjects, we come to live again as we did as children, in close relation to primary process thinking, yet now as adults, without sacrificing the differentiation and complexity of secondary process thinking. We know simultaneously that the Blue Rabbit is not God or Spirit, but we also know it puts us in touch with them; that Cyril II allows us to traffic with death while still alive; that Pythagoras explores loss that threatens to kill, by assembling the force of aliveness that enables living. This new consciousness inhabits and enlarges the space in between fantasy and reality, partaking of both; in it we refresh and rejuvenate; the space becomes a capacity. Driving to work, we live in the deep well of existence; catching the subway, we feel the surround of the primal forest; paying our taxes, we draw existence from the archaic cave of being. As analysts, we believe in transference and simultaneously know we are not the analysand's mother, good or bad, though arranged in those relational positions that the patient needs to integrate. The transference points beyond itself to the analysand's new relation to their own subjectivity, to us as another subject, to motherly forces in life.

In relation to our spiritual subjects, we build up capacity to withstand transcendence and the freedom to relate to it. As the philosopher Berdyaev says, transcendental man lives outside the division of subject and object (Berdyaev 1953, 17). We are called to testify to the inherent limits and relativity of our spiritual subjects by virtue of the large transcendence breaking through them into the world. Our small self becomes a medium to increase the available stock of reality.

On a personal level, spiritual subjects that convey this other presence to us help us work our fate into destiny. We exercise our capacity to find and create symbols that reunite us with our deepest unconscious processes and connect us to the source that undergirds our creative process. We gain the attitude that enables us to live our unique life, whatever it is. The woman with the Pythagoras bear felt her utter dependence on it to navigate the lethal undertow of grief for her deceased husband and, as well, to keep her alive to the lavish loving that she once lived with him. Pythagoras, she said, was the channel for the loving that had lost its dear object to death. The bear made a riverbed for this force in her, to keep it flowing. Without it, she feared the force would make her ill. She could open to its unknown goal, feeling faith in its flowing.

When addressed by this presence that evokes in us the capacity to invest in life, we cross from self to soul and back again. Doing analysis opens, right there in the office, to deepest layers of psyche including phases of chaos and unintegrated bits of self, to a radical enhancement of the capacity for creative experiencing (Kakar 1991, ix). New symbols appear that help us meet the problems in our life which help us work out the attitude that enables us to live our specific individual life. These symbols, as Jung puts it, evoke a religious attitude of careful observation and attentive pondering: "Religious symbols are life-phenomena, plain facts and not opinions" (Jung 1953, 166). Spiritual objects, then, that are really subjects, make us subjects and act as envoys of reality offering itself to be lived. This advance into visibility reverses our usual perspectives. Instead of it helping us, we reverse to helping it to live in us, to give it ways to manifest in the concrete particularity of our lives. The source utters itself through us.

From the side of the transcendent, it is as if our human symbols take on sacramental union of divine and creaturely life. The two realms do not substitute for each other, nor translate into each other. They forge a union that displays reality as unceasing gift in the living meeting of the transcendent in empirical reality, that realizes and reveals it (see Lampert 1943, 111, 112, 127). We live the eternally new in our ordinary human life. Yet it goes still further, because this source, this mystery, this All, offers itself to us through the small spiritual object to address us as a subject summoning our deepest and fullest subjectivity. We feel linked up in this creaturely life to the numinous, the divine, to being itself, whatever we call it, that gently criticizes all our reifications, dissolving them, and yet makes us laugh that its splendor and hugeness can be addressed in a letter that begins, Dear Basketball.

Our tasks change. We fashion a housing for this presence, a residence in our small self in this time in history in which we live. We house it like a precious ointment in the jar of us, to be poured out sometimes in lavish loving, to be conserved and sheltered, to be squandered in simple acts of kindness to and with our neighbors. We learn from the poor here. A patient growing up in the ghetto told me once, the poor don't save a windfall of money; they throw a party for their friends and neighbors and enjoy it. This presence inhabiting us makes us unafraid of self-presence; we become its medium. We inhabit all of ourselves in order to give it a big living space. The eros of being moves us to pass it on to others, in altruisms beyond any possibility of repayment.

Paradox enters. As Thérèse of Lisieux saw herself the plaything, the ball for Jesus to throw, catch, kick, it is now as if Jesus becomes the plaything for Thérèse. The lowly bear or rabbit becomes the ambassador for our new consciousness that builds up a tenderness for each living thing, all parts of the All. The many dwell in the One and the One lives in each of the many.

By this new course, we enter an "unfenced existence" (Philip Larkin cited by Hirshfield 1998, 17). Shedding the badges of identity—class, money, poverty, health, titles, houses, successes, failures, traumas, illnesses. This kind of stripping of identity is not so much a dark night of the soul as a great light of the soul. We become nameless, a fellow citizen, a sister resident, whose forms of identity are melted off by the light, even sometimes stripped of gender. John of the Cross became a bride; Hadewijch the greatest of warriors. We surrender ordinary identity for broader intimacy and allegiance. All this is conferred by the source of our spiritual objects which reveal themselves as subjects—George, Basil, Pythagoras, Cyril II, the Companion—and make us the same, all the way down, including all the parts, and all the way up and out, including all others.

References

This chapter was originally given as a presentation to the Fall Symposium of the Psychotherapy Institute, Berkeley, California, November 2003.

Berdyaev, N. 1953. *Truth and Revelation*. Trans. R. M. French. London: Geoffrey Bless.

Cassirer, E. 1946. *Language and Myth*. Trans. Susanne K. Langer. New York: Dover Publications.

Geoghegan, W. D., with K. L. Stoehr. 2002. *Jung's Psychology as Spiritual Practice and Way of Life*. Lanham, Md.: University Press of America.

Green, A. 2000. *André Green at the Squiggle Foundation*. Ed. Jan Abram. London: Karnac.

Grossman, A. 1992. *Poetry: A Basic Course*. Eight Lectures. Super Star Teachers Series. The Teaching Company.

Hirshfield, J. 1998. *Nine Gates: Entering the Mind of Poetry*. New York: Harper Perennial.

Jung, C. G. 1916/1960. The transcendent function. In *The Structure and Dynamics of the Psyche*. Vol. 8 of *Collected Works*. Trans. R. F. C. Hull. New York: Pantheon.

———. 1952/1960. Synchronicity: an acausal connecting principle. In *The Structure and Dynamics of the Psyche*. Vol. 8 of *Collected Works*. Trans. R. F. C. Hull. New York: Pantheon.

———. 1953. *Psychology and Alchemy*. Vol. 12 of *Collected Works*. Trans. R. F. C. Hull. New York: Pantheon.

———. 1958/1964. A psychological view of conscience. In *Civilization in Transition*. Vol. 10 of *Collected Works*. Trans. R. F. C. Hull. New York: Pantheon.

———. 1971. *Psychological Types*. Vol. 6 of *Collected Works*. Trans. R. F. C. Hull. Princeton, N.J.: Princeton University Press.

———. 1997. *Visions*. 2 vols. Ed. Claire Douglas. Princeton, N.J.: Princeton University Press.

Kakar, S. 1991. *The Analyst and the Mystic*. Chicago: Chicago University Press.

Lambert, K. 1987. Some religious implications of the work of Freud, Jung and Winnicott. London: *The Journal of the Squiggle Foundation* 2: 49-70.

Lampert, E. 1943. *The Divine Realm*. London: Faber and Faber.

Ogden, T. 1999. *Reverie and Interpretation*. London: Karnac.

Segal, H. 1991. *Dream, Phantasy and Art*. New York: Tavistock/ Routledge.

Symington, N. 2001. *The Spirit of Sanity*. London: Karnac.

Ulanov, A., and B. Ulanov. 1983/1998. *Cinderella and Her Sisters: The Envied and the Envying*. Einsiedeln, Switzerland: Daimon.

Winnicott, D. W. 1963/1965. The capacity for concern. In *The Maturational Processes and the Facilitating Environment*. New York: International Universities Press.

———. 1971. *Playing and Reality*. London: Tavistock.

———. 1989. *Psycho-Analytic Explorations*. Eds. Clare Winnicott, Ray Shepherd, and Madeleine Davis. London: Karnac.

EVIL

Images of Evil

Evil is a dangerous topic to address. It is not a problem to be solved nor a condition we can fix. There is no hasty solution to evil. There is a presence to it, but one hard to grasp. In clinical work, we clinicians want to say with Winnicott, that wickedness is illness and that our modalities of treatment can be effective in healing pathology (Winnicott 1950/1959, 103). Surely that is so; but then at a certain depth, at an augmented intensity, illness blurs into evil, and we can feel in the relational field between us that the person not only suffers being held fast by something that determines their life, but now, more, something threatens to annihilate their subjective agency, their ownmost self, and through them the selves of others. For evil is never a solitary venture. More like a contagion, it infiltrates the atmosphere, until before we know it a whole nation colludes in death camps that are disavowed, a whole building hears the beatings that go on in one apartment and no one calls child services, a whole street hears the screams of Kitty Genovese and no one calls the cops. Why is that silence so pervasive? What is this subtracting power that makes us unable to speak the unspeakable? Depth psychology joins theology in perceiving evil as enigma, mystery.

Analysands bring images of it; the psyche speaks of evil in its own language of impulse, affect, image. Here are some examples: at the core of my being is fear, not being able, not being possible, not being; I feel menaced, cut off, bitter, alone; an abyss where nothing comes forth, things go out from under you; a gap I've fallen into; I cannot start; cast off, discarded; not a subject but a disposable thing, dust, gone; violation at the core; a void; disregard of all persons for me; falling into little pieces; wanting to hurt, to kill; trapped in the grip of something, a need to defeat, to humiliate, to wreak unending revenge; berserk rage; blank despair, no hope; it is everything and I can't get out.

We can describe effects of evil—its power to degrade truth so it is unrecognizable; to refuse to acknowledge accountability; to extinguish agency; to evade, avoid, deny, forget, conceal, go numb, retreat, withhold, withdraw, vitiate. In the grip of evil our mind is stunned; we cannot speak of what was done; we dismantle the good; all emotional links with others are severed, so even if we repent and make reparation, it is not the perpetrating part of us that rejoins the human community, but the part that felt remorse and accepted forgiveness. The perpetrator-us we must carry in our memory and it perpetually casts us outside the circle of mutuality, "beyond intersubjective recognition" (Grand 2000, 160). Evil is like an indelible stain, or a scar, that cannot be erased.

Even if we get away with an evil act, we pay for it. For as Jung says, "Evil cannot be eradicated once and for all. . . . The thief whom the police do not catch has, nonetheless, robbed himself, and the murderer is his own executioner" (Jung 1963a, 202). Winnicott notes the murderer is the other side of suicide (Winnicott 1950/1959, 171). Veterans speak of the heavy cost the psyche pays in war: "Killing an adversary removes part of your soul. Your 'kill' turns out to be a young kid much like you, armed, in uniform, sent forth by his country into battle. As time passes, feelings of guilt, sorrow, and remorse accompany the odd, displaced feeling that you have become the person you killed. You see his family, his face, you feel his loss. You see him in your sons, and you wonder if fate will someday take them from you to settle the score" (Schauer 2004, 5).

Logic and Location of Evil

Once we are infected, evil imposes its own logic. Hurt, damaged by evil inflicted, we want to hurt and damage in turn, to pay back, to retaliate. If we cannot injure the one who harmed us, then we find a surrogate and pass on the injury, multiplying its effects. Justification accompanies our action: it is the hurt that makes us do it; indeed it is our duty to express that pain, our right, our justice. Once set loose, such logic replicates relentlessly until all of us are addicted to its rhythms. Wounded, aggrieved, we disable access to the good.

Depth psychologists have located evil in different places in the psyche. For Freud it erupts from the id; for Klein it is the death instinct that can trap us in the paranoid-schizoid position; for Bion it is the cutting of links thereby repudiating the alpha function, that is, our capacity to process the beta elements of experience into human thought and image, thereby exposing us to a force of destructiveness that goes on forever destroying time and space (Bion 1965/1983, 101). For Bollas evil annihilates one's subjectness and then one administers that killing on another's self (Bollas 1995, 188-89). Winnicott focuses on destructiveness and the necessity that the transitional space between infant and mothering one contain the infant's aggressive impulses and that the mothering one survives out of her own resources and accepts the gestures of concern the child offers to repair the hurt done (Winnicott 1971, chapter 6). Intersubjective and relational analysts write about making dead the space between us.

Jung stands out as the depth psychologist who took up the fact of evil with the most persistence, venturing even into theological precincts with his own answer to Job (Jung 1952/1958). Clinically I find them all useful, but Jung's perception of psychic reality adds a significant perception about evil. The psyche, and thus the evil it suffers and enacts, cannot be reduced to developmental history of object relations nor to social constructions alone, influential as those are, but also includes a depth dimension, what

Jung calls archetypal, that is quite other to the domain of ego consciousness. Hence addressing evil we would not do but nonetheless commit,
takes us through our personal situation into the larger collective context
where we experience evil as ensnaring all of us, indeed in what the New
Testament calls the principalities and powers, as if we are all caught in an
addiction. Then forgiveness is not the first need, but liberation, something
coming in from the outside to free us from enthrallment.

Evil from the Psychoanalytical Perspective

The perspective of depth psychology leads us to look first to the
responsibility we have for evil, to look to our contribution, to the wound
that holds us fast, even though someone else originally inflicted it. Our
dreams portray our part in the mess in which we find ourselves, even
when we feel most persecuted. For example, a man dreams he is riding his
bike swiftly on New York City streets, as he does in reality, but this dream
bike is fastened to another man's bike pedaling right alongside him. The
dreamer feels menaced by this shadowy stranger connected to him and
aims his bike to dart through an opening between a truck and other cars,
too narrow for the other biker who will be smashed against the truck. Or
a woman dreamed that on the subway she donned a cap on which a sign
blazoned, Shoot Me! Another woman dreamed she and her sister were on
an airplane and her sister took an ice-pick and walked up and down
stabbing the people in the aisle seats.

Where do we put such destructiveness? What do we make of it?
Something within us that we do not originate, nor does the analyst
author, nor a textbook, though all these sources add to our understanding, speak to us about what we suffer, where we have gone off, giving clues
to where healing will generate.

Jung took his vocabulary from the images the unconscious offers of
itself, instead of imposing conceptual formulations of secondary process
onto its primary process. He wanted to let the psyche speak in its own

terms as much as possible. I find that a good clinical method, more useful to the patient than theoretical jargon or the nomenclature of the *Diagnostic and Statistical Manual of Mental Disorders* because it is a less judgmental discourse and preserves the subjectiveness of the analysand in relation to the objectivity of the psyche. As Alice Miller showed, even our psychoanalytical vocabulary can convey contempt on the part of the clinician. What begins as helpful classification can degenerate into labels—the borderline, the narcissist—as if we do not share these disorders or have more flamboyant ones of our own (Miller 1981, chapter 3).

The psyche puts forth images of itself. We all, for example, have dreams of being chased by a shadowy figure. Jung uses this image of shadow to symbolize the unknown or little known attributes, impulses, qualities that lie in our unconscious that can become conscious. Like our shadow, all this stuff follows us around and we do not see it as easily as do others. We are less aware of these traits in ourselves than we are of those belonging to our neighbors, qualities we dislike or envy, that introduce shame, unease, ethical doubt, that we rationalize away in ourselves by saying, these don't matter much, no one notices them, and besides, everyone else does it too.

Jung was particularly alert to recognizing shadow complexes and bringing them into consciousness. This depotentiates many of them, much as a dog when locked in a closet going hungry becomes vicious, and when liberated and fed, becomes part of daily living. Reckoning with our shadow complexes is a lifelong task, best described as where do we put the bad. We can be sure that if we do not anchor its source in our own denied, split off, repressed attitudes, they will transgress our neighbor's lawn, or children.

Personal shadow material can be traced to family prohibitions and cultural mores about what is acceptable and what is rejected as bad. Greater consciousness introduces more freedom of choice about including shadow contents and attitudes in our daily adaptations, and helps change collective shadow attitudes in society, too, witness greater acceptance of women's ambitions, of sexuality in its many forms, of ethnic groups. Similarly, greater social acceptance in laws presses us individually to reckon with our shadows, and admit more of them into consciousness. ✓If we go deep enough in clinical work, the personal level of what to do with the bad soon mixes in with the collective, and inevitably leads to the archetypal. Dealing with trauma of molestation, for example, where an older person commits sexual theft against a younger one, leads inexorably to Job's question, why do the innocent suffer? Struggling with the effects of such theft, where someone else's disorder invades and leaves a mark forever on our own psyche, leaves us struggling with the shared dimension of evil, its communal aspect, that spawns discrimination, injustice, oppression.

Evil, Psyche, and Society

✓   Clinical work uncovers the dreadful chain of causality between personal shadows and social injustice (Ulanov 1999/2005, chapter 3). Where we repress our grudge-holding, our wish to make someone pay for what has happened to us, to infect an other with what makes us sick, to take all the money or power for ourselves—that repressed shadow does ✓ not just go away. It goes unconscious and remains alive with instinctual impulses, images, emotions, but far out of reach of modification by social or personal reality testing. It regresses to more primitive form, unchecked by what Freud calls the procrastinating function of thought. A repressed grudge, for example, regresses to more archaic form, and sullies everything else in the unconscious whose primary process admits no distinction between inner and outer, you and me, then and now. Everything is ✓ everything. So the petty grudge waxes into all-out rage, and also taints our conscious attitudes and actions. A genuine sweetness now is contaminated with an ulterior motive to discharge a bit of venom in gossip; or our ability to channel aggression to take a stand, now carries a smell of wanting to extract payment for this unacknowledged grievance, even if discharged against a bystander. We pass it along as vengeance.

The chain of causality does not stop here, however. Like all unconscious contents, the repressed offense-taking seeks conscious expression in lived life. From repression, regression, contamination, comes return of the repressed in projection, projective identification. We put onto others what we do not own in ourselves and identify them with this rejected bit of ourselves. The personal becomes social. But then this live bit of shadow menaces us from the outside. This other person or other group carries part of ourselves and we feel compelled to manage them, restrict them, eliminate them. Thus blooms the ugliness of prejudice, discrimination, persecution, oppression, even genocide. Even if the tables get turned and the shadow record gets turned over, the tune plays the same. What was repressed becomes oppressor. Only the intercession of consciousness introduces new alternatives (Ulanov and Ulanov 1975, chapter 11).

A deadly version of this splitting and projective identification spins out of religion because religious images galvanize the deepest archetypal energies of the psyche. Here we fall into identification with our God-images and then want to foist them onto everyone else. Those who do not identify with them, we cast out as damned, as infidel. But further, our God-images get identified with God, and now we speak for God and it is our duty, our religious devotion, to expunge those who do not take up not just our truth, but God's truth. Only with reference to the transcendent can we arrive at the conviction it is our duty to kill others in the name of a living God (Ulanov 2001/2004, chapter 12).

The Hinge of Evil

Greater consciousness, however, takes us down deeper into the mystery of evil. Really knowing our own shadow drops us as if through a trap door into collective evil, and through that to evil *per se*, its mystery in itself. Grudge may be your trap door, mine avarice, someone else's sloth. The seven deadly sins list the usual pitfalls through which we get ushered into evil in the large. An example comes from a woman who stole something from her hotel room in a foreign country. She discounted its seriousness at first, saying, Oh, it is just taking a souvenir, we do it all the time in America. Not until she heard on a tour that theft was the most prevalent crime in that country and exacted prison sentences, did it come crashing in on her that she had done something wrong, careless, inconsiderate, and what it was that she did.

Working on it in analysis, she faced into the moment of theft. She said it was like a blank space, a know-nothing state where what she knew made no difference: rules did not apply to me here, only what I wanted. I was in a zone where it was even as if I had rights to what I wanted, the world belonged to me.

Listening to this, I was mulling over Winnicott's notion that delinquency is a sign of hope, a reaching again for the good-enough mother that had been lost (Winnicott 1975, 228-29). Stealing is reaching over the gap to the mother one has rights to as a small child. And this kind of good mother initially makes the world available to her child, as if reality matches the child's wishes, thus lending her child the illusion that the objective world concurs with the subjective creative impulse. This woman had missed that kind of mothering; it had not been available to her. She did not always face the big suffering that acknowledgment of that lack made her feel. That was the bit in the shadows—the lack, the emotional poverty, the No-thing place in her own forming ego. That bit of still forming ego, left in the shadows, made itself known through behavior in which her stealing displayed a child's attitude that she had rights to the world as there for her taking.

When she realized she had in fact stolen something, and such acts were considered a crime, punishable by going to jail in that country, and that maybe the hotel maid might be held responsible, anxiety came crashing in and self-attack. How could she be so unaware of the culture in which she was a guest, so thoughtless of the maid, acting like an ugly American, especially in the current geopolitical climate, so grandiose to think she had all the rights and that rules did not apply! She saw in herself how stealing could just happen. She made amends by paying for the item (and getting a receipt) but remained sobered, stopped, arrested by this blank space she had found in herself where anything could occur, and she could be arrested in the outside world. The blank space was the ⌣ unmothered child in herself reaching out to claim the mother, acting as if the object were the mother there for the taking. That was the hinge, the trap door between her personal development and the collective problem of stealing.

Once she was aware of this hinge, she noticed it in her all the time. She did not have to go to a foreign country to discover this alien shadowy part of herself; it was no longer so far away from her consciousness. In the cosmetics displays in department stores, she wanted to reach out and take a glittering, cut-glass bottle of perfume. In a grocery store she felt the impulse to take one of the fat dates on display or plump figs in a basket. Did she know that would be stealing? Yes and No. Yes in her observation that she would look around to see if any clerk was watching; No ⌣ in the almost trance-like self-state, a zone out of time and space, moved by desire and the impulse to satisfy it. The world was her oyster, there to feed her yearnings.

That sense of the world as a subjective object, in that moment not existing external to oneself, but existing to reflect me to me, to refer to me, to belong to me and support my coming into being, much as a mothering one does for a child, gave me a clue. She had missed this utterly, and ⌣ through this irrational impulse, this anti-social desire, she was reaching back to take what had belonged to her as a child entitled to a mothering one bringing the world to feed and support her growing into a self. From an ego point of view she was in danger of shoplifting; from a deeper Self point of view her psyche moved her to reach for a left out part, the sheep that got lost, an impulse to go out and find it and bring it in, to make for greater wholeness. Both views are true: the ego's living in community says this is illegal and a violence against neighbor; the Self view, as center of the whole psyche, not just consciousness, says this behavior, this disorder, makes sense in the whole and is struggling to repair the whole.

Another example carries this point further. A woman left by her husband, in what she called a hit and run divorce, that is, with no processing between them of what led up to this rupture—he just said I want a divorce and was gone—felt so devastated that she forgot her own dissatisfactions with the marriage and was rendered powerless. In compensation for being thrown into an abyss of rejection, suicidal ruminations, and despair about the aloneness of her destiny, she constructed what she called Ninja runs. Hidden in the cover of darkness, including clothing and mask, with care taken not to be tracked through toll booths or license or phone, she spied on his new abode and committed vandalism to his property. I analyzed and analyzed the compensating see-saw of powerlessness and power, of hurt and rage, and felt the ethical dilemmas of aggression unbounded toward herself in suicidal temptations and toward him with what threatened felony of breaking and entering, and even said I'd bring her soap in jail.

Her consciousness grew; she stopped herself from breaking and entering and experienced it as a definite line, a boundary she chose not to cross though the temptation was great. Slowly, she contained the riotous opposite emotions she suffered, and the opposition of collective law and order against the disorder of committing felony, but she, and I, could see how easily psychological pain can verge into wickedness against another who has grievously hurt us.

This was a great wrestling we endured; the outcome was positive but not without the wrestling. And the outcome included an amazing surprise. In the worst of her despair about the aloneness of existence, that included suicidal emotions, she began writing poetry. Creativity began in the dark of pain. Her husband brought a court order against her in response to a poem she had written and sent to him. The poem was a good one and configured in bold imagery his denied aggression that savagely attacked others. Enraged, he took her to court to get a restraining order. She saw the irony of this: brought to the law for a creative act, and getting away with illegal acts of vandalism. She prepared her defense carefully and hired a lawyer, thus accepting her dependence on another person, and on the limits of the legal system. The suit was dismissed. What surprised and deeply impressed her, and me, was that she was supported by a bigger rule of law that before she had broken. Working on her own hinge of shadow and evil ushered her into feeling supported by collective justice that before she had felt exiled from. In gratitude, she terminated her Ninja runs.

These examples are small put up against genocide, robbery of pension funds, rape camps, starvation campaigns, street violence, and all the other vast evils we do to each other. But these small acts or omissions contribute to the possibility of the large happening at all. The small and the large evils share in common the rendering of the subject as a disposable object, unrecognized, insignificant. And when we reach the size of terrorist acts that always require the authority of a group and a link to the transcendent, the murdered victims are dismissed as infidel, dust, or as deserving what they got.

Rage at such helplessness ensues, but only wears us out. Evil sneaks into the crevices, the cracks; personal evil acts spawn evil acts on a large collective scale. When military leaders do what is morally wrong, it breaks the spirit of the soldiers and atrocities occur that destroy the sense of continuity in values. Motivated by rage and revenge, it is impossible to distinguish atrocities from acceptable military conduct (Shay 1994, 165-66, 189, 201). Betrayal of what is right, and use of drugs and alcohol to self-medicate, lands many veterans in psychiatric hospitals suffering post traumatic stress disorder. Their sleep for decades is shattered by nightmares that are usually ignored by medical institutional care, yet in fact constitute the psyche's attempt to bring to consciousness and heal this soul-murder (Wilmer 1985, 10ff.).

When a government system draws its vulnerable citizens into its corrupt racial policies, such a person becomes the visible executioner as leader of the hit squad of what the group silently endorses (Gobodo-Madikizela 2003, chapter 4). When church officials reassign to another parish priests guilty of sexual abuse, a virus is let loose into the new community, polluting the innocence of new children, and abandoning the priest to the ravages of his compulsion.

Clinical work can help with these issues of evil on the personal and collective levels. As one psychiatrist put it, I don't believe anyone is crazy; they are just caught up in a faulty premise. About her own treatment she said she felt forgiven by me a lot of the time, meaning, it was not so bad what I did; I did it for a reason. Clinically, we can trace the missing bit that has remained in the shadows and restore it to the community of consciousness. We can help differentiate and endorse the effort to do what we can to address, alleviate collective shared evil. Wrestling with our bad contributes to society. We may remove a drop of venom from the collective atmosphere, but even if we do not solve it, we carry it and do not load it on our neighbor.

Archetypal Patterns of Evil

But what of evil in itself? What of dreams that mix up our personal contributions, even our cultural inputs with evil that is vast and beyond our powers to help? Destructiveness exceeds personal and shared boundaries and pushes over into impersonal destructiveness, gratuitous, beyond the causality of personal motivation. To find our own hinge between the personal and collective allows us to work on our part and not be overwhelmed by senseless violence. But what of the rest? Where is that bad to be put?

What remains repressed in us makes us more susceptible to secret acts against each other that can flood into terrible actions becoming possible on a large scale that we then feel powerless to combat. Almost like a poison leaking into the water, something savage leaks into our social life. Imagery changes. We can see this force in the mocking faces of Jesus' tormentors in Hieronymus Bosch's painting of the scourging of Christ. That envious gleam in the eye betrays the appetite to destroy, that takes over the one who taunts as well as the victim who suffers his jeering. We can feel this force in the hacking to death of a whole people by the rival people, or when horsemen gallop into a village, burn its huts, chase down its inhabitants, running them to death in the dust. We can sense this force when a system of government, or a group, a society, a nation, promotes an abstract position paper and refuses to look into the effects of this policy on actual people, whole groups of them, who will be excluded if this position is endorsed. We can see it in the body posture that turns away, the eyes that refuse to meet others' eyes, conveying a sense we all are descending into the "cheerless, dark and deadly" of *King Lear* (Stocks 1988, 116).

Once we take up evil, it takes us down through the clefts and fissures to the gap where its force is felt and we find ourselves in line behind Cain, and Job, and Jung, too, to ask where does this come from and how are we to respond? It helps to learn we can work on our shadow bits and retrieve on the personal level what has been repressed so it need not regress to primitive form that we act out on self and neighbor. It helps to see that this repair in our individual lives reduces the collective threat of evil in our shared life; by withdrawing our projective identifications of the bad onto others we lessen the acting out of prejudice and violence on a group scale. But what of this impersonal force of evil, what of this vast bad, this seeming evil in itself? What are we to do with the evil force that exceeds personal motives and collective locations?

We know different archetypal patterns of evil—mythologized as chaos, fall, tragic flaw, exiled soul, social dysfunction, rebellion, defile-ment (Ricoeur 1967, 321-24; Stivers 2001). These archetypal symbols are not things in themselves nor end points, but our attempts to describe evil's enigmatic reality. By taking up the question of evil we are inex-orably led to ask, what do we believe about reality and evil's place in it? And belief is now the issue for nothing explains evil away, nothing erad-icates it once and for all. The issue now is not the definition of evil but how we shall live with it. And that means an expanded kind of consciousness that admits evil as well as good, admits unknowing, not knowing as well as knowing, faith as well as doubt.

We are pressed to express how we see the place of evil in relation to our images of the All and Vast, to our God-images, to whatever we call our relation to reality as both here and now and transcendent. Whatever view we hold affects our clinical work, for it is the place from which we hear this particular analysand resonating through all the levels of living—personal, cultural, archetypal. We do not speak of our view, nor does our patient necessarily agree with our view, but we need to be aware how our perspective affects the treatment we offer. We could investigate it through our countertransference to evil and good.

One position, and I would see Jung here, is the tragic view—that evil and good are elements of being itself that inescapably vie with one another as two eternal parts of the whole (Ricoeur 1967, 310ff.; Jung 1960/1964). Jung symbolized this whole as the Self which he described as the center of our whole psyche, conscious and unconscious, and, drawing on St. Augustine's image for God, as whose center is everywhere and whose circumference is nowhere (Jung 1988, 1048). The Self as archetype has good and bad poles, and Self images, Jung says, are indistinguishable from God-images, so God has good and bad, dark and light sides (see Ulanov 1997/2005, 157). Jung answers the question, where, finally, do we put the bad, by putting it in God, that God, or Self, wrestles eternally with opposing poles. Our service to God who seeks incarnation in us is expressed in our willingness to wrestle with the conflict in God of good and evil, by wrestling with good and bad in ourselves and in our world, to bring them into reconciling conjunctions instead of warring opposites (Jung 1963b, 338).

In opposing the notion of evil of Augustine and Aquinas as the privation of good (*privatio boni*), Jung fights for the reality of evil, that it exists and cannot be thought to be a nothing, somehow less substantial than is good (Jung 1960/1964). Jung wants to preserve the unity of the

Self, and he is afraid that as long as evil is a *me on*, a different substantiality than is good, that no one will take the shadow seriously and a Hitler or a Stalin will be seen as representing a mere accidental lack of perfection. Jung fights against splitting off evil from consciousness, a distortion we find too often of the Judeo-Christian message that somehow we must not register evil thoughts and emotions but overcome them by not experiencing them. Jung fights to admit these shadow contents into consciousness and to work to assimilate them, as that depotentiates their projections onto others and makes their energy available for personal and social relationships. Jung fights against moralizing about good that really ends up being a disguise for evil—producing, for example, hardness of heart, smug self-righteousness, the bullying of a good cause, the gossip, the deadly dull goodness devoid of zip, color, and joy, a religion drained of sex and aggression (see Ulanov 1976/1986, 107, 111ff.). Jung fights against the ascription of all evil to us, as that makes us indulge in a miserable worm theology, reducing evil to our fault and that lays the door open to theological sadism.

My view agrees and disagrees with Jung's. At the archetypal level, Jung is right, I believe. Good and evil vie with each other throughout all of life, opposites constantly in contention, neither one vanquishing the other. They do not comprehend each other but split apart and cause splits in us and between us. Insofar as Jung's God-image is his image of the Self, then God too has good and evil sides. This is Jung's God-image: Jung's is an archetypal God. To endorse this tragic view of reality is to gain reassurance that our struggles contribute to the whole, that we are serving God by working to reconcile the opposites of good and evil that persist as conflicting forces from beginning to end. But what of the Self as a symbol, pointing beyond itself to reality? Does God dwell beyond this archetypal God-image?

For me, the Self is not God but that in us that knows about God. Like a navel of the deepest layer of the unconscious, the Self process links to reality that transcends the psyche. All archetypes are bivalent, exhibiting positive and negative poles. The Self is no different and is a compelling God-image precisely because it makes space for destructiveness. In those processes of centering, of symbolizing wholeness, the Self acts as bridge to all-encompassing reality that all God-images denote. Self images and processes, then, extend toward reality that all God-images point to, a reality transcending the psyche in which ordering is spontaneous, whole, unified.

But at the ego level, that is, ordinary conscious level of life, both individually and collectively, we experience the bivalent archetypal field as good and evil fighting against each other, neither fully victorious nor defeated. In every order is disorder. The Gospel of John's ringing words describe this conflict. The light comes into the world and the darkness does not understand it and does not conquer it. If we use blackness as the symbol of the Holy, we can say the gleaming blackness in which the Holy dwells is never subdued by the light. However we use light and dark to symbolize good and evil, they compete forever. The light never outshines the darkness, and the dark never blots out the light (see Frank 1989, 126).

At the depth level, or the height level, depending how we envision the All of reality, another possibility obtains. As Ricoeur says, this is the realm of unverifiable faith; we can believe it, but not prove it (Ricoeur 1967, 321, 328). At the ego level, good and evil, light and dark, always fight. At the depth level, so Christianity proclaims, the light has already conquered; we have been brought home to a healing darkness. Here the heart of reality takes into itself evil and the endless suffering that streams from it. Judaism symbolizes this as the suffering servant of Isaiah, Buddhism as our being ushered into compassion for all sentient beings. Christianity symbolizes this as the figure of Christ who takes the suffering of evil onto himself, saying in effect, the buck stops here. Though innocent, he suffers as if guilty and ends the logic of evil by taking our suffering onto his body, and not being destroyed by it nor by the death it inflicts (Marion 1991, 13, 15, 17, 19, 21). The abyss of love is revealed as stronger than the abyss of death, the power of love as stronger than the power of hate.

To endorse this unverifiable faith ushers us into new opposites in addition to good and evil. On the ego level, we register we are all but blips on the radar screen, not mattering in the larger scheme of things, exchangeable objects; from dust we come and to dust we return. At the depth level of reality that transcends the psyche, and to which our symbols, our language, and our God-images point, each of us is known, cherished, irreplaceable. We know this by faith, unverifiable by the senses, surpassing logic. It is a gift, and gifts can only be received or refused. To receive this gift means to live in paradox, in different spaces or states of consciousness simultaneously. And it is meditating on the mystery of evil that brings us to this new awareness.

Our consciousness admits the reality of the psyche, that though we experience it as ours, the psyche is also objective, not reducible to our subjective experience, nor to social constructions, nor to our historical object relations, any more than the body is. We continue recognizing that our conscious choices, our cultural conditioning, our object relations still influence who we are and can become, but we also see this reality of the psyche. We live in the paradox of discovering the objectivity of the psyche through the subjectivity of our own psyche.

Under the shadow of evil we paradoxically commit wholeheartedly to our lives, grounded in what we are living and believing as if it is the ultimate, and simultaneously disidentify from our path because it is not the ultimate. The ultimate is bigger; we are employees in a larger firm.

That paradox of commitment and nonattachment means we live with knowing and not-knowing, unknowing. Meditating on the evil we do and that is done to us, we go on struggling for more justice, greater charity, and push through to the inevitable mix of order with disorder, good and evil in all things. We sacrifice the ultimacy of our plan for peace, our political vision, our action for justice, at the same time we go on working for it, to put it in place. The mystery of evil abides as mystery in the face of our action. We hold these opposites, suffer their tension, sacrificing the certainty of our knowing, doing, solving, fixing, at the same time we try everything in our power for the good as we see it.

It is only if we remain solely identified with our view of the good that we can split off the bad to put on our neighbor's lawn to be perse- cuted and killed there. Sacrificing our total identification with our ego view of the good, while at the same time endorsing it, working for it, indeed, offering it, even suffering it, admits us into the whole as a strong citizen seeking to align with the wholeness of reality.

The hinge I spoke of, where our personal shadow bits tip us into the collective and archetypal states of evil, also works the other way. If we take seriously the evil we do and the evil done to us both individually and as groups, we are pushed into the bigger question of how evil is part of existence, how we see reality and the place of destructiveness in it. Winnicott worked on the transformation of destructiveness in personal terms, that it establishes the externality of the other as a subject inde- pendent of our projections, and that it feeds our unconscious imagination to see daily events ever afresh (see Ulanov 2001, 116-19). Jung worked on the transformation of destructiveness in God, and saw our struggling with opposites as a service to the divine which anchors our personal and social struggles in meaning.

For me, I see destructiveness finding its proportionate place in the larger whole of reality as channeling aggression through consciousness to build up strong ego and cultural identity and symbols, and at the same time delivering us to the edge of our identities and symbols, pointing beyond them to the larger completeness of reality. We hold to our identity and our symbols at the same time we know this one variation on a larger theme of human identity, this one set of symbolic renderings, is not the whole story. We are anchored and let loose from our moorings simultaneously.

Using our aggression to form images, words, and constructs of how we see the totality, the company for which we work, and seeing that those images and words are destroyed because they are finite and cannot grasp the unoriginated infinite, gives a place to destructiveness within the whole. We project our visions on to the Vast and All, we create God-images, and reify those perceptions into ritual and dogma, and also see that these are what moth and rust doth corrupt. Our precious beliefs are not the ultimate, but they do usher us toward it. The narratives we create are also the narratives that are destroyed, because they are only stories, not the mysterious subject of the stories. But we need the stories to see the mysterious subject.

And so the dance of Aha! I see it, got it, and No! It is not it. The ladder that got me this far is kicked away by reality itself, as if it wants to be immediately experienced by us, not mediated by all we need to symbolize it. The living encounter with mystery destroys our descriptions of it. As Wittgenstein says, "There is indeed the inexpressible, this shows *itself*" (Wittgenstein 1955, 6.522, cited in B. Ulanov 1973/2003, 260).

References

A shorter version of this chapter was originally given as a presentation at a conference on evil sponsored by the Metropolitan Center for Mental Health, New York City, May 2005; and was published in *Quadrant* 36, 1 (Winter 2006).

Bion, W. R. 1965/1983. *Transformations*. New York: Jason Aronson.

Bollas, C. 1995. *Cracking Up*. New York: Hill and Wang.

Diagnostic and Statistical Manual of Mental Disorders IV. 1994. Washington, D.C.: American Psychiatric Association.

Frank, S. L. 1989. *The Light Shineth in Darkness*. Trans. Boris Jakim. Athens, Ohio: Ohio University Press.

Gobodo-Madikizela, P. 2003. *A Human Being Died That Night*. New York: Houghton Mifflin.

Grand, S. 2000. *The Reproduction of Evil*. Guilford, Conn.: Analytic Press.

Jung, C. G. 1952/1958. Answer to Job. In *Psychology and Religion:*

West and East. Vol. 11 of *Collected Works*. Trans R. F. C. Hull. New York: Pantheon.

———. 1960/1964. Good and evil in analytical psychology. In *Civilization in Transition*. Vol. 10 of *Collected Works*. Trans. R. F. C. Hull. New York: Pantheon.

———. 1963a. *Mysterium Coniunctionis*. Vol. 14 of *Collected Works*. Trans. R. F. C. Hull. New York: Pantheon.

———. 1963b. *Memories, Dreams, Reflections*. Ed. Aniela Jaffé. Trans. Richard and Clara Winston. New York: Pantheon.

———. 1988. *Nietzsche's Zarathustra*. 2 vols. Ed. James L. Jarrett. Princeton, N.J.: Princeton University Press.

Marion, J-L. 1991. *Prolégomènes à la Charité*. Paris: La Différence.

Miller, A. 1981. *Prisoners of Childhood*. Trans. Ruth Miller. New York: Basic Books.

Ricoeur, P. 1967. *The Symbolism of Evil*. Trans. Emerson Buchanan. Boston: Beacon.

Schauer, T. G. 2004. *The New Yorker*, August 2.

Shay, J. 1994. *Achilles in Viet Nam*. New York: Athenaeum.

Stivers, R. 2001. *Evil in Modern Myth and Ritual*. Athens, Ga.: University of Georgia Press.

Stocks, K. 1988. *Emily Dickinson and the Modern Consciousness*. New York: St. Martin's Press.

Ulanov, A., and B. Ulanov. 1975. *Religion and the Unconscious*. Louisville, Ky.: Westminster John Knox Press.

Ulanov, A. B. 1976/1986. Disguises of the good. In *Picturing God*, 107-26. Einsiedeln, Switzerland: Daimon.

———. 1997/2005. Jung and religion: the opposing Self. In *Spirit in Jung*. Einsiedeln, Switzerland: Daimon; also in *Cambridge Companion to Jung*, chapter 15. 1997/2007. Ed. Polly Young-Eisendrath and Terence Dawson. Cambridge: Cambridge University Press.

———. 1999/2005. The double-cross: scapegoating. In *Spirit in Jung*, chapter 3. Einsiedeln, Switzerland: Daimon.

————. 2001. *Finding Space: Winnicott, God, and Psychic Reality.* Louisville, Ky.: Westminster John Knox Press.

————. 2001/2004. When religion prompts terrorism. In *Spiritual Aspects of Clinical Work.* Einsiedeln, Switzerland: Daimon.

Ulanov, B. 1973/2003. Mysticism and negative presence. In *Creative Dissent*, chapter 22. Eds. Alan Roland, Barry Ulanov, and Claude Barbre. Westport, Conn.: Praeger. Originally published in Columbia University's *Journal of Ancient Near Eastern Society* 5 (1973): 411-20.

Wilmer, H. 1985. War nightmares: a decade after Vietnam. In *Vietnam in Remission.* Eds. James F. Veninga and Harry A. Wilmer. College Station, Tex.: Texas A&M University Press.

Winnicott, D. W. 1950/1959. Aggression in relation to emotional development. In *Through Pediatrics to Psychoanalysis.* New York: Basic Books.

————. 1963/1965. Morals and education. In *The Maturational Processes and the Facilitating Environment.* New York: International Universities Press.

————. 1971. *Playing and Reality.* London: Tavistock.

————. 1975. *The Child, the Family, the Outside World.* Harmondsworth, Middlesex, England: Penguin.

Wittgenstein, L. 1955. *Tractatus Logico-Philosophicus.* London: Cambridge University Press.

CHAPTER 7

THE THIRD IN THE
SHADOW OF THE FOURTH

The notion of "the third" has captured the minds of many psycho-analysts in recent years. Taken together, different theorists see the third as the mutative agent in treatment, as that mysterious something that brings about healing. The third puts the participants in analysis in touch with regenerative process, ushering them into creative aliveness that undoes deadness. In addition, focus on the third transcends binary oppo-sitions so antithetical to postmodern thinking, giving evidence of the fresh paradigm of our new century and millennium, where either/or positions yield to open-ended constructions of meaning.

Brief Review of Literature

Winnicott focused attention on the space between mother and infant, infant and beloved bear (the transitional object), analysand and analyst, finding there, in that transitus between I and other, that our self is both found and created. We do not get the one without the two. Indeed, the external subjectivity of the other (including the world) gets established by its capacity to survive our destructiveness (Winnicott 1971, chapter 6; 1963/1965, 76-77). The third space between self and other enables the one—the self—to be and become, and the two—the other—to be and become real, a resource for living.

I see Winnicott's transitional space as replicated in subsequent relationships throughout life, particularly in their beginnings, for example, in love, in creativity, in prayer (Ulanov 2001a). In the beginning of a relationship two kinds of bonds are inaugurated—to the other without, be it lover, mentor, child, idea, musical sound, color, or spiritual object—and to the other within, that is, a specific psychic content aroused in response to the object without, like erotic desire, a dissociated self-state, an animus figure. It is in the space in between the outer and the inner other that growth flourishes, discoveries surprise, suffering roots in meaning, destructiveness finds its proper proportion.

That space-in-between is the third which facilitates oneness and twoness and their interaction. We can diagnose difficulties of analysands in terms of not enough oneness—a self not big enough to include destructiveness; or not enough twoness—another not big enough to meet our dependence and survive our destructiveness. An example of not enough oneness is a middle-aged woman of two cultures, American and Near Eastern, enmeshed in her family. My countertransference alerted me to how grave the entanglement was. Listening to her I felt myself going to sleep; not feeling sleepy, but pulled under, conked out, no space to get air or my footing. This particular countertransference was unusual for me (my complexes veer in the opposite direction). I was experiencing, I believe, and was eventually able to use in interpretation, the analysand's absence of space for an experience of herself as an independent subject.

An example of not enough twoness comes from a consultation after I gave a public lecture. The man told me he fell asleep with his eyes open when I started speaking, that he did not want to hear what touched something deep inside him. The only thing he remembered from my lecture was my phrase, "it is never too late." What emerged in our conversation was what I called an emotional catastrophe. At the age of ten, his family moved away from the old neighborhood that he experienced as loving and full of friends, to what was called a better house and community. He experienced the move as a frightening rupture, all the friends taken away, his world lost, so painful that he shut off all feelings thereafter, and still lived in that sealed-up state now as middle-aged man. He said he lived in fear; I could also feel the unacknowledged hostility. Prognosis for healing turns around how much the third space can be regenerated in between analyst and analysand.

André Green asserts that the third locates in the mind of the mother involved with her infant and, analogously, in the mind of the analyst engaged with the analysand. The infant is one, the mother (or analyst) is two, and the third is the mother's consciousness of the father who symbolizes the concrete partner in making this infant and also the mother's own subjectivity. The third is what is in the mother's mind not to do with the baby, though it will affect her relation to the baby (Green 2000, 25). If this third is "radically excluded" from the mother's mind, this is fateful for mental illness for then there is no space in between mother and infant, or analyst and analysand, in which the fertile No-thing space can become symbolized (ibid., 45). Green sees symbolization as the reuniting of two parts that were separated, rebinding this broken unity by a third element distinct from the two parts in reunion. Green summarizes: "Firstness is being, secondness relating, and thirdness is thinking" (ibid., 63).

My response to the analyst being like the mother who thinks of the father is that the third is what is in our minds not to do with analysands specifically, though it affects them because we bring it with us into the work in our orientation. The third is what we relate to that supports our work, what helps us contribute to patients; it is what we rely on, such as passion about our theory of analysis, or a love of art, or of poetry, or a devotion to God, or a practice of meditation.

We all know of therapeutic situations where this gap between analyst and analysand does not emerge and no back and forth in the space-in-between to flex imagination and symbolization occurs. Instead, the analyst's mind is blotted out; the analysand registers no associations, nothing clicks. In one such case, the analysand endorsed the reality level to the exclusion of the imaginal, attacking me as saying incomprehensible things.

159

For Lacan the third is speech, represented by the symbolic father interposed between mother and infant, and between analysand and unconscious. If the third does not interpose itself (Lacan's "le mot"), nothing interrupts the potential merger of mother and baby, analyst and analysand, I and unconscious. Without this third space in between the two, one can kill or be killed, for example, in the image of the mother nursing forever and then turning and eating the baby. Or we could cite analyses that go on for decades, years and years, erasing the hard fact that an analytical couple does not substitute for a real couple. Lacan and Green locate the third in the analyst's mind, a point of observation removed from the immediate here and now incarnate reality of analysand and analyst. This removal to an observation point that only the analyst has privy to, introduces a hierarchy into analytical work, as if only the analyst knows, dispenses insight and healing.

The intersubjectivists, Atwood, Stolorow, and Orange, and the more recent relational group of analysts, see the third as a system of reciprocal influence in which the analysand comes to recognize the analyst's subjectivity. Instead of the impassive objective neutrality of the analyst who knows, here the analyst discloses subjective responses and facts. The third builds up as the one and the two communicate their subjectivity. I agree with Jessica Benjamin that the third is more of a process than a structure, more of a process in motion, in the making and breaking down that the two people create, destroy, and repair in endless repetitions. The third is not a structure in which the two are situated, but a capacity to surrender to in the living relationship of analysis (Benjamin 2003).

Thomas Ogden understands the third as an intersubjectivity growing from the unconscious permeability between analyst and analysand. The analytic pair construct an "intersubjective third," a "third subjectivity" that is distinct from the subjectivities of the two. The analytic pair experience the third as an unfolding flux transformed by their separate understandings of what is happening between them (Ogden 1999, 25n, 30). Each participates in the new analytic objects created between them, but asymmetrically, with more emphasis on the inner object world of the analysand. But the analyst pays close attention in each analytic session to his own reverie as a clue to the drift of the unconscious of the analysand (ibid., 109-10, 190).

Ogden remembers, for example, his annoyance with his garage man, or his noticing the fancy label of his client's coat that she carelessly tossed on the floor, or his evasion of his dying friend's loneliness. Through this shadow route, that is, affects that fall outside our preferred analytic attitude, he traces connections to his patient's irritations, spyings, and evasions. What may look like the analyst's failure to be receptive but instead being preoccupied, turns out, upon examination, to be specific to a particular moment in a particular analysis and a shift comes about into joint creation. Ogden rarely speaks about such reveries to his patient, but urges analysts to speak from that space (ibid., see 158, 162, 175, 187). The analyst's unconscious process gets elaborated in specific ways by what is going on unconsciously in his analysand. This intersubjective unconscious process generated between the analytic pair creates new intersubjective events that have not existed before for either party (ibid., 190).

This is an example, I think, of what has been called objective countertransference. The analyst gets informed through registering his unconscious experience about what is going on unconsciously in the patient. Ogden describes what Jungians might call shadow meandering, that is, affects and contents that conflict with the persona we believe appropriate as analysts. Yet it is always our inferiorities that link us together, knitting us all into the human family like so many fellow refugees. The archetypal shadow is not illustrated by Ogden and that bears on a criticism Benjamin has of Ogden's view, that his is the negative of the third, rather than a true third, because the space in between the analytic pair gets erased, blended, merged (Benjamin 2003).

Jessica Benjamin sees the third as the process the analyst and analysand create between them. Each surrenders to the flow of feeling linking them as two subjects, only then to split apart into a subject reduced to an object, then to repair the breach and become again two stronger subjects in recognizing and forgiving each other (Benjamin 2005, 197-98). When an impasse in communication occurs, each feels treated as a mere object by the other, feeling alternately helpless to mend the disconnection and blaming the other for the rupture, or accusing oneself of failure. Repair begins when each lets go of ego stances to discern their own part in the breach and appreciate again the subjectivity of the other. This rhythm of connection, breakdown, repair is the process of the third to which we yield. Any of us who have been mothers of infants recognize this rhythm, now transposed into analytic work. Although Benjamin wants to transcend binary dualism, the implicit model of mother-infant reasserts a power hierarchy.

As long ago as 1959, the theologian Paul Tillich posited the third as the source of healing, saying there is "essential goodness, existential estrangement, and the possibility of something, a 'third,' beyond essence and existence, through which cleavage is overcome and healed" (Tillich 1959, 199). In short, the "third" is a vision of "reconciliation"; "the third is Life" (cited in Lowe 1984, 250, 253). Theologically, we could say that the third partakes of the Holy Spirit, that source and force that digs up the secrets of the heart and the depths of the Godhead.

All of these theorists call our attention to this crucial space-in-between, to the third. I want to suggest that we cannot see this third, this space-in-between, except in the shadow of the fourth, something Jung explored decades ago, yet is at once astoundingly postmodern in its implications for clinical work and for understanding reality.

Jung and the Third

In 1916 Jung wrote a pivotal essay on what he called the transcendent function which is where he locates what is now called, and what he called then, the third (Jung 1916/1960). Our conflicts split us into two: consciously we want to diet, unconsciously gobble. Consciously we want to free ourselves from enthrallment to a fetish; unconsciously our behavior of fascination endlessly repeats itself. Consciously we want to commit suicide; unconsciously a dream reveals that a part of us is already dead and should be buried (see Ulanov 1992a/2004, 45; 1996a, chapter 3; 1997/2005, 161). Our conflicts also split us apart from other people, each of us insisting on opposing views, a splitting we see in analytical groups, religious traditions, political parties, nations. The transcendent function is a natural psychic process of going back and forth between opposites to create a third out of the two.

In analysis, the analyst often must at first carry one of the contrary points of view warring in the patient, bringing the left out opposite into steady conversation with the analysand's ego position, until the analysand can consciously bear the tension of carrying both opposites. The analyst, at first, does not know about the adverse position but finds herself arranged within the transference-countertransference field to embody it. For example, the patient enmeshed in the conflicting cultures of her heritage suffered opposing tendencies in herself—the American one saying, have your own life and speak up with your point of view (as a teenager she wanted to become a cheerleader); and the Near Eastern one saying, gently facilitate a pleasing environment for others to feel in harmony. Her life as an independent subject combining both these cultural imperatives had not steadily awakened, but only blinked off and on. I had at first to descend into almost unconsciousness to know firsthand what she did not yet know, that she was ensnared in the family unit and, like the sleeping princess, needed to be awakened.

For Jung, the third locates in the space between the opposites within us and among us. In analysis we find the third working in the transference-countertransference space between analyst and analysand, and also in the space within each of them, between conscious and unconscious opposing viewpoints and behaviors. Jung writes, "We are crucified between the opposites and delivered up to the torture until the 'reconciling third' takes shape. . . . A life without inner contradiction is either only half a life or else a life in the Beyond, which is destined only for angels. But God loves human beings more than the angels" (Jung 1973, 20 August 1945, 376; see also Ulanov 1996b, 194).

⌄   The third for Jung also locates in the spontaneous appearance of a creative solution to the tension of the opposites which emerges if we can bear that tension consciously. Jung writes, "The solution, seemingly of its own accord, appears out of nature. Then and then only is it convincing. It is felt as 'grace.' Since the solution proceeds out of the confrontation and clash of opposites, it is usually an unfathomable mixture of conscious and unconscious factors, and therefore a symbol, a coin split into two halves which fit together precisely" (Jung 1963b, 335).

For example, the bi-cultural woman woke up to the fact she was behaving as if she was still a child, ceding to everyone else grown-up authority superior to her own. As she began consciously to relate to the child part of herself instead of falling into unconscious identification with it, a new confidence in her own depths grew, and new images appeared. She confided about an anal itching that had persisted for years, that she would resist scratching (which she also called itching) until it woke her up at night. Then she would indulge in a frenzy of scratching ("itching"), and return to sleep. Itch means "a peculiar tingling or uneasy irritation of the skin which causes desire to scratch the part affected" (*Random House College Dictionary* 1975, 711). She was awakened from unconsciousness to desire, and indeed, this nether location included sexual excitement, which, along with vaginal pleasure, comprised part of lovemaking with her husband. The desire now was psychic. She exclaimed, Something comes alive in me! It's fighting for my soul; I want to go after what I want; I do not want to do things as I have done them; what is my task? What is my soul to be doing?

She had pursued for years a sincere spiritual practice of meditation, reading, prayer, but she felt she became disembodied; the practice did not translate into more living in the world. We began to see the urgency of the anal itching as the exact compensation, bringing her down into her body in an unmistakable way. Contrary to Freud's essay on the anal character, she is not overly orderly, parsimonious, or obstinate, but just the opposite, though it may be, as Freud says, that "one may expect to find but little of the 'anal character' in persons who have retained the erotogenic quality of the anal zone into adult life . . ." (Freud 1908, 32). Also relevant to her is the anal stage in Erikson's schema that centers around the task of developing will and autonomy versus self-doubt (Erikson 1959, 65-74).

As she held in consciousness both opposites of daily spiritual meditation and nightly anal itching, new images emerged that reconciled them. The new images pictured a woman with an elephant trunk. She drew her face framed by her big feet stretched out straight on either side of the face. She has strength, my analysand said, and there is something sweet about her; the trunk is for sniffing, and the weight of her grounds me. She connected this image with her long-standing meditation practice, saying the elephant's sensitivity to tremors in the earth through feet and trunk (for example in the coming tsunami in Southeast Asia) was also response to the cosmic Om vibration of universal consciousness. At home, she imaginatively enacted being the elephant, she said, on all fours with my rear in the air, aware of my rear, as if with big feet and pressing into the floor, with primitive grunts from my gut, and solid deliberate walking.

Her drawings of the elephant woman showed massive legs and buttocks. She would bend over backward before a mirror and look through her legs to see reflected, she said, my animal body, that whole anal/genital area. She said, I am an animal, a human animal; I go back to something I lost, and get consciousness of that whole area. I am allowing myself to experience it. The pictures were strong: the buttocks, thighs, anal and genital area dominated, and her breasts hanging down between her legs look, with their nipples, like eyes. She drew herself seeing herself looking at herself. The last elephant picture featured the vagina as the central focus.

This whole eruption from the unconscious was previewed by a dream of "horses being hung over wires; their legs are hanging down for 'pedicure' (being shoed). Then they slowly begin to fall, to come to the ground. The wires break. It is like a stampede. There are many of them. I am caught in the middle and at first frightened, but then decide not to be afraid. The horse starts kissing me and I say, I love you too."

The dream pictures a huge amount of animal energy coming down to be lived. The high voltage of her spiritual practice where, she said, she was always going up, has ensnared the animal horse energy that must get shoes to run on the ground. The dream-ego decides not to be afraid, but to receive this energy that could stampede, to love it. In the transference, she exclaimed, I am an adult with you, myself, not a child pleasing. I want to break out! I like who I am with you. She felt, she said, that coming into my body is shaking me at my foundations, waking me up to my essence so I don't squander it, but to be a presence that the divine presence works through. The third thing here is the animal body energy coming into her living, and connecting her up to life at its center, symbolized by divine presence.

Not only does this marvelous third thing—a new attitude, a new symbol, a new behavior—help resolve the bedeviling conflict of the two, it also makes us feel thread into the center of life itself. Our little opposites pass us through the great opposites of life itself. Jung writes,

> What the union of opposites really "means" transcends imagination. . . . *tertium non datur.* . . . we are dealing with an eternal image, an archetype. Whenever this image is obscured [our] life loses its proper meaning and consequently its balance. So long as [we] know that [we are] the carrier of life and that it is therefore important for [us] to live, then the mystery of [our] soul lives also—no matter whether [we are] conscious of it or not. But if [we] no longer see the meaning of [our] life in its fulfillment, and no longer believe in [our] eternal right to this fulfillment, then [we have] betrayed and lost [our] soul, substituting for it a madness which leads to destruction. . . . (Jung 1963a, par. 201)

Healing psychological conflicts thus transforms the soul.

Decades of clinical work have convinced me that people's experience of this transcendent function working within them brings direct experience of something transcendent beyond them. Jung makes this connection, saying the creative solution "represents the result of the joint labors of conscious and the unconscious, and attains the likeness of the God-image in the form of the mandala" (Jung 1963b, 335). Our personal clash of opposites reveals that it, and we, live within a greater whole: "The clash, which is at first of a purely personal nature, is soon followed by the insight that the subjective conflict is only a single instance of the universal clash of opposites" (ibid.). "Nature consists entirely of such 'thirds,' bridging the gulf between the opposites just as a waterfall mediates between 'above' and 'below'" (Jung 1963a, 674). The third reveals the larger fourth, emerges from the fourth, is sponsored by the fourth.

For Jung, then, healing locates within the third in the process of the transference-countertransference field in the space between analyst and analysand. Healing locates within the third space within each person between conscious and unconscious opposing perspectives. Healing locates in the third that reveals the fourth; indeed, it yields to the fourth as the author or source of the surprising solution to the bedeviling conflict. Our personal third creative solution that comes to us like grace, gift, a mysterious something that shelters our sorrows, extends from and gives perception of a larger fourth—a whole reality, of which our experience of the third is a tiny example.

Connection to the transcendent function working in us by which the third is created, a kind of everyday transcendence, opens us to the *Deus Absconditus*, the God hidden in and yet beyond the depths of our own psyche. Like a wild animal crossing our path, that comes when it chooses, this "wild wisdom" just appears, like "a living thing . . . that reveals its presence to you" (Jung 1988, vol. 2, 876). Appearance of the third feels like release into a new reality, like a river that flows in us, through us, beyond us, back to its source. But questions loom. Who or what is its source? Who or what is the giver of this creative solution? Is it connected to us personally? Can we personally be in touch with it? The third raises the question of the fourth. Each of us must grow toward our own answer to such questions. As clinicians, we must mull over our answers because what we believe to be the source of the mutative agent of healing directly affects our work with analysands.

Jung and the Fourth

Jung explored such questions and traced the third to its archetypal roots. We can feel those roots in an ordinary analytic session as we feel arranged by our analysand's unconscious to play certain roles in the treatment. We can feel those archetypal roots with our analysand as a couple, so to speak, when we see we two get arranged to perceive what emerges as a third in the space between us to be lived for its own purposes. For example, contacting the child part in the bi-cultural woman opens to *the* child in all its archetypal varieties from orphan to wonder at the new. When the archetypal child, this pattern of energies, gets constellated in treatment, access to renewed energies, youthful zest, a sense of rebirth moves the patient, appears in the dream material, in the transference/countertransference. On the negative side of the child image, a kind of abandon of communal and ethical standards can get constellated, a free-for-all-do-anything-that-you-desire air because the child sees only its own point of view.

In a patient's presenting symptoms, we can spot the ancient mystery of three and four. Masud Khan gives the example of a successful young pop-musician who sought analysis because he was an onlooker, not really living his life. Only in sleep and in his frequent drug trips did he feel intense aliveness; he wanted to capture it into his daily life. In his description, we hear of the three and the four: "When I hear the right tune in that state, I *am* that tune which I am also hearing. . . . There are four of us: the tune, me listening to the tune, and the tune and me as one. And yet again we are also all one. That is the joy of it" (Khan 1983, 48).

Jung researched the same joy in the axiom of Maria Prophetessa, the Hebrew prophet taken to be the sister of Moses, the Copt, the seer of alchemy, who "cried without restraint, 'One becomes two, two becomes three, and out of the third comes the One as the fourth'" (Jung 1967, 209; 1963a, 619; 1953, 152). Her axiom runs through seventeen centuries of alchemy, acting as an undercurrent to Christianity, filling in the gaps left by that dominant religion (Jung 1953, 26). Jung cites Plato speaking of the three/four mystery in the *Timaeus*: "One, two, three . . . but where is the fourth?" and Goethe in *Faust* as well, where the Nereids and Tritons exclaim, "Three we brought with us, the fourth would not come. He was the right one. Who thought for them all" (Jung 1948/1958, 243).

We are familiar with Jung's emphasis on symbols of the fourth and the quaternity as a spontaneous manifestation of psychic structure within the human psyche—the psychological functions of thinking, feeling, intuition, sensation—and as an ordering image of the cosmos itself (Jung 1938/1958, 62-63, 90, 98, 105, 107; 1953, 31). As an archetype, "this quaternity . . . can be interpreted in any number of ways . . . ," says Jung (Jung 1967, 207), and gives examples of the four seasons, the four quarters of heaven, the four "roots" of Empedocles, the four rivers flowing from Eden, the four animals in the vision of Daniel, the four cherubim in Ezekiel's vision.

The fourth is not the ultimate end number, witness the research Jung did on the fifth, the quintessence or quincunx, that also appears in people's dreams (Jung 1953, 327; Ulanov 2001b, 74) and has been associated with the center crown of Christ's cross uniting its four beams. Jung writes, "The process of transformation does not come to an end with the production of the quaternity symbol" (Jung 1963a, 264), but we are still catching up with the fourth that symbolizes getting into daily living the healing locus of the third.

This is where we are now, I believe, individually and socially. Our work personally and collectively, I suggest, is sorting out the fourth that engineers the third wherein healing locates. For all the stuff, the *materia prima* that does not get included in conscious living, bundles into the fourth. Just as we cannot find the healing third except in the shadow of the fourth, we cannot get to the fourth without going through the shadow of undifferentiated life stuff lying in the unconscious. Jung speaks of it as "the recalcitrant fourth," adversary of the Christian Trinity, hence all that lies missing outside the model of conscious social and individual integration (Jung 1948/1958, 280).

What do we find in the fourth? The bad, the destructive, whatever is evil, what not only competes with our ideals of the good, but seeks to dismantle the good, exterminate it (Jung 1953, 123, 297). We see this in any fundamentalistic approach, be it to religious truths, political positions, environmental causes, neurotic complexes. Those who fall outside our definition of the good are to be banned, put outside our community, even killed, as epidemics of genocide horribly illustrate. That kind of splitting off of what we find bad, and projectively identifying it with those whom we then scapegoat, is the solution of the two. If we can only get rid of the bad, kill it, that is, keep the one for ourselves and export the evil two onto others, then the third—its precious value symbolized by the land, the religion, the safety—can be secured.

We find as well in the undifferentiated fourth the missing feminine that stands for the earth, the Virgin out of whose material body the savior is born, the *Mater Dei*, the matrix from which the Trinity issues, symbolized in the wooden carvings of the *Vierge Ouvrante* where Mary houses the Father, Son, and Holy Spirit (Jung 1938/1958, 103-4, 107, and n. 52; see Neumann 1955, 234, 331, plates 176-77 for illustrations; Jung 1963b, 563; Jung 1976, 1552). The feminine in its own right, not less than the masculine, not even thought of as equal to the masculine, but *sui generis*, a mode of being human, still lies too much in the shadows despite all the advances made through feminism. Jung saw the conjunction of feminine and masculine as the encompassing symbol for all divisive oppositions (Jung 1953, 192; see also Ulanov 1971, 144).

We also find in the fourth what Jung calls the inferior function, that which is archaic, primitive in us and which, surprisingly, plays a pivotal role in the process of individuation and, more surprising still, acts as the stable in which the deity is born: "the mystery always begins in the inferior function, that is the place where new life, regeneration, is to be found" (Jung 1988, vol. 2, 954). For when the inferior function is constellated in consciousness, it drags the whole of the unconscious with it (Jung 1948/1958, 184, 185, 290; 1953, 31, 193, 269; 1971, 763-64). It also pushes us into the mob: "If you understand your inferior function, you understand the collective lower man, because your inferior function is exceedingly collective. It is unconscious, archaic, with all the vices and virtues of the collective man. . . . That is the reason why we have such a resistance against the inferior function. We have a feeling of being soiled. . . . there is something dangerous about it; it can overwhelm the conscious existence of the individual" (Jung 1988, vol. 2, 1022). The inferior function refers to capacities that lie undeveloped in us, outside conscious ego control and hence outside the modifying influence of personal and social reality: "It refuses to come along with the others and often goes wildly off on its own." Its "roots reach back as far as the animal kingdom . . ." (Jung 1948/1958, 244; 1963a, 276, 277). I think of this function in each of us as an unlockable door through which the lowest and the highest can barge at any time, bringing with it the tremendous energy of our animal root-impulse (see Ulanov 1998/2004, 289-300). As Jung puts it, the lowly origin of our inferior function lies in the dark, yet it also "dwells with and is friends with the gods . . . always to be found both below *and* above. . . . It seeks, and itself is, what I have elsewhere called 'the treasure hard to attain'" (Jung 1967, 205).

This amazing and precious treasure is found through the human psyche and connects to what lies far outside us. The mysterious fourth leads, writes Jung, "straight to the Anthropos idea that stands for [our] wholeness, that is, the conception of a unitary being who existed before man and at the same time represents [our] goal. The one joins the three as the fourth and thus produces the synthesis of the four in a unity" (Jung 1953, 210; 1963b, 619). In this way the fourth acts like the "life force (*vis animans*)" or the "glue of the world (*glutinum mundi*) which is the medium between mind and body and the union of both" (Jung 1953, 209). The fourth, then, speaks of human wholeness and serving the whole of reality, of finding where we fit in and feeling joy in contributing our bit to the entire mosaic, thereby experiencing the unity underlying our multiplicity. Religion speaks of this experience as loving God; alchemy speaks of it as perceiving the link between psyche and matter, beholding the *unus mundus*, that the stuff of matter is the stuff of psyche and vice versa.

In the clinical practice of analysis the symbol of four often turns up in patients' material. Jung saw the fourth, the quaternity, as representing "the parts, qualities, and aspects of the One" (Jung 1938/1958, 98), thus acting as "a vehicle of the synthesis in which the individuation process culminates" where the goal of individuation is "symbolized by the putting together of the four"; hence Jung took the quaternity as "a symbol of the self . . ." (Jung 1948/1958, 281). Yet our Self experience links to what transcends us, exists as the center of reality far outside us because Jung also recognized that the age-old pre-historic quaternity symbol has always been "associated with the idea of a world-creating deity. . . ." Jung found that his patients, in the face of such symbols of the fourth arising in their symptoms and their dreams, "took it to symbolize *themselves* or rather *something in themselves*. They felt it belonged intimately to themselves as a sort of creative background, a life-producing sun in the depths of the unconscious" (Jung 1938/1958, 100). Jung sees the quaternity as "a more or less direct representation of the God who is manifest in his creation. . . . We might, therefore, conclude that the symbol spontaneously produced in the dreams of modern people means something similar—*the God within*" (ibid., 101).

Thus we find both from clinical work with analysands and from theoretical research into the history of symbols, that the small and great are united. Jung says, "This mystical idea is forced upon the conscious mind by dreams and visions. . . . My observations date to 1914" (ibid.). For Jung, the symbolic concept of the Self links the inner psyche and outer reality. We can look at the "God-image aspect of the quaternity as a reflection of the self, or, conversely, explain the self as the *Imago Dei* in man. Both propositions are psychologically true, since the self, which can only be perceived subjectively as a most intimate and unique thing, requires universality as a back ground . . ." (Jung 1948/1958, 282).

Images of the God within that appear right on the border between oneself and the cosmos suggest that, in borderline behavior, we need to look at what the border discloses, and not just at the one side or the other, but the conjunction of the two sides in a third and pointing to the fourth as the total picture. The crazy behavior of a person afflicted with a borderline condition seems so when viewed from first one opposite and then the other. Seeing such behavior from the inclusive perspective of both-and, the personal and the universal, yields better clinical results, I have found (see Ulanov and Ulanov 1994, 270-80).

Living the Fourth

All very well and good, interesting. But what of living? Here is the rub. Like Adam Phillips who recognizes the unconscious as the interrupter (Phillips 1995, 7), Jung calls the unconscious the "fly in the ointment, the skeleton in the cupboard of perfection, the painful lie given to all idealistic pronouncements, the earthiness that clings to our human nature and sadly clouds the crystal clarity we long for. . . . But at the same time is . . . the basis for the preparation of the philosophical gold" (Jung 1967, 207). To find that gold, we must house the fourth, or rather, find the fourth housing us in the ordinary living of our lives, for healing of suffering lies in finding its meaning if not its resolution. Meaning is found in the spaces of the third sponsored in the shadow of the fourth.

Shadow is the operative word here, for to incarnate, to make real the insights that promote individuation, means accepting the imperfect, the cloudy, the earthy, the disordered, the opposite of our ideals. This acceptance is crucial in our new century and millennium for it applies to nations and world religions as well as to individuals. If the basic question of the twentieth century was being versus non-being, the paradigmatic shift into the twenty-first century turns on the question how to be committed with all our hearts, souls, minds, and strength to what we believe as the true, good, and beautiful and, simultaneously, to admit and accept that our neighbor, near and far, engages a similar commitment to a different spiritual object, a different vision of the good. As Jung said, if we lose the soul, madness substitutes for it, only destruction will follow. Having a soul commitment and honoring others' builds social space between us, the third, where peace may flourish. But that space of acceptance is made possible only by our notice of the shadowy fourth advocating, advancing, promoting the third.

Our old way of handling difference is to split into good versus bad, better versus worst, a hierarchy of superior to inferior. Under splitting of good and bad is an opposite blurring, from falling into identification with what we believe, and then unconsciously insisting that others identify with it, too, or be exiled outside the permissible. Our groping toward a new way in this new century means recognizing difference as a step toward differentiation, that though we do not agree on the vision, we all are looking to the same origin point. If devoted to our particular way, deeply, we can sense the same depth of devotion in others. Together we can take an interest in what each has to tell about the mysterious center around which we all circle (see Cousins 1992, chapter 6).

But this means wrestling with our own efforts to house our perception of the fourth as we seek the spaces of the third. Here shadow takes on at least two meanings, one destructive and the other constructive, protective. We are familiar with the destructive shadow as those undeveloped, unintegrated impulses and desires that burst into our behavior or attitudes that oppose our conscious values. This destructive shadow is the other side of what we hold to be good. For example, we see it in collective form in the other side of the three great monotheisms that can explode into fundamentalistic jihad, not now as struggle to follow Allah but to exterminate all those outside our faith as infidel; or as Christian crusade against all others who are seen as evil; or as a chosenness of Judaism over against the unchosen. The huge task we face in our new century is finding processes of acknowledging instead of exterminating the opposite.

Less familiar is shadow as protective. The Psalms speak of our finding shelter under the shadow of God's wings (Ps. 63:7: "For thou hast been my help, and in the shadow of thy wings I sing for joy" [RSV]). Light can be glaring, parching, and trail with it inadvertent racism, as if dark always means less, or bad. We forget the necessity of growth beginning in the dark, sponsored by what a little patient of Marion Milner's called the lovely black, that Gregory of Nyssa and St. Bernard took to be the acme of spiritual perception. In clinical work, as Loewald put it so well, the analyst holds the patient's core until the patient can grow it. Hence things are allowed to dwell in the dark, finding there a kind of nutriment, like the airy ebony of compost. Our holding something of the analysand in the shadows, insulated from the light of premature interpretation, protects us as analysts from impinging our agenda on the analysand (see Ulanov 1992b/2004, 250).

What is undeveloped in us, what lies in the inferior function, grows at a slower rate than our developed functions. The darkness of shadow slows us down, allowing us the delights of the body in contrast to the swift angel wings of insight. The shadows of death, when we lose one we love, also offer protection for life despite the power of grief to pull us across into a deadness zone, where, though alive, we do not embrace the pleasures of orange leaves, tart apples, soft evenings with katydids chanting, the bright clearness of winter air, the rollicking laughing with friends, the thrill of sexual release. Yet the very darkness of death can vault us to a ruthless choice to live and set the beloved other free to be other, that is dead, or living a life with God, whatever we believe happens after death.

The shadow of the fourth applies both to us as individuals and to all of us as groups, tribes, societies, nations, the human family. In such groups, the danger, again, is to be dragged into anonymous affect, collective emotion, the shadow of the group, and it is very hard then to remember our puny ego has a vote. For example, we can understand Tillich's recognition that though he consciously stood against Nazism, refusing to raise his arm to the Führer, he feared that unconsciously, because of the pressure of the group all around him, he would find his arm saluting (Tillich, personal communication; see also Pauck 1976, 127, 131ff.).

We want to belong to each other, be part of the large whole, enjoy the holding context. The collective can also be a resource and a shelter, the Self within us and outside us as community. Examples of political prisoners refusing, for years, to give a false confession, or surviving decades of unjust incarceration and then emerging back into the world whole, benign, are astounding. They drew upon communities to which they belonged, the Ignatian exercises of the Jesuits, or the breathing meditations of the Tibetan Buddhists, or figures of tradition embodying truth and honor, or on the love of spouse, children, mentors, ancestors as imaginal presences, what Mary Watkins calls invisible guests, who are more persuasive than present suffering (Hillman 2004). This inner city, inner community is Self in the sheltering shadows that becomes enacted in personal freedom to choose faithfulness to community at the same time it endorses, indeed makes possible, such freedom. The negative alternative is to feel this inner crowd of others as a fragmenting force, yanking us first this way, then that, until frayed, we feel no center at all.

The link between the individual and collective shadow is found, I believe, in what I call the hinge of our own shadow (see chapter 6) that trips the trap door through which we fall from our personal penumbra— what we experience as stain, blight, shackling, blind spot, petty meanness, fault—into an abyss of numbing psychic nullity where any atrocity becomes possible. The fourth lurks in the shadows because all the left out parts are bundled there—the bad, the feminine, the earth, the inferior, the body, and the hidden God coming into the world through a bush bursting into flames, or through stable muck, or the confusion of hearing voices calling one to be a prophet, or the flight from luxury into misery to discern the true nature of existence. The *Deus Absconditus* differs from accepted God-images.

Think, then, of each analysand we work with, and think of our own lives. Where does the specific hinge lie, that trap door that suddenly opens and our personal shadow fault or lack or envious resentment gives way to the collective version of the same, where whole classes of people feel entitled to loot neighbors' stores or homes; where gangs of men feel justified to rape females, even imprison them in camps for future sexual abuse; where kids feel no qualm when eating on the city street of dropping wrappings, napkins, garbage on the sidewalk, thus adding to the waste amassing all over the world; where refusal to hear another's need for silence turns up my radio to top volume; where our pent-up humiliation finds catharsis by dumping rage on our parent; where our need for clean air, water, or soil extends only to our neighborhoods and we send the toxic waste to pile up in other sections of the community; where our refusal to see others' need for help in psychic or physical pain joins in the collective refusal to see the happening of death camps, forced marches, starvations, destructions of villages in different parts of the world?

Facing our particular hinge between personal and collective shadow makes us three dimensional and grounded in this world, facing obstacles to the values we hope to live by and to contribute to our shared existence in society. For example, the bi-cultural analysand suffered weeks of shadow stuff between the horse dream and the image of the elephant woman. She felt hurt and rage at being criticized for a job she did, at not being valued enough by colleagues on the job, of being seen as childish and vulnerable. Her shame and self-doubt alternated with bouts of fierce anger. This passage where she often felt shut up in semi-darkness led to her forming her own critique of the job and a determination to go back on her own terms with something specific to offer, instead of giving all power away to others. I do not think she would have found the elephant woman image rising up in her, let alone the unfolding of the itching into desire to be what her own soul summoned her to be, without having descended into the shuttered parts of herself.

Three and Four

Perceiving the fourth that advances the third leads to a new kind of consciousness that the fourth seems to be inaugurating. The two levels of thinking Jung described so long ago (Jung 1916/1956, 4-17, 25, 32, 39) as nondirected (unconscious) and directed (conscious) parallel Freud's concepts of primary and secondary thinking. Unconscious thinking, as one, proceeds by fantasy, associations, daydream, affect, impulse, and image piled on image. Effortless and expressive of our psychological state, this nondirected thinking is not communicable to others, admits no distinctions of time or space; no inner-outer, me-you; past-present-future blend and merge, separate and coagulate. Consciousness, as two, admits distinctions of inner-outer, me-you, past-present-future. Directional, purposeful, willed by the ego, such consciousness is goal-oriented, using reason and language, capable of delay of gratification, communicable to others. These are two modes of mental functioning, two ways psychic energy gets patterned.

A third kind of thinking lies between the one and the two as a union of nondirected and directed thinking, neither just associations, nor just linear seeking a goal, but a shifting combination of both. Such third mentation circles around a central image, for example, elaborating it in a network of expanded meanings. Drawing on both conscious intent and unconscious expressiveness, this sort of thinking is process, to-ing and fro-ing from center to circumference of the issue or image at hand, building up a content (see Ulanov 1996/2004; 1997/2004).

This third mentation partakes of all the descriptions I gave in the review of literature of the third; it is intersubjective, conscious and unconscious, including reverie, gaps, impasses, and reconciliations. Yet here I want to pin down its relation to the fourth, that our perception of the fourth, however shadowy, makes possible our living in the third. The fourth engineers the third. The fourth is the whole thing, the wholeness of reality which flows into and through this moment. In the third the circle of our focus is opened, not bound, and the sense of agency which shifted from the one versus the two into both in the third, now shifts again. The two held in the third are moved to perceive they together are enlivened by the circulating fourth. The sense of not me or you but us that the third conveys, opens still further to us beheld by the fourth. The fourth is all—it is us, through us, endorsing our living in the third which it sponsors. If, in Jungian jargon, we think of the fourth as Jung's notion of the Self, that Jung symbolizes the fourth as the Self, then this sort of mentation expresses our ego's relation to and experience of the Self, and perhaps, the Self's experience of the ego, too. This conversation between ego and Self comprises a process of communication between these two psychic centers within us, asserting the claims of each and their collaboration. Like lovers, the more communication, the more distinct each center becomes, and that generates more conversation. A new kind of consciousness assembles, igniting passionate and steady attention.

This conversation occurs in a psychic location different from directed linear thought, that proceeds straight from A to reach the goal Z; and different from unbounded nondirection of just being moved by what flashes up from the unconscious; and from circumambulational thought where we combine the first two kinds of thinking and circle around a central affect or image. This new way draws on the first three and adds a stillness, a dwelling at the still point, with an awareness of moreness. It is as if we are seeing the whole of reality to which we all belong through our specific focus, task, problem, or insight, listening to this person, this dream, struggling with this grief, compulsion. In that center is No-thing, no-I, yet our tiny I is standing by in readiness to respond to what emerges in this non-knowing place. This circled space forms an instantiation of time in space, and a space in time, an eternal now. Entering from the whole circumference into and through the ego is communication of personal, archetypal, known, not yet known affect, image, idea, all anchored in tempo of the conversation.

This fourth kind of consciousness "knows" immersion in the unconscious (primary, nondirected thinking); and knows abstracting from it and formulating conscious thoughts and language (secondary, directed thinking); and knows the mixture of the two (circumambulating thinking). The fourth includes all three with its own consciousness of the whole of them. This consciousness can be likened to the witness-awareness of Buddhist meditation, to the affective hovering of attention in prayer, to the being in, definitely in the world, but not of the world, that is, non-attached, of spiritual engagement illustrated, for example, in Kierkegaard's knight of faith. We live paradox: completely here, present, engaged; and also there, aware of presence. We live again, as we did as children, in the fluid interconnectedness of the unconscious, that erases subject-object divisions, but now we live there as adults with a beholding, participating consciousness.

Where does this kind of consciousness turn up in sessions? Here are a few examples. A man whose serious suicide attempt two decades earlier (he was found by a roommate and saved) discovers a legacy of that suffering in his determination to insist upon emotional honesty from himself and his partner in their unfolding love. A man suffering from sexual compulsion all his adult life finds his spiritual practice now symbolically includes that compulsion that caused him and others so much grief and missteps, that it, too, as he says, is in the light and the light is in me. A woman meditating on her lifelong doodled drawing that has in it a dot, discovers first that she is now standing on that dot and it becomes a terrain, and next, that the dot has moved, like a knight's move on a chess board, she says, and that this expansion and movement opens to her a whole new way of perceiving the block between herself and her husband. A woman dreams that she is in the water and sees two laser beams like search lights on the shore emitting powerful light. She swims toward them and crouches next to them as if a campfire. She says in the dream she realizes she can think. She sees it is not good to be in laser light and moves to a safer distance. Her discovery of light is accompanied by her discovery of her capacity to think with her own consciousness. What turns up in analysands' sessions is a sense of a bridge, with all its personal idiosyncrasy, to the beyond.

Where has this kind of consciousness been described in human culture? Often in spiritual texts—the empty consciousness of the Buddhist, no longer attached to external things, but as Jung says, "open to another influence . . . of a non-ego which has the conscious mind as its object." Christianity describes this new state of consciousness in St. Paul's proclamation, that another presence, Christ, lives in us. Our mode of perception shifts. Jung puts it, "It is not that something different is seen, but that one sees differently" (Jung 1939/1958, 891; 1943/1958, 949, 574). A new window frames our view of reality.

We experience the fourth as a capacity operating within us to generate dynamic intercourse between consciousness and a center deep within us which connects to the center of reality. We are at once the carrier of life with a sacred uniqueness of inestimable value, and one of countless others in the city of a greater center, a there there with its own process and transformation. This feels intensely alive, an inclusion of animal root-impulse and spiritual insight, of earthly bodily life here and now connected to the transcendent, living *sub specie aeternitatis*.

One image Jung gives for this aliveness is "the blessed greenness," expressing "the secret immanence of the divine spirit of life in all things" (Jung 1963a, 623). Interpersonally, we experience this connectedness as the interdependence of all peoples, that in our tiny subjectivity dwells as well an ecumenical spirit thrown open to all cultures, languages, laws. Imaginally we are citizens of the world, where everyone on the city street, the rural path, the far-away nation is our neighbor because they, too, are subjects of this subject within us, this power far outside us.

Living in this third space sponsored by the fourth is tremendously dynamic without being manic, energized and meditative, active and contemplative, specifically personal and yet universal, for we can see that this state in between, this third living in the shadow of the fourth, belongs to everyone. Like good music, layers of meaning can be heard simultaneously. This makes for richness, quality of living.

A kind of asceticism accompanies our living in the third, for we renounce our need to explain, which often masks a need to control. We yield to the larger whole, not knowing how evil is justified, for example. We continue to be knower and wanting to know, yet accept that we are known, an object of a greater subject. If we align ourselves in response, the greater subject verifies us as subject. That perception moves our ego out of center stage, acknowledging that the Self, or whatever we call this other, must fulfill its own function and transformation, that everything does not circle around our ego values and projects. This means living also in shadows—of not knowing, of unknowing. Our consent to experience this darkness makes visible the sparks of light dwelling there; our willingness to see through a glass darkly helps the light to be seen and is one of our individual contributions to the social collective.

In clinical work, I agree with von Franz that "the right to practice this profession must be earned again and again within oneself" (von Franz 1993, 281). In each session we are exposed to the unknown in each dream that expresses something new, in the symptom that shelters some dissociated part of the personality, in the transference-countertransference impasse that heralds the arrival into the treatment of some left out suffering. Can we stay open to the new year after year? Can we submit to what she calls "reduction to skeleton, to bones, to what is indestructible, the eternal in the human being" (ibid., 278, 281)? Then we see the shadowy fourth that promotes the space in between of the third through which healing generates.

References

One version of this chapter was given to the analysts of the C. G. Jung Institute of Los Angeles, 2005; a revised version was given to inaugurate the Annual Seattle InterInstitute Guest Lecture Series, 2006.

Benjamin, J. 2003. Presentation given to the Association for Psychoanalytic Medicine, New York City, December 2.

————. 2005. From many into one: attention, energy, and the containing of multitudes. *Psychoanalytic Dialogues* 15 (2): 185-201.

Cousins, E. 1992. *Christ of the Twenty-first Century*. Rockport, Mass.: Element.

Edinger, E. F. 1995. *The Mysterium Lectures: A Journey Through C. G. Jung's Mysterium Coniunctionis*. Trans. and ed. Joan Dexter Blackner. Toronto: Inner City Books.

Erikson, E. 1959. *Identity and the Life Cycle*. New York: International Universities Press.

Freud, S. 1908. *Character and anal eroticism*. In *Character and Culture*, chapter 11. Ed. Philip Rieff. New York: Collier Books, 1963.

Green, A. 2000. *André Green at the Squiggle Foundation*. Ed. Jan Abram. London: Karnac.

Hillman, J. 2004. Psyche in the world. Presentation to New York C. G. Jung Institute, January 26.

Jung, C. G. 1916/1956. *Symbols of Transformation*. Vol. 5 of *Collected Works*. Trans. R. F. C. Hull. Princeton, N.J.: Princeton University Press.

————. 1916/1960. The transcendent function. In *The Structure and Dynamics of the Psyche*. Vol. 8 of *Collected Works*. Trans. R. F. C. Hull. New York: Pantheon.

————. 1938/1958. Psychology and religion. In *Psychology and Religion: West and East*. Vol. 11 of *Collected Works*. Trans. R. F. C. Hull. New York: Pantheon.

————. 1939/1958. Foreword to Suzuki's *Introduction to Zen Buddhism*. In *Psychology and Religion: West and East*. Vol. 11 of *Collected Works*. Trans. R. F. C. Hull. New York: Pantheon.

————. 1943/1958. The psychology of Eastern meditation. In *Psychology and Religion: West and East*. Vol. 11 of *Collected Works*. Trans. R. F. C. Hull. New York: Pantheon.

————. 1948/1958. A psychological approach to the dogma of the Trinity. In *Psychology and Religion: West and East*. Vol. 11 of *Collected Works*. Trans. R. F. C. Hull. New York: Pantheon.

————. 1953. *Psychology and Alchemy*. Vol. 12 of *Collected Works*. Trans. R. F. C. Hull. New York: Pantheon.

————. 1963a. *Mysterium Coniunctionis*. Vol. 14 of *Collected Works*. Trans. R. F. C. Hull. New York: Pantheon.

————. 1963b. *Memories, Dreams, Reflections*. Ed. Aniela Jaffé. Trans. Richard and Clara Winston. New York: Pantheon.

————. 1967. *Alchemical Studies*. Vol. 13 of *Collected Works*. Trans. R. F. C. Hull. New York: Pantheon.

————. 1971. *Psychological Types*. Vol. 6 of *Collected Works*. Trans. R. F. C. Hull. A revision of the translation by H. G. Baynes. Princeton, N.J.: Princeton University Press.

————. 1973. *Letters*. Vol. 1 of 2. Eds. Gerhard Adler and Aniela Jaffé. Trans. R. F. C. Hull. Princeton, N.J.: Princeton University Press.

————. 1976. *The Symbolic Life*. Vol. 18 of *Collected Works*. Trans. R. F. C. Hull. Princeton, N.J.: Princeton University Press.

————. 1988. *Nietzsche's Zarathustra*. 2 vols. Ed. James L. Jarrett. Princeton, N.J.: Princeton University Press.

Khan, M. M. R. 1983. *Hidden Selves: Between Theory and Practice in Psychoanalysis*. New York: International Universities Press.

Lowe, W. J. 1984. Innocence and experience: a theological exploration. In *Evil: Self and Culture*, 239-67. Eds. Marie Coleman Nelson and Michael Eigen. New York: Human Sciences Press.

Neumann, E. 1955. *The Great Mother: An Analysis of the Archetype*. Trans. Ralph Manheim. Princeton, N.J.: Princeton University Press.

Ogden, T. 1999. *Reverie and Interpretation*. London: Karnac.

Pauck, W., and M. Pauck. 1976. *Paul Tillich: His Life and Thought*. Vol. 1: *Life*. New York: Harper & Row.

Phillips, A. 1995. *Terrors and Experts*. Cambridge, Mass.: Harvard University Press.

Random House College Dictionary. 1975. Revised edition.

Tillich, P. 1959. *The Theology of Culture.* New York: Oxford University Press.

Ulanov, A., and B. Ulanov. 1994. *Transforming Sexuality: The Archetypal World of Anima and Animus.* Boston: Shambhala.

Ulanov, A. B. 1971. *The Feminine in Jungian Psychology and in Christian Theology.* Evanston, Ill.: Northwestern University Press.

———. 1992a/2004. Mending the mind and minding the soul: explorations toward the care of the whole person. In *Spiritual Aspects of Clinical Work,* chapter 1. Einsiedeln, Switzerland: Daimon.

———. 1992b/2004. Unseen boundaries, dangerous crossings. In *Spiritual Aspects of Clinical Work,* chapter 9. Einsiedeln, Switzerland: Daimon.

———. 1996a. The perverse and the transcendent. In *The Functioning Transcendent,* chapter 3. Wilmette, Ill.: Chiron.

———. 1996b. Vicissitudes of living in the Self. In *The Functioning Transcendent,* chapter 10. Wilmette, Ill.: Chiron.

———. 1996/2004. Countertransference and the Self. In *Spiritual Aspects of Clinical Work,* chapter 14. Einsiedeln, Switzerland: Daimon.

———. 1997/2004. Transference, the transcendent function, and transcendence. In *Spiritual Aspects of Clinical Work,* chapter 13. Einsiedeln, Switzerland: Daimon.

———. 1997/2005. The opposing Self: Jung and religion. In *Spirit in Jung,* chapter 7. Einsiedeln, Switzerland: Daimon.

———. 1998/2004. Dreams: passages to a new spirituality. In *Spiritual Aspects of Clinical Work,* chapter 11. Einsiedeln, Switzerland: Daimon.

———. 2001a. *Finding Space: Winnicott, God, and Psychic Reality.* Louisville, Ky.: Westminster John Knox Press.

———. 2001b. *Attacked by Poison Ivy: A Psychological Understanding.* York Beach, Maine: Nicolas-Hays.

Von Franz, M-L. 1993. *Psychotherapy*. Boston: Shambhala.

Winnicott, D. W. 1963/1965. The development of the capacity for concern. In *The Maturational Processes and the Facilitating Environment*, 73-83. New York: International Universities Press.

———. 1971. *Playing and Reality*. London: Tavistock.

CHAPTER 8

WHAT IS THE
SELF ENGINEERING?

Years ago when lecturing in Atlanta, my late husband, Barry Ulanov, and I went to the High Museum, a favorite. A special exhibit for children displayed the city, but from the bottom up. We went too. We climbed down a manhole and looked up at moving images on film of passing buses, walking feet, buildings reaching into the sky. Looking from beneath street level cast the city's reality in a fresh light, calling us into new relation to it.

Our work with the people who come into analysis reorders when we look at everything from the perspective of the Self, from the bottom up, so to speak, or from the center outward, or from behind through, however we spatially imagine Self space. This departure point differs from our usual ego stance. A gap always remains between ego and Self viewpoints; they speak different languages and breed different kinds of consciousness. The ego is personal and the center of consciousness; the Self impersonal, the center of the whole (conscious and unconscious) psyche. The ego uses reason and words; the Self conjugates in instincts, affects, images. Ego consciousness offers a sense of belonging to oneself, and to community; the Self a sense of belonging to the ages. They never merge completely, except in illness (in mania for example), but approach each other as if from different worlds. In Rilke's words, two solitudes salute each other. The gap between them can be a place of madness where the ego falls in and loses its foothold in reality, or where the unconscious can be so invaded by conscious ambition that it seems to withdraw forever, leaving the ego functioning mechanically but joyless.

Mapping the Self

Self is process and content; it is the doing of the analysis and is what gets done. As process, it promotes the analytical relationship, the relational context, the experience the two have of the third space as if arranged to do so in the shadow of the fourth. As content, the Self is constructed as we go along, not a prefabricated entity that drops upon us, nor a fixed ideal we seek to achieve, nor a coherent greater personality dictating from behind the scenes. Yet, as content, something is there, as if in the shadows, that cannot be reduced to what goes on between interpreter and interpreted, nor to the provisional meanings the analytical couple create. Like an objective something, it nips at our heels, barking at us, wooing us, steering us through the narrow gate to do, to meet, to arrive, at what? Whether content or process, Self is Jung's symbolic concept to describe what drives an analysis and presents itself as the goal. Self is what distinguishes Jungian analysis from other schools of depth psychology.

Jung's description of Self is familiar to us, the circle whose center is everywhere and circumference is nowhere (Jung 1938/1958, 92). He speaks of Self as "a borderline concept," hence

> a symbol because it expresses something we cannot express otherwise, because we simply do not understand it. The self is unknown ground. . . . the self is a living symbol because it designates something we know exists; we know there is a totality of consciousness and unconsciousness because we are the living examples of it. The self expresses our acknowledgment of a thing that is actually in existence, but of which we do not know enough. It overreaches us, it is bigger than we are. (Jung 1988, vol. 1, 413-14)

Because Self is unknown ground, our experience of it always begins in muddle, blankness, even dis-ease, deconstruction of narratives and meanings dear to us. But left unknown, unacknowledged, we experience it as fate determining our future, instead of as aliveness, invitation to conversation, culminating in conjunction.

The Self points to a pattern of energy that gathers the bits of psyche around a center big enough to include all the parts of us, and small enough where it meets the ego when we connect to this energy, to feel as if we uniquely are being addressed. We register such moments in a sense of having come home to where we belong, or in such questions as, What am I to be doing in this life? What matters, and am I living toward it?

A Guiding Question

Over the years of work as analysts, and as patients with our own psyches, we each develop a guiding question that scopes out the territory, the frontiers, the borders of known and unknown. For me, the question that emerges to guide my work has been, What is the Self engineering? This query opens to what I do not know, and focuses on the particularity of each analysand's problem and potentiality. Something is being engineered, for example, through this woman's stubborn animus criticism against anything she says in meetings as "shallow and obvious," despite her many degrees; something is being engineered through this man's repetition compulsion of masochistic abasement before prostitutes, through this woman's suicide attempts. Something very specific is communicating—that the first woman does not go far enough down into her own depths to speak her own voice but instead says what she thinks is expected, and she discovers that it is not what she knows that is asked for but what she is; that hiding in this man's perversion, and sheltered all these years by it, is a small boy wounded in both his aggressiveness and his need to venerate something beyond himself; that this woman's suicide attempts were something to fall back on when her ego gets exhausted (see Ulanov and Ulanov 1994, 344-45; Ulanov 1996a/2004; 1996b/2004, chapters 3 and 10).

The Self is an archetype by which Jung means "instinctual forms of mental functioning. *They are not inherited ideas, but mentally expressed instincts*, forms and not contents" (Jung 1975, 16 November 1959, 521). Another word for archetype is primordial image which has a collective generalized quality and expresses our human tendency to picture our instinctive life in mythological motifs, fairy tales, folk-lore, religious symbolism. An example that surprised me was an analysand describing his desperate experience of his overwhelming work schedule. It is like being chained to a wheel, he said, just relent-lessly grinding you down. I registered a small shock of recognition, but had to go look up the myth to be sure. It was Ixion tied to the wheel in punishment for trying to seduce Hera. That bore on an element in our transference-countertransference field and helped me see more clearly the meaning of his not appearing for sessions (because of work deadlines) but paying for them, saying, I pay for availability, hence having me but not actually being with me and the work with the psy-che. I too was bound to a wheel going nowhere. Jung says, "I don't know whether the archetype is 'true' or not. I only know that it lives and that I have not made it" (Jung 1975, 13 June 1955, 258).

The Self is not only an archetype but the centering archetype of the layer of the psyche Jung calls objective, as that pattern of energy that gathers the various primordial images that turn up in a person's psyche into a coherent whole. In his long study of Nietzsche, Jung gives the example of Zarathustra as the old man archetype that appears "in times of trouble, when mankind is in a state of confusion, when an old orien-tation has been lost and a new one is needed" (Jung 1988, vol. 1, 24). (We might say this characterizes our time now, the beginning of this new century and millennium.) "In that moment the father of all prophets, the wise old man, ought to appear to give a new revelation, to give birth to a new truth." But Nietzsche could not metabolize this powerful image, could not relate to Zarathustra, by balancing it with integrating what he called "the ugliest man" (ibid., 702) that he had to "swallow the toad" (ibid., 255). Jung thinks Nietzsche intuited his end while writing this book, "that it was going to finish him, and in fact his disease began soon afterwards . . . and that he felt it as a catastrophe" (ibid., 724-25). Behind, so to speak, the constellation of the old man archetype the Self operates to unravel the old and inaugurate the new, through announcing a truth beyond the God whom Nietzsche proclaims is dead.

The Self engineers centering, decentering, recentering of the individual and collective psyche and promotes our recognition of itself in ordinary life: "If the self has no real feet in this world, it might just as well be a ghost . . ." (ibid., 709). Recognition of the Self, and the archetypal world through which it speaks, distinguishes Jungian analysis from other schools. In clinical work, the Self engineers the constellations in which the ego finds itself located. The goal of analysis can be described as the ego becoming strong and supple enough to engage in steady conversation with this other psychic source, this resource of energy and pattern-making that promotes its own transformation into living and supports the ego aligning itself with this transformation.

Usually, however, we live unaligned, out of sorts, not fed by this basic spring of our psyches. The waters get wasted, flow only underground, do not irrigate our neighbor as well as our own little patch of land. We set up dams, troughs, grow stagnant, only to overflow in the flood of mania, or fall into the drowning of depression, or the anxious panic of dispersal. As Jung puts it, our ego attitude often feels "the Self is such a disagreeable thing in a way, so realistic, because it is what you really are, not what you want to be or imagine you ought to be and that reality is so poor, sometimes dangerous, and even disgusting, that you will quite naturally make every effort not to be yourself" (ibid., 99). Yet seeing our poverty includes us in those who are blessed. For the least of the brethren turns out to be ourselves; we discover that in visiting the split-off parts of ourselves in the prison of our rigid defenses, bringing a cup of feeling to the parched soul, proffering understanding to clothe our defenselessness, we have been aligning with this other center. The treasure hard to attain lies under our own stove.

In response to the analysand's distress, I am asking, what is being engineered in this bedeviling problem? For we succumb to repetition compulsion when the archetypal core of a complex cannot release into its own living, but gets squeezed through the personal material of the complex our ego suffers. The archetypal energy has nowhere to go and must keep presenting itself through the too-small opening of the ego complex (see Ulanov 1996a/2004, 404ff.). It is like getting alcohol out of the liver, so the liver can function properly; we must deal consciously with our drinking problem and not project it into the liver.

For example, a patient was caught in what we came to call a burdened ego, a posture of just pushing through (see chapter 1). Life was only chores, endless lists of them, like treading water in a viscous medium, at best keeping her chin up above the level of depression threatening to drown her. This complex deadened her richness of living with a husband and children she loved, a meaningful profession, and a remodeled apartment. The depression's repetitious insistence was fueled by the archetypal energy having nowhere to go in its own terms, so to speak, hence it inflated the deflation of her ego. Hard work slowly opened the unconscious depths and a series of images climaxed in her recognition, when seeing a painting, of new possibility for herself. The painting's image released her into what she and I kept between us for months, like a glowing jewel we beheld, what she came to confide to a friend in the sentence, I have never been happier; and what released the archetypal energies from captivity in the depression. The image in the painting, that she eventually went into debt to buy, was of a door ajar. The point was not where the door led, but that it opened. Something in her unsealed.

Ego and Self Tasks

Two kinds of tasks present themselves when we pay close attention to ego and Self patterns of living in our analysands (and in ourselves).

Specific undertakings are presented to the ego, particular to each analysand. For this doctor the ego task was, what is it like to live unsealed, unshut? What threatens to close up the door again? How can she respond to its opening? Our clinical focus shifts to new questions away from the old ones of how can I survive the chores and burdens? She said, I am interested in loving better, which way to approach it, what gets in the way? She fell back and forth into depression, but now felt it as if from below, as a symptom, not as a surrounding condition which she inhabited. For another patient, who survived a New York ghetto where all his childhood friends, by the time they were eighteen, were either dead or in jail, the issue was how to be creative, not work himself to death to save the children of the world, but to relax into joy. For another woman, who died before this could be faced, it would have been to confront the hostility in her low self-esteem and the chaos it spread into her children.

At the archetypal level, our task in relation to the Self, so to speak, is recognizing that it is as if the archetype has a life of its own, its own projects to pursue, and our job is to enter conversation with it. Can we tolerate not knowing what that archetypal project is, to inquire as if to a stranger? Or do we fill up with resistance to this unknowing, wanting to decode instead of respond, feeling compelled to make sense, and that holds back healing? Think of our pet. Our cat is not thinking about us every minute every day. It has its own thoughts—mice, bugs, chases, lazy snoozes. Can we tolerate its otherness, its ownmostness that intermingles with its affection for us? Similarly, the anima, for example, leads its own ventures toward the wise old woman or man, to speak mythologically, and must not always be lumbered with a man's ego deficits as if her only reason for being is to fill in the blanks of his developmental wounds. Or, again to speak mythologically, repeated animus attractions even though one is happily married, celibate, single, that is, anchored in one's ego reality in what we experience as an appropriate life pattern, may not be aimed to disrupt the relationship we built so that we keep starting over in a new one. That is a typical negative animus fantasy that the ghostly lover, the

Flying Dutchman, tempts us to leap into with the idealized partner as so much better than the real person with whom we live. That conclusion would be to look at these animus attractions only from the ego's point of view. More is asked of us. Animus is the name for a pattern of strong energy that lures us beyond ego boundaries toward something undetermined, unguessed. Libido is summoned through sexual imagination toward the Self, to engage in a back and forth there with as much intensity, doubting, flirting, power, excitement, fear, as if it were a new love affair. Who, what, is this other pattern of energy that calls me out, beguiles me, offends me, woos me? The sexual metaphor is the tried and true one to get the soul in gear (Ulanov and Ulanov 1994, chapters 11 and 17).

Another typical example of facing a Self task is a woman's repeated outbreaks of rageful accusing of her partner of failing to do what she wanted, of not honoring her sufficiently. Archetypal affect bursts into the ego level of relationship because it does not yet have an appropriate channel of expression except the narrow eye of the ego complex, so to speak. The way through this is to take seriously the ego objections that not enough homage has been paid and return that projection (onto the partner) to where it belongs: we need to expand our awareness to pay honor to the Self. It is owed the daily respect, the devotion of ego energies to the reality the Self discloses. We need to be paying attention to this bigger center and what it conducts into our awareness.

What does this feel like, to set the archetypal psyche free? It feels like energy, electricity contained within insulation, going somewhere to alight the world. What is this world? For the woman who felt shallow, it was finding her voice, her destiny which meant moving to another part of the country, to her climate, to her combination of professional and private work. For the man with perversions, it meant exchanging a lifetime collection of fetish objects for love of the previously split-off boy part of himself, that is, growing his own aggressiveness on the ego level, and on the Self level discovering a little anima girl who grew up during the analysis. For the woman who fell back on suicide as a symbol of something to depend on if all else failed, it was discovering the symbol was too small and negative and she set about growing toward a new one. For the woman lured to ever new relationships, and for the woman furious that not enough respect was being paid her, it was returning this projection outward to its inward locale: the ego was attracted to a center beyond itself, a center which demanded respect and devotion. Left unrecognized, the attraction compelled her outward for what needed to be enlarged (engaged) inwardly, the ego connecting to the Self.

Self tasks have a collective dimension as well as an individual one. This archetypal dimension set free to its own channel of expression feels like a fruitive gleaming dark, a fertile soil in which society grows. Individuals living toward the Self nourish community, transforming it from collectivity. Yet the Self also gathers people together and establishes a bond: "The self, the very center of an individual, is of a conglomerate nature. It is, as it were, a group. It is a collectivity in itself and therefore always, when it works most positively, creates a group" (Jung 1973, 30 September 1948, 508). An example is the astounding fact that of all the schools of depth psychology, only the Jungian has local societies across the world, of laypeople mixed with clinicians, that meet regularly to discuss matters of psyche. There are no "Friends of Freud."

The Jungian perspective bridges the gap between professional and lay audiences because it reaches to the impulse of Self common to all of us. We experience Self patterns of energies as the urge to individuation ✓ which we register as both release to be all of ourselves, and also with dread, as if "the psyche, as an objective fact, hard as granite and heavy as lead, confronts [us] as an inner experience . . . saying, 'This is what will and must be'" (Jung 1947/1964, 471; see also Jung 1932/1954, 303). We experience Self energies as a primordial image that arrests all our attention, not only to compensate the level on which our egos live, but mysteriously to mark us with what Joyce calls epiphanies, and Marion Milner calls the inbreaking of the gods. We may not understand this primordial image breaking into daily life, but we never forget it.

We experience Self energies in periods of dismemberment, when all containers that held life are loosened; they are shred and we float unplanted, to tumble in a chaos of affects. I think of a poem by Paul Celan that describes this suffering and its surprise (especially poignant after 9/11):

THERE WAS EARTH INSIDE THEM, and they dug.
They dug and they dug, so their day
went by for them, their night. And they did not praise God,
who, so they heard, wanted all this,
who, so they heard, knew all this.

They dug and heard nothing more;
they did not grow wise, invented no song,
thought up for themselves no language.
They dug.
. . .
O one, o none, o no one, o you:
Where did the way lead when it led nowhere?
O you dig and I dig, and I dig towards you,
and on our finger, the ring awakes. (Celan 1972, 153)

Healing

It is precisely the reality that Jung calls Self that centers his perception of healing. For me, the method of analysis is dictated by the question, what is the Self engineering? Jung describes three steps. In the chaos of affects where we feel tossed and torn, distressed, seeking help, images appear expressing the counterposition, the compensation of the Self attitude, so to speak, to our ego position. In the midst of such tumult, an analysand said to me (and then I saw the counterbalancing effect of the work we were doing together), you are my magnetic north. Such primordial images order the chaotic affects, bundle them into portraits of the instincts, upon which we can meditate, and eventually we translate the affect/image into language we can use and share in daily living. Thus ego meets Self; our ordinary I in daily life receives and responds to what feels as if outside time and space, and the mixture of the two creates a larger sense of living, and of living in relation to something we do not invent but join.

The Self needs the ego, and the ego finds its placement with the totality of the psyche of which the Self is the center. Jung writes:

> The self is by definition, the totality of all psychical facts and contents. It consists . . . of our ego consciousness that is included in the unconscious like a smaller circle in a greater one. So the self is not only an unconscious fact, but also a conscious fact: the ego is the visibility of the self . . . as if the self were trying to manifest in space and time. (Jung 1988, vol. 2, 977)

The Self "needs" the ego to manifest in our here and now life and that is not always pleasant:

> We must say to the self, "Now don't be blind . . . be reasonable. I shall do my best to find a place for you in this world, but you don't know . . . what military service means or tax collectors or reputations. You have no idea of life in time and space . . . if you want me to help you manifest . . . you should not storm at me. If you kill me, where are your feet?" That is what I (the ego) am. (ibid., 978)

It is this conversation the Self is engineering, seeking to inaugurate, sustain, further it our whole life long. In addition to Jung's methods of reductive analytic and prospective synthetic analysis, in addition to circumambulating the image by giving first our directed associations to the specificity of this particular image of dog, for example, not to dogs in general, and then amplifying the image by giving examples of dog in other settings, Jung offers a synchronistic approach to the image where all the levels of experience speak at once. We submit to discovering what the image means, allowing ourselves to grow toward a new totality (Bright 1997).

A tremendous advantage of this notion of healing lies in its releasing us from shame of being humiliated by compulsive behavior, because at the heart of repetition compulsion lies an archetypal image that persists in getting our attention. Hiding in the compulsion is some alive energy that insists on being lived. Our finding it releases the compulsion and shifts the clinical task to how to relate to this energy presenting itself in the imagery. For example, the woman caught in the compulsion of pills and wine and going to bed in oblivion who then felt discovered by the new image of "liquid in me," shifted, in the remainder of her analysis, into the task of how to go on living in relation to this new spring of aliveness (see chapter 2). Several years after she finished her analysis, a life crisis brought her back for a few sessions. It was clear the work she did in analysis had held. At this time a dream showed her old complex, in muted form now, not between her mother and her but between two women friends. In the dream the two women chatter about having to get new careers. In the past, that was the kind of duo that made her feel excluded, inferior, exhausted. Here, though not yet doing it, they at least entertain how to become better employed. In the dream she does not get caught in feeling left out by her friends, but instead focuses on beautiful stone tables made by a fourth woman who remains in the shadows. When you work in stone, the dreamer thinks, you work in material that you must respect and that will only let work be done at the pace it can go. Commenting on the dream, she said, I know this about words (her medium of creativity); I believe it. You pay attention to it; you're not self-involved, but other-involved, putting all your energy into this relationship.

Finding what specific tasks the Self is engineering us toward heals because we feel we contribute to the whole human family. We contribute to the whole by bringing into accessible living our particular solution to this particular human problem. How do we know this? Not by the analyst thinking it up, nor by the patient needing or wishing it to be so. But by the psyche producing an image of the problem's resolution or at least the direction to go that all people recognize. Jung goes even further, saying our problem may be part of God's problem, and our tiny solution a contribution to the transformation of reality at its heart (see Jung 1963b, 335; 1988, vol. 2, 904-5).

Individuals working on psychological problems build up society; it is a form of social action, and even of religious devotion. We build up a middle realm of society where children can experience but not act out murderous impulses against their classmates, where snipers can find shelter instead of shooting strangers in a McDonald's restaurant, where opposing groups can use their aggressiveness to hammer out a peace proposal without resorting to suicide bombing or missiles that inevitably hit civilians, too. Between denial and acting out, this middle imaginal realm grows (Ulanov and Ulanov 1994, 249ff., 366ff.).

The Ego's Role

Our ego's willingness to converse with what the Self engineers is the ✓ *sine qua non* of transformation. Puny but essential, our ego always includes the dependency and the destructiveness we would prefer to omit, or at least outgrow. Dependency means on both ego and Self levels. On the ego level we depend on someone taking interest in us—our suffering, our gifts, what we make of our experience and what deadens it. We need someone who has in mind our mind, and who holds the core of us in being. This line of thought is in keeping with the insights of Loewald who sees the mutative agent to be the analyst offering himself as a new object to the analysand who then revisits and reorganizes his psyche's past into the present, benefiting from the influence of this new point of view (Loewald 1980, chapter 14; Lear 2004, 36-37). Kohut's idea of self-objects also applies here, where we know the lavish inflowing of energy from another's concentration on us, our experiencing the other as a mirror to our own self understanding and as an ideal to emulate (Kohut 1971, chapters 2 and 6). What the other is in himself or herself is not yet a live question.

✓   This other engenders in us a witnessing attitude. We begin to listen into ourselves as we experience this other listening to us. Roots take hold in our own depths. Our ego, now supported firmly, fattens, grows supple and, above all, interested, with warm loving attention to the neglected parts of our psyche that get enacted in the transference-countertransference field. This other putting faith in a different part of ourselves which is more creative than the part with which we have identified, helps us refind the generative state of mind we have lost. This other who survives our destructiveness out of their own resources and willingness to stay in relation to us without retaliation or withdrawal, establishes this other as outside our omnipotent control and our projected self-object state. The other emerges as other than our projections, an independent subject who symbolizes resources in the world that can feed us.

Dependency usually circles around the analysand depending on the analyst. Sometimes it reverses. I remember when a woman's analysis was interrupted because of my nursing my husband who was dying. She said to me, "I will carry the analysis for the time now. I will do it," meaning I could depend on her to sustain the connection between us and the work we were doing. A real gift.

The Self's Role

On the Self level, the analyst depends on this something that is the doer of the analysis and what gets done. We discern vectors of the Self by attending to how we get pushed around to witness to what is present and what is absent in the archetypal field of transference and countertransference, to what roles we get arranged to play in terms of the analysand's personal object relations, and what roles the two of us together enact. We can analyze levels of countertransference to the Self complex—our idiosyncratic responses to Self energies, our abnormal reactions that require us to analyze them, and what is induced in us by the unconscious in the analysand. In addition, we can inquire into our countertransference to Self motifs in the analysand's material, in the transferential field, and in our own lives that influences our patients because it is part of who we are and how we approach the work (Ulanov 1996b/2004, chapter 14). This is analogous to what Barbara Pizer calls the non-analytic third which she describes as the analyst's unique relationship to something "other" that she brings into the sessions that helps generate surprising new thoughts and affects. For Pizer it is poetry (Pizer 2003). Our particular relation to the Self will cast the vector of the style of analyst we will become.

Consciously to depend as analysts on the Self engineering the analysis brings benefits and dangers. One benefit is the relief it yields in no longer overly conscientiously believing everything is up to us, a kind of deflated omnipotence. Acknowledging the Self also punctures our inflated omnipotence and quiets power complexes. We two, analyst and analysand, are also engaged by a third. When impasses occur with analysands, we can inquire what meaningful purpose they also hold, and work on them by working on our relation to the Self in this deadlock. The danger is that the analyst might duck out, saying in effect, don't put that negative mother on me, you must deal with the archetype. Jungians are rightly criticized for such avoidance dressed up in archetypal language. Harder, but more useful all around, is to inquire how your negative mother complex inflames mine, and how we both fall in the soup and must work our way not only to connect to each other again, and to the archetypal energies themselves, but also to what is being engineered through them, that is, what specific reality addresses our work together through this particular complex constellated for us as an analytical couple.

Attending to the Self dimension of the work keeps us alive year after year, for we never know what adventure this analysis will herald. The symbolic language really bridges to something real which we see only if we believe in the reality the symbols represent. The Self is called into being by passionate ego-attitudes of inquiry and interest in Self life—what it would be like to live in touch with the reality the Self images conjure. The images of liquid in me, of the stone's beauty and pace, of the shut-up door now ajar, are what the analyst pours interest into, and then the analysand does, too, and then the psyche responds, and the conversation takes off. A general sense of purposiveness—that this work goes somewhere and that it matters—gives the analytical pair a sense of ultimate reality in every session.

What I have called double vision ensues—the ego's view, including society's (the collective ego consciousness), and the Self's view happen simultaneously, breeding a new consciousness best called synchronistic (see chapters 2 and 9). But a lot depends on the analyst's dependence on the reality of symbol, and the reality to which it points. We serve that reality. We cannot accept the symbols that arise in the transference-countertransference field as really real if we do not accept the being that the symbols configure. That being is embodied in the analyst's belief in this reality as constant, present, involved with us, as if in conversation back and forth.

Precisely here is where destructiveness enters, not only on a personal level between analyst and analysand, but on a Self level, too. On a personal level, if we leave out aggression and its destructive forms, we never reach the independent reality of others and the world. Winnicott has shown in his terse style that only when the object we created is destroyed and survives destruction does it become really real to us (Winnicott 1968/1989, chapter 34). Avoiding moments of misunderstanding, challenge, anger, and impasse in analysis makes it go dead, the energy of aggression gone underground.

The Self perspective helps us move from focus on the analyst's anger versus the analysand's anger to see as well the anger in the room, as a third in which the two are intimately caught up. But go further. We now have your anger, my anger, anger itself as a real energy flowing in and through and beyond the two of us to create a third intersubjective reality, and through that a mysterious fourth in the shadows engineering us both to see a double vision, that is, our personal issues in the larger human issue, and still further, maybe even God's issue, namely, what to do with destructiveness? Where does it find its place? It must find a place in every analysis if the work stays alive.

What is being engineered here challenges our whole analytical enterprise, as if to pull us loose from the very theory that guides us, as if to conduct us to immediate experience, no longer mediated by Jungian concepts (Ulanov 1990/1996, 183-84). The work of this negative is to bring in what our theory left out, to bring in more of the All. And we each must find a way to name the reality the Self engineers us to see that gives destructiveness its place if we are to stay alive in this work and in relation to this reality.

Why do we need names? Because we are dependent creatures with an ego consciousness in space and time; we need forms to make relatable the formlessness in which we dwell. We personify in order to relate to; we conceptualize and symbolize to apprehend. For anything to be real, it must become incarnate; that is the lot of an ego living in a human psyche-body. Otherwise we sink, vaporize, drift off into outer space, outside of time. I think of Stravinsky's form when he said: music is our way of digesting time.

Naming

Winnicott helps us see that our personal destructiveness, when survived by the other, establishes the other and the world as resources for living independent of our projections. Jung helps us see that the archetypal dimension of destructiveness, what he calls the dark side of the Self or of God, that cannot be reduced to developmental failures, nor appeased by propitiatory gestures, establishes the realness of reality, or God, independent of our projections (see Ulanov and Ulanov 1975, 40). To insist on our projected images and forms of apprehension for transcendent reality is the solution of Job's comforters, who try to lasso archetypal reality into explainable ego terms—Job did something wrong, therefore his suffering is punishment. Job saw that the explanation had been burst by numinous energy and he is the only one who addresses it, the only one in the whole book who prays to God. Seeing this energy, which is like a tornado or hurricane, is what faces the twenty-first century. Can we find forms, symbols to hold it, like the bush that burns but is not consumed, or the Virgin who contained God, without being destroyed?

Our response, I suggest, is helped by Jung's recognition of Self, which is his name for that human capacity that connects with reality that creates, sustains, and transcends us. For Jung, images of Self and images of God are indistinguishable, but he makes clear that "the self never at any-time takes the place of God though it may perhaps be a vessel for divine grace" (Jung 1959/1964, 874).

The Self is Jung's God-image; for me the Self symbolizes our human capacity to apprehend God, or whatever name we give to the transcendent. The names people create for this reality are wonderful, varied, intimately personal, and always embody their personal nature and the society in which they live. Teresa of Avila calls it His Majesty who dwells in the interior castle which reflects her social-political context; her prayer of union reflects her sexual nature. Hadewijch of Brabant sees a vision of a tree whose roots are in heaven and branches extending down to earth. She hears an angel summoning her to climb "all the way to the profound roots of the incomprehensible God!" which reflects her aggressive quality (see Ulanov 1998/2004, 200f.). Catherine of Sienna sees the great ship of the church descend upon her shoulders which reflects her political skills in negotiating the split in the papacy. Alchemy gives us the image of the stone. A Buddhist master speaks of going into Mu, nothingness, which is absolute freedom. Others write of waves of love, a still point, ineffable fire, radiant light, coming home, a scent of sweetness, rhythmic surges of energy, isness, suchness, thatness, blessing.

Our names for the ultimate even include our personal problems (Ulanov 2001b/2004, 466ff.). This means that our craziness, our complexes, participate in the visions of that transcendent we create, the theories we devise, the beliefs we endorse. Hence all the parts get included, the weak and disreputable, the shameful and weird, along with the genius, the fresh, the talent. This makes life, and analysis, endlessly interesting. For example, in the midst of Bion's mapping psychic transformation as a grid is evident his schizoid withdrawal, at one time so great he said his soul had died. From the midst of Jung's tumultuous relations to mistress and wife, including destructiveness to both, emerges at the end of his autobiography his paean to love as the force in all of life (Jung 1963b, 354). Freud's genius to create a rational vocabulary for the irrational unconscious also exposes his fear of its overwhelming power that makes him faint when beholding St. Peter's Square at the Vatican. Winnicott's brilliant insight that destructiveness establishes the externality of the world and the other betrayed his own vulnerability to destruction when the New York Freudians questioned this paper and he did not defend himself, and fell ill. Melanie Klein's trouble with her mother and with mothering her own daughter that erupted into public fights in the British Psychoanalytic Society with her daughter on one side and Klein on the other, turns up in her giving preeminence to the death instinct in the child (i.e., not problems in the mother-child relationship) as the root of persecutory anxiety. We can take heart from these creators whose complexes may have helped lead them to the new they uncover and make available to us. There is room for our complexes, too, in what we create.

The collision of ego and Self is monstrous, like the command to Abraham to sacrifice his only son, beloved Isaac; or like an analysand identified with the mother archetype, who is a very good mother to children and patients alike, suffering illness which cuts off her breasts, and faces her daughter suffering the same illness and removal of her breasts and the mother can do nothing to protect her child. Now these two are vaulted into a new relation, as sister sufferers facing death (see also

Marlan 2005, 151-55ff. for examples). Such suffering if we survive it, summons our ego to make what is unconscious conscious, to drag into bits of insight, image, concept, and symbol what is being engineered here, to give our warm-blooded animal response, even if we just howl and curse.

We need forms, personifications, narratives of meaning to face such crises, such violence to all we hold dear. Such work of mourning and creativity is how our ego slowly makes a collision, a *coincidentia oppositorum* into a *coniunctio oppositorum*. Our ego gives this monstrous combination animal blood and warmth, making a conversation through symbols, names, images, with this unknown breaking in upon us. Such names make the reality the Self invokes real in space and time. Then it lives, we live, all together. We serve life.

Livingness

Destructiveness thus finds a place in aliveness. On a personal level of ego life, symbolic death is required, "*the experience of the self is always a defeat for the ego*" (Jung 1963a, 778) that we must submit or consent to, renouncing our centrality as if in charge of our lives. We are defeated; we cannot hold off death; we cannot cure our addiction; we cannot see through the fog of our confusion; we cannot save our daughter; we cannot guarantee peace; we cannot cure outraged resentment at gratuitous injustice. We must go into unknowing and both allow and attend to the life flowing through us. We must shoulder the burden of relating to the Self. That means witnessing the inflowing of aliveness that transcends our human boundaries; finding forms for it, bridges to it to share with one another and to cross into conversation with it, itself. These forms are precious, jewels, treasures hard to attain. Yet these treasures are as dust.

For, as Jung says, "the Self wants its destruction as symbolic reality . . ." (Jung 1997, vol. 2, 1314). On the Self level destructiveness also is included. We need forms to relate to the reality the Self conveys, yet the reality bursts through any locked up reified form. Postmodernism

emphasizes that we construct meanings, pictures for God out of the stuff
of our immediate locations in history, ethnicity, politics, family, language,
religion. We cannot spring free of such conditioning to reach a set universal truth. However, we can so overemphasize the many narratives of
truth-making, that we lose a sense of its abiding existence. All seems relative. To spot how we construct truth does not destroy it; what get relativized are our versions of it, our images for it, concepts and symbols of it.
Theologies still function as signposts pointing toward the transcendent.

Jung was highly sensitive to this gap between our symbols and the
transcendent reality they convey. I believe he did not care much, was not
preoccupied much, with the controversy about names versus reality,
because he was caught up in the It itself. He said, "The main interest of
my work is . . . concerned . . . with the approach to the numinous" (Jung
1973, 20 August 1945, 377). The Self destroys itself; it will not be reified,
stuck fast into one form; it will not be iconized, for it, too, is but a
signpost, Jung's God-image, if you will, but not the reality itself.

We are familiar with deadness in analysis, and in our psyches, when
we fall into identification with an archetypal image, with one point of
view, with one symbolic representation of truth. Then we bully others
also so to identify, and power replaces witnessing. The symbolic death
then gets acted out concretely, for example, in suicide or murder, genocide or terrorist acts (Ulanov 2001c/2004, chapter 12). Yet it is a necessity, an inevitability, that we make tangible symbols concrete enough to
support our weight as they bridge to reality that transcends us. The bridge
directs our gaze to the other side as we are living on this side. That
paradox contributes to our double vision (see chapter 2).

Analytical work contributes the perception that we experience
something objective in the midst of our subjectivity, summoning us into
relation with itself. We feel pulled toward something that transcends our
reason, our culture's forms, toward what Ricoeur calls a horizon where
illusion is both necessary and destroyed (Ricoeur 1970, 530). Our projections now function to embody the new, to give us a way to grasp hold of

what exceeds our grasp. We might call these integrative projections, not now to expel the bad we cannot metabolize, but rather to make perceivable, through our projected symbols of the good, the new assembling itself to be assimilated by us (see chapter 9; Ulanov, 2001, 106).

Such double vision, where we depend on our symbols and see them destroyed, includes the dependence we feel on Jungian theory. It is our temenos; and contact with the living psyche will destroy it (Ulanov 2001a/2004, 443ff.). We are ruthlessly engineered to go through the narrow gate into livingness, an alive living in relation to the reality to which the Self, or all the other names so wonderful in their variety and specificity, point.

Such double vision includes seeing we have been engineered to see what is seeing us. This double mirroring occurs in every one of us, across divisions that usually separate us. We are the material for it to become whole just as it engineers our moving toward greater wholeness. Livingness abounds in all directions.

We feel self-communicating objective reality flowing into, through, and beyond us. This is where we arrive; this is what the Self is engineering; not products, however precious, like health, peace, money, books, jobs. Important as these ego values are, livingness is different, and available to us even if ill, poor, healthy, rich. It is aliveness that has the scent of joy. We contribute to a wholeness we share.

References

Versions of this chapter were given to analysts-in-training at the C. G. Jung Institute in San Francisco and Seattle, and to analysts of the C. G. Jung Institute in Los Angeles.

Bright, G. 1997. Synchronicity as a basis of analytic attitude. *Journal of Analytical Psychology* 42 (4): 613-36.

Celan, P. 1972. *Poems of Paul Celan*. Trans. Michael Hamburger. New York: Persea Books.

Jung, C. G. 1932/1954. The development of personality. In *The Development of Personality*. Vol. 17 of *Collected Works*. Trans. R. F. C. Hull. New York: Pantheon.

———. 1938/1958. Psychology and religion. In *Psychology and Religion: West and East*. Vol. 11 of *Collected Works*. Trans. R. F. C. Hull. New York: Pantheon.

———. 1947/1964. Epilogue to "essays on contemporary events." In *Civilization in Transition*. Vol. 10 of *Collected Works*. Trans. R. F. C. Hull. New York: Pantheon.

———. 1959/1964. Good and evil in analytical psychology. In *Civilization in Transition*. Vol. 10 of *Collected Works*. Trans. R. F. C. Hull. New York: Pantheon.

———. 1963a. *Mysterium Coniunctionis*. Vol. 14 of *Collected Works*. Trans. R. F. C. Hull. New York: Pantheon.

———. 1963b. *Memories, Dreams, Reflections*. Ed. Aniela Jaffé. Trans. Richard and Clara Winston. New York: Pantheon.

———. 1973 and 1975. *Letters*. 2 vols. Eds. Gerhard Adler and Aniela Jaffé. Princeton, N.J.: Princeton University Press.

———. 1988. *Nietzsche's Zarathustra*. 2 vols. Ed. James L. Jarrett. Princeton, N.J.: Princeton University Press.

———. 1997. *Visions*. 2 vols. Ed. Claire Douglas. Princeton, N.J.: Princeton University Press.

Kohut, H. 1971. *The Analysis of the Self*. New York: International Universities Press.

Lear, J. 2004. *Therapeutic Action: An Earnest Plea for Irony*. New York: Other Press.

Loewald, H. 1980. On the therapeutic action of psychoanalysis. In *Papers on Psychoanalysis*, chapter 14. New Haven: Yale University Press.

Marlan, S. 2005. *The Black Sun: The Alchemy and Art of Darkness*. College Station, Tex.: Texas A&M University Press.

Milner, M. 1957. *On Not Being Able to Paint*. New York: International Universities Press.

Pizer, B. 2003. Passion, responsibility and the non-analytic third. Presentation given at the National Institute for the Psychotherapies Continuing Education, New York, November 15.

Ricoeur, P. 1970. *Freud and Philosophy*. Trans. Denis Savage. New Haven: Yale University Press.

Ulanov, A., and B. Ulanov. 1975. *Religion and the Unconscious*. Louisville, Ky.: Westminster John Knox Press.

————. 1994. *Transforming Sexuality: The Archetypal World of Anima and Animus*. Boston: Shambhala.

Ulanov, A. B. 1990/1996. Disguises of the anima. In *The Functioning Transcendent*, chapter 9. Wilmette, Ill.: Chiron.

————. 1996a. The perverse and the transcendent. In *The Functioning Transcendent*, chapter 3. Wilmette, Ill.: Chiron.

————. 1996b. Vicissitudes of living in the Self. In *The Functioning Transcendent*, chapter 10. Wilmette, Ill.: Chiron.

————. 1996a/2004. Ritual, repetition and psychic reality. In *Spiritual Aspects of Clinical Work*, chapter 15. Einsiedeln, Switzerland: Daimon.

————. 1996b/2004. Countertransference and the Self. In *Spiritual Aspects of Clinical Work*, chapter 14. Einsiedeln, Switzerland: Daimon.

————. 1998/2004. The gift of consciousness. In *Spiritual Aspects of Clinical Work*, chapter 8. Einsiedeln, Switzerland: Daimon.

————. 2001. *Finding Space: Winnicott, God, and Psychic Reality*. Louisville, Ky.: Westminster John Knox Press.

————. 2001a/2004. Hate in the analyst. In *Spiritual Aspects of Clinical Work*, chapter 16. Einsiedeln, Switzerland: Daimon.

————. 2001b/2004. After analysis what? In *Spiritual Aspects of Clinical Work*, chapter 17. Einsiedeln, Switzerland: Daimon.

————. 2001c/2004. When religion prompts terrorism. In *Spiritual*

Aspects of Clinical Work, chapter 12. Einsiedeln, Switzerland: Daimon.

Winnicott, D. W. 1968/1989. On the use of the object. In *Psycho-Analytic Explorations*. Eds. Clare Winnicott, Ray Shepherd, and Madeleine Davis. Cambridge, Mass.: Harvard University Press.

CHAPTER 9

BEYOND THE SELF: NO-THING: ABYSS AND BEGINNINGS

What is the Self engineering? Livingness. If analytical work succeeds, it ushers us into a zone where aliveness blazes up and invites quiet
communion. We feel inwardly glad. We have been set free in the sense
of unshackled. Conflicts still exist and our old complexes, but we are
released to live from another center of being. First things come first, so
choices get subsumed to this major focus that feels like an unfurling, an
advancing into visibility of an unimaginable dimension of existence that
nonetheless we house. We house it as it houses us. It lives embodied in
the world, incarnate in us. We feel a freshness, a bounce, a rhythmic possession of space in time and time in space. We grow roots yet also spring
free of entangled insistencies.

People describe this livingness in different ways. One woman said,
"I have a sense of great vastness, as if looking at my life from a great distance and space, not so much a withdrawal or fear of falling into the void,
but as giving me a bigger view of my life in relation to life." Another
woman said her dream filled her with jubilation in existing; in the dream
she had begun to dance, "to step, bow, raise my leg, step, bow and raise
my leg; I get it! A whole new world opening!" Another woman said, "I
had the distinct perception of the nearness, the presence all the time of
the fire, the breath, the energy of God. It is there between the moments,
the tasks, the everything, and I was attentive to it." A man spoke of looking down into the "depth of space and moving color in the bright whiteness

of space. I sense this is penetrating to the point from which all originates."

Analysts try to describe this mysterious center which we experience as process, pattern, image, energy. It amazes us that this mystery lives with us in our own psyches, and between us when with other people. We circle it with our symbols and concepts, point to it with our ideas. Freud speaks of the unplumbable navel of the dream; André Green of instinct as the bud of being; Neville Symington of the lifegiver we must choose in order for it to unfold in us; Bion speaks of O, the ineffable ultimate that directs every session; Grottstein of arrival at the transcendent position; George Bright of synchronistic approach to clinical work, where we let all that appears at this clinical moment come into awareness; Rosemary Gordon of investing in the links between personal and archetypal, thus making sturdy our access to beyond-ego patterns of energy; Jung of the Self that drives us to accept the influx of our unlived life and consent to put all the parts together, including this mysterious one that resists all our definitions.

Questions loom. What is this power in us, beyond us? Must we put it outside us, depending on objects to carry it so that we can perceive it? Do we need this reality to be embodied in definite forms in order to relate to it? Do we try to give it away, or install it in a religion or a political party or a psychological theory, because it is too hot to handle in ourselves? We seem to need to make rituals to relate to it and express its relation to us. Are we afraid to see this presence living in us, through us, carrying us beyond ourselves? We can catch ourselves, and see our patients, too, resisting this presence. Too big, too much, it is like talking to a comet. Jung's notion of Self makes a bridge to the reality the Self points to, but that reality we fear can burn us up if too near, and burn us out if too far away.

As analysts, we take interest in each analysand's psyche—what patterns, vectors, vertigos occur (that block inner freedom) in the face of this ultimate that engineers us toward itself? As teachers, we take interest in each student's kind of mind—is it mythic, grasping the whole but needing to find the parts? Is it reductionistic, finding a freedom, an expansion by distilling to bare bones? Is the student's mind intuitive, bid by unseen possibilities that can only be smelled? Is the student's approach through thinking out the basic structure of the material studied?

Illness is finding only what we expect, hence boredom, lassitude, and trauma suffered in the past continues into the present. A man in his forties told me in an early session that at the age of eight he knew he was too old to learn to play baseball. The analyst must carry for a time the resistance to the Self, this O of Bion's, this mysterious energy that makes everything go. And the analyst in herself joins the human fear that Pascal describes, "Le Silence de ces espaces infines m'effraie"—the silence of these infinite spaces terrifies me (cited by Bion 1965/1991, 171).

Resistance

Resistance springs from fear that our connection with the infinite could blow us up into megalomania, a grandiosity that could burst our finite limits. We could go mad and lose the preciousness of this world, be so outsized we would explode all relationships—to our own body through orgies of eating or drinking, through intensities that burn out our capacities for sex or conversation or working. We would so overdo in manic ecstasy that we would short circuit (see chapter 3).

Or our resistance wells up from fear we would disappear into the void, be lost in the most abased nothingness, losing not just the alternation of pleasure and pain that gives us the semblance of control over our lives, but lose the very thought forms, the imaginative shapes through which we perceive life. We would go out of our minds. So we resist by holding on to what we know and to knowing itself.

As clinicians, we resist the darkness and pain of our ignorance and so make premature interpretations, what would be for Bion conversation stoppers (column 2 of his grid), and for Winnicott would be theft by too much interpreting, stealing from the patient the joy of arriving at insight (Winnicott 1971, 57, 86). We cannot descend all the way down to the No-thing place that feels so dark, where we live in the blackness of ignorance, to the unknowing that feels like no-knowing.

We resist the ascesis required, that renunciation of knowing, being, doing, that cannot grasp the infinite from our finite point of view. We balk at the otherness of this reality, we tiny to its big, so we retreat into the small. Or we foil relating to it by becoming it: let it replace our ego. Then we are certain, clear; we know the truth. We feel safe knowing we do God's will and inflict theological sadism toward others who threaten our safety by not identifying with our point of view. Such fanaticism results when we let the Self substitute for the ego. We see all around us this moralizing bullying that would ostracize or even kill others who differ from our conception of the true way to follow. How, then, can we live in this century when so many truths rival each other? How can we commit wholeheartedly to a path and also accept that others find and create very different, even opposing paths?

What, then, does recognition of the reality the Self points to require? Jung talks about it as symbolic death (Jung 1963a, 64, 778; Jung 1956–57/1976, 1661; see also Edinger 1996, 111-13). In alchemy it is the passage through dismemberment (Jung 1967, 87n, 91, 97, 111, 304n; Jung 1963a, 64, 259, 361, 493, 607; see also Edinger 1985, chapter 6). In Job it is the moment of theophany, a new perceiving of God that so rearranges the ego's position that he cries out, "I had heard of thee by the hearing of the ear, but now my eye sees thee; therefore I despise myself, and repent in dust and ashes" (Job 42:6, RSV). So great is the shift, that the religion of the ear changes to the religion of the eye. The ego, that eye in which consciousness is located, through which consciousness beholds reality, now becomes a means to look at consciousness, an organ through which consciousness—its place and its limits—is perceived. Through such perception, consciousness proves "indispensable to the self because it is the organ of awareness of the self" (Jung 1988, vol. 1, 408).

Bion says this reality cannot be known: "Reality has to be 'been'" (Bion 1965/1991, 148). He seeks to capture this being we can only become one with but never know through mathematical formulations. Geometry with its points and lines, for example, associates with the presence or absence of an object; and arithmetic associates with the state of the object, whether it is whole or fragmented into fractions; and calculus with patterns of movement of the object (ibid., 151 ff.). But Bion recognizes that religious formulations of mystics such as John of the Cross or Meister Eckhart come closest to transformations in O. Bion himself raids religious vocabulary to say we can only enter at-one-ment (atonement) with O but never know it (ibid., 163).

We can look at theology as a record of how the formless, unknowable Godhead makes transitions to knowable forms, such as Trinity. God is described as taking up residence in the Holy of Holies in Solomon's temple as "a cloud [that] filled the house of the LORD," who "set the sun in the heavens, but has said that he would dwell in thick darkness" (1 Kings 8:10, 12, RSV); and a second translation emphasizes God's choice: "You, LORD, have placed the sun in the sky, yet you have chosen to live in clouds and darkness" (1 Kings 8:12, GNT). This theophany is repeated by the anonymous author of the Christian classic *The Cloud of Unknowing* on how to pray, as if through a cloud to the One who communicates through a cloud. We can inquire of all theologies and spiritual practices whether they further or impede our reaching this O, this ultimate, this reality. The point is that the ineffable is ineffable.

On the opposite side of our ego resistance is the remarkable nonresistance of the Deity. God is called all kinds of names, and thrown out altogether, and no thunderclaps fell us; we are not killed or burned up in flames; no frogs or locusts invade our houses (see Jung 1988, vol. 1, 39). We can freely go off in all directions without penalty, but that does not excuse us from what Jung calls the symbolic death if we approach the reality behind our pictures and theories of the ultimate.

Symbolic Death and the No-Thing Place

Symbolic death awaits us; it is the transitus, the space of darkness in time, the time of searing light in space, the gateway to what our symbols symbolize. And it is of utmost importance for our community too: "We are threatened with universal genocide if we cannot work out the way of salvation by a symbolic death" (Jung 1956–57/1976, 1661). Images of this symbolic death terrify: mortification, putrefaction, blackness of despair, wounding, torture, dismemberment. It comes in many forms, all of which include destructiveness of some kind, each of which convicts us of our little size. We are relativized in relation to the larger whole. Instead of feeling this a liberation into postmodern thinking where we freely explore many constructions of truth, we shudder at the shaking of the foundations, the loss of ground to stand on, and hence our utter dependence on what Jung calls the Self, which we experience as our ego's defeat (Jung 1963a, 778).

✓ We fall into that circle "whose centre is everywhere and the circumference nowhere" (Jung 1938/1958, 155 n. 6). We feel as a woman did when she dreamed she had "gone into missing places and got tossed about" or as another woman did when she dreamed she was in outer space with no markers for north, south, east, or west; or a third woman who in group therapy amazed her compatriots by how utterly still she sat. She told them it was not poise, but going back into nowhere, as if suspended again in the incubator after her premature birth, waiting to arrive in life.

Gap

This route to the No-thing place opens from the gap between what we hope and what we realize, what we need and what we get (see Ulanov and Ulanov 1991/1999, chapter 2). For some of us the gap persists from our sense of our beginnings, describing the lack or deficit that results from dependency not met, the loss of the mothering one or never having that solid earth in the first place. One woman describes visiting her original family as going into bleakness; there is no malice, she says, just a lack of oxygen and I will go unconscious from lack of air. I feel as if I am going into a void, deadening. Then all by myself I must get re-generated to come alive again. What struck me, listening to her, was how sad she was, as if so used to being disappointed that it did not bother her much now. She felt very much alone even though I was in the room, too. I could feel how apart she was, the past around her in our present relationship, like a moat of sorrow. Abandoned in her castle, no door opened to what we were living together right now. I thought of Khan's notion of cumulative trauma and Symington's description of the trauma continuing to live in the present, going on traumatizing self and others (Khan 1963/1974, chapter 3; Symington 1993, chapter 7).

Another woman traced her phobia of computers to terror of being swallowed up in an abyss. She feared the machine, by some mechanical error or her own touching the wrong key, would erase what she had written, her poetry, and thus "eradicate my voice which I have worked so hard to find." For her this was not a technical problem she could learn to solve, but a demand to face the devouring mother who could make her text, and thus herself, disappear. On the ego level, she must learn how to work her computer; on the archetypal level, she must descend to this place where she becomes nothing in the face of the abyss.

There is no way out. We suffer the psychotic anxieties Winnicott lists, of falling forever, fragmenting into pieces with no home in our body, and cut off from reality of others and of the world (Winnicott 1962/1965, 57-58). What to do? Nothing. There is nothing to be done but to be there. In it. Another woman described her starting to cry and she could not stop. She wept and wept and felt she went down and down, hurtling, nothing to stand on, nothing to hold her, nothing to support her. A motherless child. Exhausted, she slept and dreamed her mother was driving her and her own child home and finds a fast way and also goes into the fast lane to the left while all the other traffic is crawling along in the right lane. We speed along, she says. It is gorgeous, with reddish brown earth and cliffs and the road goes under them. A huge primeval falls of rushing water appears on the left. But where is the road?! A steep descent appears; the road goes down at almost a ninety-degree angle, and is covered with thick ice from the huge spray of the immense waterfall. Packed ice, straight down, and no guard rail at all. We cannot turn back because we have crossed the lip of the hill. The dream ends with her asking, Will we slip off or will we reach the bottom next to the turbulent waters?

I mused on the mother who was not there as also the mother who takes her to the depths, to the depths where the waterfall returns. Through the lack, the gap, the complex of non-mothering, this dreamer is conducted to the deep place. Consciously experiencing the No-thing place in her great weeping, constellated the psyche's image of that place. Odd to say, we depend on the complex to deliver us to its archetypal core; here the negative Self-image of the missing mother delivers her to the primordial falling waters. We depend on that Self image to make a bridge to the reality that lies beyond it. The psyche pictured this woman's task as navigating thick ice, fast descent, danger of flying off into space, or reach the bottom. Would she drown there? Find a road? A shelter? Relate to this primordial water?

Shadow

The gap of the No-thing place for some of us opens through a shadow route of our rage, resentment, envy, refusal. These emotions often boil up in reaction to the blows of life where we are felled by loss, death, illness, war, rape, theft, injustice. We are helpless to bring the loved one back to life and feel intense anger at the basic plan that anyone should have to suffer and die. We feel powerless to bring back to life the dead relationship to lover, or parent, or God, and fill up with suspiciousness about the durability of any kind of love. Rage overtakes us in battles with insurance companies who will not grant a medical test for what causes us or our child pain or, worse, death. The injustice of some policy we are impotent to change in a crisis of poverty or bad schools can make us feel murderous. Sometimes murder gets committed and we want to kill the murderer who killed our sibling or parent or child. Or we want to torture the rapist, to wound with everlasting hurt the one who spewed their fury all over us.

Recognizing parts of us that lie in the shadows means "accepting the thing which is loathsome, difficult, terrifying . . . to accept one's own negation, the side which is against one . . . whatever is beyond or behind the present condition . . . you must go out of the known into the unknown, out of the light into the shadow . . . you leave the recognized truth for the absolutely unknown . . . There is nothing: you step into empty space and it is dark and cold. You touch nothing, you see nothing, nothing meets you . . ." (Jung 1988, vol. 1, 257).

Sometimes the shadow surprises us. As if in a trance, an unthinking, unidentified place, we say or do something without realizing fully that in fact it was swindling, or meanness, or gross usage of another person. Oblivious to the implications of our action, or nonaction, we later awake to its full weight that presses down on us making us panic: Will we be caught? Publicly humiliated? Made to pay? What will people think of us? We feel like a bad person and wonder how long we will suffer guilt. Should we just kill ourselves? Not only do all these left out bits fall on us at once, but we are frightened by the fact we were so unconscious, indeed as if in a daze, in an anonymous unknowing place. Our lack of relation to our action and to our surroundings makes us now experience those surroundings with the full force of persecutory anxiety, as if we will be annihilated.

The personal shadow piece, idiosyncratic to ourselves, thus acts like a hinge that pivots us into a collective shadow realm (see chapters 6 and 9). Our rage at losing a loved person or faith or job plunges us into human rage at death, at loss, at injustice. Our personal theft drops us into the larger world of crime where persons and reciprocity do not count, only acquisition; no mutuality, only the isolation imposed by compelling impulse. Our personal injury by another hurtles us into universal victimhood, transmogrified into a disposable object. We join the ranks of those who cannot get their red-blooded life flowing in their bodies again but wander like ghosts in netherland, shadowed by the hurt done them.

What is to be done in this shadowland? This No-thing place into which the hinge of our own shadow drops us? Nothing. No-thing can undo it. We sit there not knowing, giving up that we know a way out. We enter again that blank space, that spell-like state where the shadow moves into the light. Can the analyst sit there too with us and not try to fix it, but to be there, just there, not knowing from the ego source how to help? The ego sources get routed, and clinging to them, even those of analysis, postpones regeneration and draws out suffering. If we sense the fourth engineering this descent, then we can wait on its rhythms. We depend on that fourth in the shadows to create the work of the third.

Still another way the gap yawns wide and we hurtle into the No-thing place is through dismemberment. This is truly terrible. We feel we are being destroyed, torn apart limb from limb. Here the symbol of the cross can grow deeply meaningful, for it bespeaks an order in agony, an engineering of suffering for a meaning. Fra Angelico's fresco of the crucifixion in St. Mark's Monastery in Florence shows it is God's angels who hammer in the nails on Jesus' cross. But on the human level in dismemberment we do not know this; we feel we are chopped into bits, the pieces of our lives all detached from each other, no longer making a whole.

Our home may be disrupted, what we have knit together over the years, now unraveling. Given up to the mortgage company, adding shame at bankruptcy, or just having to move, the nest we created now destroyed. Our relationship may be over and the identity we knew within it now dissolving. Our job may end or necessary retirement force us to disidentify from being the worker we were and now not know who we are to become. Our health may change and our body is no more the animal we loved and trusted, but now a menace, a beast hiding in the thicket, springing dread diagnoses on us. How to go on living up to the moment of our death?

Our fortunes may change and we lack money to support what we believed was the good life; or money may pour in and we are disillusioned, torn from our former belief that more money would solve all problems. Now we have it, we feel empty, poor, undirected. We may have to give up our analysis, the one place we felt accompanied, recognized for what we are going through (see Jung 1997, vol 2, 1357; see also Ulanov 1992/2005, 71-72). Or the once good analysis no longer works, and we cannot avoid this end by repeating the process with a new analyst or new school of depth psychology. What was of a piece is now in pieces; what was a fabric of our lives is now rent; what was a direction now is a blank; what was identity is now disidentified and that feels like a death.

What to do? Nothing. There is nothing to be done. We are there and there we must be. To be there. Like the alchemical lion with its paws cut off; like the black despair of the nigredo phase, like the drawn and quartered one, the one divided, mortified, in the tomb, dismembered, disjointed. It takes tremendous courage to be there and not flee back into what Jung calls the restoration of the persona, to do the life we had over again with a new partner, a new analyst, a new theory, a new job, a new religion, a new child. It takes tremendous courage not to turn our face to the wall and go numb. But instead to be, and there, to look around and see what happens.

My analysand Nancy about whom I wrote in *The Wizards' Gate* had such courage (Ulanov 1994). Three months before her first seizure announced that her brain harbored a malignant tumor, she dreamed terrible dreams—of her apartment being totally robbed of every single thing in it, of hearing buzzing hornets in her apartment and the dream announcing, You cannot go back there, you cannot open that door again. The last year and a half of her life, and of her analysis, she spent looking around in this No-thing place to which she had been exiled. And everything came in there—the rage and grief at her life cut short, and all that had been left out by her making a whole life for herself that was about to blossom when she fell ill. She centered now on what she felt, feared, and found as she made her way toward death.

Another patient who experienced his life as completely stopped— job cut off, marriage cut off, affair cut off, health cut off—ended the first year of analysis, in which nothing happened except his talking hard and fast about wanting to find the meaning in all this and no meaning coming at all, with an archetypal dream that climaxed with his head being cut off (Ulanov 1998a/2004, 210). What followed for him did not include actual death, as with Nancy, but did usher in the same kind of symbolic death that she experienced, of being landed in a No-thing place, of knowing nothing, doing nothing. An image came to him that summed it up: I am a piece of sea-weed drifting on the sea. The symbolic death, that confrontation with the shadow inflicts, comprises an inescapable part of meeting with the Self which acts in us as a bridge to the transcendent. Jung says:

> Anybody who seeks the self is forced into that fight with the shadow, with the other side of himself, his own negation and . . . he becomes ashes. . . . This conflagration is necessary; otherwise the self as a living unit cannot appear, otherwise it would be obliterated by the continuous fight of the Yea and the Nay. They must exhaust each other in order that we may be still enough to hear the voice of the self and follow the intimation. This is the ordinary way of the religious experience. First it is a Yea and then it is a violent Nay, and then there is a catastrophe and man ceases to exist; then he becomes willing and submits to God. Then it is the will of God that will decide for him. (Jung 1988, vol. 2, 722-23)

Beyond Self

Symbolic deaths come to each of us in our own peculiar fitting ways, but they reach beyond our selves to the society in which we live with others. Our personal struggles play a decisive part in the world's struggles. That is the meaning of Jung's statement that we are threatened by "universal genocide" if we cannot reach our provident lifeline by undergoing "symbolic death." Our personal dismemberment locates in a shared suffering of the whole human family. We contribute not just through what we achieve and create that is good and life-giving; we also contribute to others how we suffer and accept the suffering life inflicts on us. This insight does not baptize suffering as a good thing; it recognizes its contribution to meaning and to the power in humans to make something of what they experience, even what they suffer. Think of writings about the Holocaust; think of the Blues. This is the dark side of Jung's perception of healing.

Healing comes when we discover our complexes are not ours alone, but are part of a shared human problem. That insight relieves us from humiliation of being in the grip of a complex, caught in behavior that both fascinates and makes us ashamed, that makes us feel put outside the community. To see our suffering as belonging to the shared human problem of how to relate to compulsion or grandiose ambition or base greed shifts us from shame at being exposed before we are ready, into seeing that our personal struggle belongs to our common struggle. This breaks our isolation from others. Our wrestling with conflicts is our contribution to the solution we all construct. Instead of feeling banished as inferior outside the fold, we feel part of the whole, as fellow refugees, sister sojourners, all trying, and failing, trying and reaching unshackled behavior, and a vision, in the words of Micah, to do justice and walk humbly with God and neighbor (Mic. 6:8, RSV).

We are pulled through into a larger container that holds all of us, and each of us contributes to the whole reality of all of us. That is where individuation leads. Healing happens when we reach the vision that we belong to the whole, all sharing existence together. The good Buddhist, along with St. Francis, goes so far as to include insects, creepy crawly life, indeed, all sentient beings. This can heal our suffering or at least give meaning to it and that makes it more bearable. Projecting the bad outward onto neighbor is no longer an option. Projection now will function in a new way, not disappear, because we are image-making creatures. Projection now lassos in visions of our wholeness in community (Ulanov 2001, 102-4).

Jung goes further in his vision of how healing takes place, what the mutative agent is in our analytic work and in life itself. We may not only be working on our problem and also on a human problem, but in addition, we may be working on what Jung calls God's problem. The All that sacrifices its vastness to take up residence in each of our small beings is too big a foot for such a tiny shoe. Incarnation means suffering, for the foot and the shoe. How to get archetypal affect into daily living, transpersonal energy into the personal ego material world? To come to earth, to become embodied, to enter consciousness, means a way must be created and found to bridge the gap between huge and tiny, between divine and human, between psyche and matter.

We experience such big archetypal opposites in our personal conflicts of love and hate, self and neighbor, conscious and unconscious in all the myriad forms of our problems. But our personal tasks get charged with archetypal energy. If we take that archaic energy as our own, if we overpersonalize our complex as if it originates only in our personal misbehavior or in that of our parents, for example, then we will be rent apart by the archetypal energies of the opposites in our own problems. In theological terms, we cannot reduce the scandal of sin to the scandal of fault. But if we see the outsized energies as God's problem, we can take our smaller place as employees working for the good of the firm.

For example, a woman relying for her sense of security on a glamorous persona social life that looks alive with exciting celebrity but which leaves her feeling alone and unseen, faces the choice of letting that go, to side with her real self and the friends it attracts. For those of us who do not have a glamorous persona this seems like a superficial problem. It is not. It is a life choice, a choice for aliveness over the appearance of aliveness that is in fact deadness. But that persona has been security, the world she has known. She will be reaching for the trapeze without a safety net. What will she choose? Which way will she endorse and so strengthen it for the rest of us—to go with soul, to go with surface? But soul and depth are unknown paths for her socially and she does not know the route; it is all in the dark. Her choosing to take her road into the dark makes it lighter for the rest of us, and for God too. Jesus is an alive symbol for her. I found myself thinking of the words, he has no place to lay his head. At that moment she said, I will make a place for Jesus in my heart; he who has no place to lay his head attracts to himself all the souls of the world.

What is healing is to see that struggling with a persona problem contributes not just to our neighbors but also to the reality the word Self or God or Jesus points to. This analysand is saying, I can make a place in my heart and in my daily living for the one who has nowhere to lay his head; that mysterious presence can live in me. Her choice bestows a bit of freedom on us too, for we see we are shifted from being immersed in the intractable problem besetting us, where we feel stuck, to see that we are working on our small part of a larger task. Someone else is running the bank and we contribute to its business, helping it succeed in resolving a big obstacle. This attitude of objectivity—that we did not originate this problem, it came from on high and is a problem in its own right—admits slivers of gaiety into our suffering, moments of humor, a pleasing ease in the midst of tribulation.

In each of our personal situations, we face the task of making a whole out of conflicting opposites, to gather their coincidence and complexity into conjunctions that last and irrigate the whole of existence, our own and the nations'. Whether our descent into the No-thing place is sponsored by a blow from fate, a heartbreaking loss, a shadow crime, a dependency not met, a dismemberment of the identity we have built up, we must ask, Is the Self engineering this? Is the mysterious fourth in the shadows luring, pushing, exposing, guiding us toward this place where No-thing is, and doing none of the above?

Jung has the idea that the Self undoes itself, dismembers itself. That places our dismemberment in a bigger bowl, so to speak. We are not just breaking down old forms in our lives, we are breaking through to this inclusion of destructiveness in life itself. We are participating in a reality that supervenes our problems. We are in its process and adding our personal dot of contribution to its line of unfolding (transformation). This lends meaning even to our wreckage.

Deus Absconditus

Jung writes, "The Self as the *Deus Absconditus* can undo its own symbolism for a certain purpose. When an individual has been swept up into the world of symbolic mysteries, nothing comes of it, nothing *can* come from it, unless it has been associated with the earth, unless it has happened when that individual was in the body. . . . the Self wants its own destruction as a symbolic reality . . ." (Jung 1997, vol. 2, 1313-14). If the Self as an image or concept becomes either too ethereal without embodiment in personal human life, or too reified into earthbound forms of prescribed behavior, the reality the Self points to will undo its own symbolism. Like us, or we like it, it too will undergo symbolic death. Destructiveness will be used to free up the reality our Self images or God-images point to. That reality will not be trapped by spiritualizing or concretizing. It wants livingness, not deadness of unrealized spiritual meanderings, nor of being boxed up into moralistic rules.

This plowing up from the depths, this destroying our God-images to free God is the work of the *Deus Absconditus*, the God of the Depths, from the dark, from the light so bright, it blinds. It is here I understand Jung's notion of the Self having an evil side. He refers to Luther, "who recognized that God was not always good . . . he allowed for . . . a concealed or veiled god that is a receptacle for all the evil deeds . . ." (Jung 1988, vol. 2, 1031). It is evil because it falls outside our image of the good. It destroys it. But it goes further and destroys itself. The Self is a mere symbolic concept, a bridge to point beyond itself to the whole of reality of which we are a part. It defeats the ego, and itself too, as a human construct.

From our conscious perspective, this *Deus Absconditus* differs greatly from our personal God and the collective God-images of religious traditions. It is hidden; it makes off with our images; it absconds with our notions of fair play, of ethical behavior; it steals our visions of the whole. Of course, then, we want to contain it, box it, insulate it from our direct experience, or alternatively, install it in religious authorities, political leaders, eternal verities.

Early in her analysis, Nancy pictured this absconding God, the one who runs off with our dearest images for it, as big black horse's hoof and leg coming from the sky planted down on the earth below (Ulanov 1994, 21 and picture 2, 49). If as a child we have ever been stepped on by a horse's hoof we know the aptness of this image. The horse is not bad, or intentionally evil. It is huge, and it breathes over us. Watch it, get out of the way, get into relationship with it, even get in step, learn to ride it.

At the archetypal level all archetypes have a negative and a positive pole. That is their nature; like animals who have fur, archetypes have evil and good sides. Jung's God-image, in my thinking, is the Self and it, as archetype, has an evil and a good side. But the archetype itself bridges to a reality beyond Self, what Jung called god, and there a different reality obtains. Is there a God beyond the archetypal god?

The point I am making here is that destructiveness is included even in our symbols and concepts for the vast reality they convey. From the perspective of meditation, spiritual practice, religious belief, comes the same insight as this one about the Self destroying itself as a symbolic form. Our images for God will get smashed, whether by the blows of life's harshness, or by the success of the images which we exhaust because they are finite (Ulanov 2001, 21-40). Our Jacob's ladder to God comes to an end; a big gap, a space, a No-thing place lies between us and what the ladder leads to. No image or concept, no psychological theory, no semiotic discourse, no plan for education or policy to install justice, no political platform or religious credo can cross that gap because these are all finite, human creations, precious treasures, but finite and human, mixed with inspiration toward the divine, but limited, mortal. Even our prophets die, even our god-man is killed. Nothing crosses that gap from our side. Our images for the whole, for the Vast and the All, for the It and the suchness of reality cannot span the gulf.

What does? Our answers to this question define the particular influence our psyches will bear upon the analytical work we do with our analysands. How we conceive of the reality the Self symbolizes, how we name it, what our countertransference is to it in our patients' material, all influence our work with each person.

Jung's view, as I discussed earlier (chapter 6), holds that Self and God-images are indistinguishable. The Self as an archetypal pattern of energy displays, as do all archetypes, a good and an evil pole. Hence God has a good and an evil side and needs us to work on their conflict. Yet Jung is ambiguous. He also distinguishes between the Self (as the centering archetype in the unconscious) and God: "The unconscious is the immediate source of our religious experiences. This psychic nature of all experience does not mean that the transcendent realities are also psychic" (Jung 1997, vol. 2, 1538). This ambiguity, so frustrating to Jung's critics, is also a source of the aliveness of the notion of Self. It takes us to the frontier:

> The self is a borderline concept, which I call a symbol because it expresses something which we cannot express otherwise, because we simply don't understand it. The self is really unknown ground. The psychological definition of the self is the totality of consciousness and unconsciousness, and that sounds pretty definite: we seem to know what consciousness is. . . . But to say we know the unconscious is going too far; we only know *of* it. (Jung 1988, vol. 1, 413)

> The unconscious is essentially unknown. (ibid., vol. 2, 983)

> The self is by definition the totality of all psychic facts and contents. . . . The self consists . . . of the most recent acquisition of the ego conscious-

ness and on the other side, of the archaic material. The self is a fact of nature and always appears as such in immediate experiences, in dreams and visions . . . it is the spirit in the stone, the great secret which has to be worked out . . . because it is buried in nature herself. (ibid., vol. 2, 977)

Jung presents us with the necessity of attaining symbolic life, of reaching a discourse arising from our experience of living in relation to the Self which we know and do not know: "A symbol is not a sign for something of which I know. . . . A symbol is an expression for a thing of which I only know that it does exist. I don't know *it* . . . symbols are irreducible to literal explanation. So the self is a living symbol because it designates something we know exists; we know there is a totality of consciousness and unconsciousness because we are the living examples of it" (ibid., vol. 1, 414). The names for this symbol are varied and amazing: the self is "expressed by the figure of Christ . . . the *lapis philosophorum* . . . the womb . . . the gold . . . the *Tinctura magna*, the *quinta essentia* . . . the Grail . . . the cross . . . the king . . . the god-man . . . on lower primitive levels it is a fetish, an object that is inhabited by the divine breath, or by mana, or by extraordinary magic effect" (ibid., 416).

But the living experience of this unknown presence is the real thing, spanning from our animal to spiritual nature, for they form one arc along which we experience aliveness: "as soon as you deal with the self as an experience, the whole changes and wild things come up, because you are then confronted with mountains of obscurity; it is just like being actually in the midst of an excited herd of elephants" (ibid.).

What crosses the gulf between us and the transcendent reality pictured in our God-images can be described, then, as the influx of terrific energy—the elephants, the wild things—that come through the unconscious. Other images to describe this crossing fill religious traditions. To take just one, Christianity pictures the God who enters human suffering as the Christ figure who gives himself to stand with us and for us in the No-thing place. The gap is crossed from the other side. This can be believed, be real to faith, but it cannot be certified.

Not only does Christianity want to assert the wholeness of the whole—the monotheism that contains the tragic conflict of good and evil; it also changes the terms of the discourse. For in the *kenosis* of Jesus, described in Philippians 2, the son who is also the father (as manifested in the Trinity) voluntarily empties himself to become the servant. The one who is both bridge to the All and is the All, the Everything, the Source, becomes the human and the least of the human to show us how the All, the Source, lives in our lives here in this world. The One takes on the suffering of the many. The Powerful takes on the position of the helpless. The Creator regains the No-thing place, entering the deepest recesses of the human state to be threatened there by non-being, nullity, nothingness, death. This is the symbolic (and sacramental) death, renouncing identification with the Source of the Source to be the ugliest man, the most abased woman, to serve us. He undoes the death-instinct of Freud and the notion of a superego god that judges and punishes our transgressions, by freely entering our state of suffering and death. The old god is dead. This new god comes back from the god who is dead, refashioning God's statement: Behold! I made all things new.

The new reality shining forth links back to the tree not chosen in the original Eden. The focus now shifts from the tree of splitting—the eternal tragic conflict of good and evil where the ego is rent asunder by identifying with the good and fruitlessly trying to get rid of the bad—to the Tree of Life that does not deny the warring evil and good, but recognizes them, holds them, and transcends them.

This god-man rearranges the whole way we see the human dilemma. He lets go of all we would attain—the power, the glory, the insight and soaring thought, the status, the capacity to do good—by suspending the powerful functions of God the Source. He descends to No-thing, because the servant of the least of the human. He puts suffering beyond tragic flaw, beyond fault, beyond vengeance. He lets go of resentment, blame, retaliation; he places suffering beyond desire not to suffer, beyond justice. He gives himself to enter the No-thing place to stand with us there, to come find us in prison and nakedness in this life, and to seek us out in hell in the after-life (Holy Saturday). We are released from death and splittings of good and evil and from what Kristeva calls mutilations of desire by threats of judgment (Kristeva 2006). We are freed into a living so differently ordered, it is called resurrection, a life of giving that reflects this gift of new life. Suffering is overcome by the gift of the Source of the father in the son to join us in the No-thing place which replaces the father of judgment, of law, of punishment, with the father as son of passion and compassion. We suffer with the One who suffers with us. The God who regains nothingness is the God of beginnings. Rising from the dead, the old re-presents in the new, just as our old consciousness, in glimpsing this new being, comes alive.

The One who comes brings the end of religions, pushes to the limits the religion that negotiates with the divine to secure a form of the divine in human terms, to install our human ego as ambassador of the divine, forming propitiations, lists of sins and penances, schemes of justice. We reach the limit in this No-thing place. A new giving gives new sense to meaning. Receiving the gift given, we give; entering the passion of deadness resurrects us into aliveness.

Jung approaches this same aliveness in his discussion of the mystical round dance that follows participation in the Christian Eucharist in the apocryphal Acts of John. Here the disciples, and contemporary communicants, dance around (circumambulate) "the Lord as the central point." They, and we, are urged to identify with Christ in the center for

> when you relate to your own (transcendental) centre, you initiate a process which leads to oneness and wholeness. You no longer see yourself as an isolated point on the periphery, but as the One in the centre. Only subjective consciousness is isolated; when it relates to its centre it is integrated into wholeness. Whoever joins in the dance sees himself reflected in the reflecting centre, and his suffering is the suffering which the One who stands in the centre "wills to suffer." The paradoxical identity and difference of ego and self could hardly be formulated more trenchantly. (Jung 1955/1958, 415, 427)

The movie *Indiana Jones and the Last Crusade* makes the same point about renewal of aliveness coming from the other side, not from our capacities. As long as Harrison Ford looks to the goal of the other side of the abyss, and does not look down into the agony of falling forever into nothingness, sections of a bridge display themselves across the gulf for his support. One block at a time, they shine forth like squares of light onto which he steps. But he does not know they will appear, or last after he steps past them; he does not know how they appear. They are not the point; the goal he looks to, the other side, where he is going is the point.

The same shift occurs in spiritual practice when we come to contemplate God for God's sake, not for what God will bring us. Jung writes about this movement of soul as offering himself to the psyche: "I put my trust in the thing which I felt to be more important *sub specie aeternitatis*. I knew that it would fill my life, and for the sake of that goal I was ready to take any kind of risk" (Jung 1963b, 194). Whatever form for each of us the blocks of shining light take, on which we can stand for a time, but that do not endure, we will meet at the same origin and end point, although our personal paths differ as much as one religion does from another or one psychological theory does from another. Yet it makes all the difference which way we commit ourselves.

The astounding fact is that none of these blocks can be equated with the fixed truth or the good. They manifest to conduct us toward the source of truth. Stepping on those blocks of light that appear and disappear as we devote our whole attention toward the Source of the Source begetting aliveness, is our way of living the eternal in time and the All in the tiny. The No-thing place surprises us: it is full of beginnings.

Slime

Beginnings begin in slime, not in articulated understanding. Beginnings happen in the dark; in the No-thing place. If livingness is what the Self is engineering, and destroying itself as a symbolic form so that we do not mistake it for what it symbolizes, then destructiveness is integral to aliveness.

Jung knew this, I believe, and embodied it in his reluctance to begin a school of Jungians, and in his surprise that at his eightieth birthday celebration he much preferred the many well-wishers who came in the morning over the fewer famous, international leaders of Jungian Institutes who honored him at dinner that night. The morning public were "the people who read my books and let me silently change their lives." One unsophisticated woman said, "They are bread" (Hannah 1976, 323). Jung is the only analyst who includes in treatment the destruction of the analyst and analysis itself. Once we consciously take up the conversation with our unconscious—the undiscovered self living in us—we do not need the analyst. The legacy of our analysis, by which we continue the conversation, is to work with our dreams and in active imagination. Jung is after the experience itself, not mediated (by the analyst) but immediate. No other school of depth psychology confers such an inheritance.

In the No-thing place formlessness infiltrates us and unravels our focused ego consciousness that divides things into subject and object. Surpassing dreams when we, the subject, are made the object of someone else's laughter or sexual desire or anger, in this No-thing place even this sense of reversal of subject and object may dissolve. Conscious of knowing nothing, possessing not even a compass from an ego perspective, we disseminate into the unconscious. The concept of the unconscious designates only our unknowing (see Jung 1988, vol. 2, 983; 1963b, vol. 1, 331). From whence, then, comes change? Healing? What is the mutative agent?

We do not know. But it comes. Jung writes of reaching archetypal depth where the destructive forces change into healing ones because the archetype is set free "to independent life and taking over the guidance of the psychic personality, thus supplanting the ego with its futile willing and striving. As a religious-minded person would say: guidance has come from God. . . . I must express myself in more modern terms

and say that the psyche has awakened to spontaneous activity. . . ."
Something comes up "from the hidden depths of the psyche—something that is not [our] ego and therefore is beyond the reach of [our] personal will. [We have] regained access to the sources of psychic life, and this marks the beginning of the cure" (Jung 1932/1958, 534; see also Ulanov 2001b/2004, 440f.).

But how and when and if this happens we do not know and we cannot invent its happening nor control it. It happens in the dark or, in alchemical language, in the time of the new moon, what von Franz calls "the belly of the closed house, that is, the innermost creative is secluded by nature," parallel, on a personal level, to what Winnicott calls the incommunicable core of the true self that must not be touched, whose violation makes "rape and being eaten by cannibals . . . mere bagatelles" (Winnicott 1963/1965, 188). On an archetypal level "the *coniunctio* . . . takes place in the darkest night where not even the moon shines, and in this ultimately dark night sun and moon unite" (von Franz 1980, 162). For John of the Cross, only in the blackest night, the darkest night of the soul, do we go out to the love call of the God who would unite with us. The Twenty-third Psalm heralds the valley of the shadow of death as the place we are comforted by rod, staff, and table.

I would describe this place where beginnings begin in No-thing as slime. Outside our vision and will, beyond our control, something happens. A patient dreamed, "a shift occurs, like a drop of water, and a tanker ship out to sea shifts the balance"; another dreamed of "a meeting point of all directions." Neither person had any associations, saying the dream just stated a fact. The move to the new takes place out of sight and hearing, beyond understanding, something switching at a dark level, a move from formlessness to form. Something grows—like a conception that advances into a pregnancy that changes our lives into a before and an after.

We become aware of this new emerging only gradually, and our ego response is part of what emerges. Our ego task now is to gather all the scintillae of light and witness their presence, remark their effect on us. We get nudges, flashes of ideas of what to do, insight that the question we persisted in asking is the wrong question but we would never have seen that if we had not insisted on repeating it.

Heidegger says repetitive thinking, gathering a history, making a narrative, is the *transitus* from calculative (that is ego, instrumental) thinking to primordial thinking that recognizes transcendence *"within the framework of contemporary thought itself"* (Macquarrie 1968, 57). Historical repetitive thinking means we know our story takes place within a larger community to which we belong, what postmodernism ✓ calls our location in family, ethnicity, class, gender, culture, etc., with their accompanying discourse(s). To find and create our story we need the repetition that belongs to ritual, that is, the knitting together as a community the threads of existence that span individual to group to transcendent ultimate, what has been called a *Heilsgeschichte*, a holy history of God's dealing with us. To create and find our embeddedness in this temporality, we need to repeat it in consciousness and in body which means gesture, posture, procession, kneeling, standing, gathering, and separating in relation to each other, and with all the senses that complement language.

In analysis we have such ritual of time and day of appointment, fee, even chair that we sit in and the forms through which we go about listening, speaking, remaining silent, creating and finding the work of analysis. This ritual frames the gap of knowing and unknowing in patient, in analyst, and between them, and makes analysis real and alive. The session works; we do the work and the work does us. Emotional illness shows as deadness, nothing works, and this form no longer works and we are taken down to be found and created in the slime.

Primordial thinking includes the slime from which delicate, pale, white-green tendrils of the new germinate. The *arche* of archetype that means absolute beginning, that is attributed, for example, to the four basic elements of earth, air, water, and fire that make up the material world, that in Aristotle is the form that the *materia prima* yearns for as the female does toward the male. This inaugurating energy dwells in the slime. My late husband, Barry Ulanov, favored the translation of Anaximander of Miletus of *arche* to *apeiron*, meaning "the principle and element of existing things," containing "the whole cause of the coming-to-be and destruction of the world. . . . It is eternal and unchanging; it surrounds all the worlds and is the source of all" (Ulanov and Ulanov 1994, 22).

The ritual of analysis, its form of historical thinking, links ego think-ing that wants to get the work done, the problem solved, the suffering made meaningful and brought to resolution, to primordial thinking that goes down to the *arche* and *apeiron* where the new mysteriously occurs, in the dark, outside our knowing. This principle or element lives in us like that pale white-green tendril growing up in us from and within the No-thing place. We know this new emerging by slight but persistent happen-ings—a dream fragment, an impulse to spontaneous action, a momentary clarity, a body sense of another live presence, a scent, a breaking open of space in time for a new kind of consciousness of living in the third, engineered by the fourth.

A New Kind of Consciousness

Living in the third means living consciously with the indeterminate *apeiron*. The boundless, endless, infinite, unlimited, undetermined lives within the limits of our consciousness, our body, and our history together. What an extraordinary way to live! We live in time and space under the laws of gravity and mortality connected to the unlimited in its origins and in its continuing being. Can we ride this wave without going under? Can we sustain this heart-felt love as stronger than death? Can we encompass this ecstasy—of music, of orgasm, of beauty, of kindness, of truth? Can we house in our ordinary life liv-ing all the way from animal root-impulse to spiritual contemplation? Neither burning out nor burning up (Ulanov 1998b/2004, 283)?

Who has done this? Mary who housed the god and lived through his birth and death and was not destroyed; artists whose stone or blues or late quartets, or feet and hands, shine forth, sing forth, dance forth celebration of livingness. The mystery lies in the mystery being visible; we see it, or smell it, and all the senses mix up to become senses of the soul. We touch it with our eyes when beholding the sea; we smell the coolness of blues, taste the reds; we stand on the ineffable and feel its texture as ground beneath our feet; we hear it pressing into all our pores through the cello's music. Like animals, we now have whiskers or feelers, or many legs, or ends of fur with which to spread out into and take from the surround this alive livingness. It breathes us and we sweat it out into itself. Undulating, enfolded, tacked down, and sprung wide open, it is, and is in and through us, between us, in our dreams, welcomed in food, traversing our conversation, inhabiting us through sacrament. We are the jar in which the immortal eternal substance lives (von Franz 1999). In alchemical terms we discover we are the material to build up the precious stone, to become, as the poet Jimenez writes, the "diamond hard consciousness" (Jimenez 1987, 15).

What can be said about this consciousness? It spans the animal to the gods. The instincts stir us up and we extend into the spiritual meaning of this eruption. Spiritual insight quickens animal warmth, a root-impulse to action that pins us into living, not withdrawing. What used to be split into dichotomies dwell together in a larger whole. The question of external and internal realities relating to each other, or splitting into subject and object, changes into a wide vision of a world of shared subjectivities, that what we thought of as external, is mediated always by someone else's subjectivity. This perspective yields the possibility of building up complementary experiences of truth, that together we construct a spiritual universe with ample enough space for all of us to share in common our differences. We emerge into a webbed interconnected whole where disturbance in one part affects the experience in other parts.

On a personal level this means we grow nimble enough to hold to our view of the best psychological theory, for example, and to entertain others' views of their best theory. We risk wholehearted commitment to our god and recognize similar commitment to a different god in our neighbor. Together we share this combination of identity and disidentification, here and now living the limits of our belief, and our conviction that others' belief as well as our own points to unboundedness, transcendence, source. Our identity as Jungians, Muslims, plants us in this earth in this life; our disidentification from these beliefs is the spade that makes space, digs up matter to let spirit circulate. We live a disidentified consciousness. We are housekeepers together, housing the infinite in the finite; we are earthworms together, aerating the soil.

A similar rhythm displays itself in our creating the third space of illusion where reality matches fantasy, where we project images of the other, of the good society, of God, and simultaneously destroy those images as falling short of the reality they symbolize. For projection reveals a new function. We go on with our image-making (or according to different typology through our other senses) and now with the knowledge that it is image-making, representative at best, but never the real thing. But we cannot find the real thing except by sending out these tendrils, these tunes, these hunches that we work up into ideas or inventions or creative attitudes toward what we love. We must help create the good in order to receive the good that is there. We must envision the best self of our child in order to receive the unfolding of the best self that is there. We must theologize about the gifts of God in order to receive all that would be given us, and offer all that would be received from us. This is integrative projection. We do not go out to look for the lost sheep to bring it back. This is a new sheep that appears out of the wilderness for our receiving.

Still another aspect of this new consciousness presents itself. We withdraw our projections onto the other person, especially if we have loved and lost them to death, or to death-dealing experience, or to their own life in another direction. The work of bereavement includes releasing the other to their own livingness, whatever that is, whatever we believe about life after death. Whether the relationship ended because it could not survive, or because of death, our task toward the other is to let them loose, unbind them from our need for them, from the destroying power of our grief, from our overwhelming sorrow in losing them, our anger at them for not staying, our dependence on them.

We work toward setting them free to circulate into their own independent life, their journey here or in the hereafter. This is a great act of love; it makes a big space in us and strengthens our inner capacity to love. We love the other in their otherness; we endorse their ownmostness, celebrate it, wish it well, herald and salute it. To do this is like the larger move to love God for God's sake, not for benefits we hope to accrue to ourselves. Then we see the other and love them in their wholeness and that makes us part of a larger wholeness too.

Experiences of the No-thing place take us into death, into the underworld, into griefs that rob us, strip us, divest us, deprive us, and leave us dispossessed. Dismemberment is just that—torn limb from limb. Only in that terrible place might we see thereby we are reduced to order, the members that make up a whole, the four cardinal directions, the cross. The slime beginnings of the new in that No-thing place usher in a bigger order that makes room for death-dealing experiences. In the spirit of Persephone who becomes Queen of the underworld, we too may come to partake of such sovereign power. That power does not deny the No-thing place, but roots in it and touches the capacity she symbolizes to reign over death-dealing experiences, experiences so terrible that we fear if they happened again they would kill us. Yet we live. In the dark unknowing place, a structure, a staying power is forged that presides over the underworld, over death. Alchemy symbolizes this capacity of aliveness in the face of deadness by the stone that endures despite mortality. We are the jar in which the immortal essence is held, freeing the God in us.

In ending I come back to the opening question: What is this power of aliveness to make something of our experience, to be found and created by the new, through even the No-thing place? Is this aliveness capacity in us, or outside us? Do we have to put it outside us? Yes. I think we do, and at the same time to find it finding us inside us. We need to reify the source of aliveness, and know simultaneously all those reifications, those forms, are dust, wind, No-thing. Its life kills our forms. Our forms make visible this aliveness source. It lives from us and toward us, and we, the same, from it, in it, through it, it through us, toward it, making it graspable in human terms and giving it back into its ownmost self.

References

This chapter is based on versions given to analysts of the C. G. Jung Institute of Los Angeles, and as two presentations to the Guild of Pastoral Psychology at St. Hilda's College, Oxford University.

Bion, W. R. 1965/1991. *Transformations*. London: Karnac.

Edinger, E. F. 1985. *Anatomy of the Psyche: Alchemical Symbolism in Psychotherapy*. La Salle, Ill.: Open Court.

———. 1996. *The New God-Image*. Ed. Dianne D. Cordic and Charles Yates. Wilmette, Ill.: Chiron.

Eliot, T. S. 1966. *Collected Poems, 1909–1962*. New York: Harcourt Brace & World.

Hannah, B. 1976. *Jung, His Life and Work: A Biographical Memoir*. New York: Putnam.

Jimenez, J. R. 1987. Full consciousness. In *God Desired and Desiring*. Trans. Antonio T. de Nicolas. New York: Paragon House.

Jung, C. G. 1932/1958. Psychotherapists or the clergy. In *Psychology and Religion: West and East*. Vol. 11 of *Collected Works*. Trans. R. F. C. Hull. New York: Pantheon.

———. 1938/1958. Psychology and religion. In *Psychology and Religion: West and East*. Vol. 11 of *Collected Works*. Trans. R. F. C. Hull. New York: Pantheon.

———. 1955/1958. Transformation symbolism in the Mass. In *Psychology and Religion: West and East*. Vol. 11 of *Collected Works*. Trans. R. F. C. Hull. New York: Pantheon.

———. 1956–57/1976. Jung and religious belief. In *The Symbolic Life*. Vol. 18 of *Collected Works*. Princeton, N.J.: Princeton University Press.

———. 1963a. *Mysterium Coniunctionis*. Vol. 14 of *Collected Works*. Trans. R. F. C. Hull. New York: Pantheon.

———. 1963b. *Memories, Dreams, Reflections*. Ed. Aniela Jaffé. Trans. Richard and Clara Winston. New York: Pantheon.

———. 1967. *Alchemical Studies*. Vol. 13 of *Collected Works*. Trans. R. F. C. Hull. New York: Pantheon.

———. 1973 and 1975. *Letters*. 2 vols. Eds. Gerhard Adler and Aniela Jaffé. Princeton, N.J.: Princeton University Press.

———. 1988. *Nietzsche's Zarathustra*. 2 vols. Ed. James L. Jarrett. Princeton, N.J.: Princeton University Press.

———. 1997. *Visions*. 2 vols. Ed. Claire Douglas. Princeton, N.J.: Princeton University Press.

Khan, M. M. R. 1963/1974. The concept of cumulative trauma. In *The Privacy of the Self*. New York: International Universities Press.

Kristeva, J. 2006. A father is beaten to death. In *The Dead Father Symposium*. New York: The Association for Psychoanalytic Medicine, Low Library, Columbia University, April 30.

Macquarrie, J. 1968. *Martin Heidegger*. Richmond, Va.: John Knox Press.

Symington, N. 1993. *Narcissism: A New Theory*. London: Karnac.

Ulanov, A., and B. Ulanov. 1991/1999. *The Healing Imagination*. Einsiedeln, Switzerland: Daimon.

———. 1994. *Transforming Sexuality: The Archetypal World of Anima and Animus*. Boston: Shambhala.

Ulanov, A. B. 1992/2005. The holding Self: Jung and the desire for being. In *Spirit in Jung*. Einsiedeln, Switzerland: Daimon.

———. 1994. *The Wizards' Gate: Picturing Consciousness*. Einsiedeln, Switzerland: Daimon.

———. 1996/2004. Countertransference and the Self. In *Spiritual Aspects of Clinical Work*, chapter 14. Einsiedeln, Switzerland: Daimon.

———. 1998a/2004. The gift of consciousness. In *Spiritual Aspects of Clinical Work*, chapter 8. Einsiedeln, Switzerland: Daimon.

———. 1998b/2004. Dreams: passages to a new spirituality. In *Spiritual Aspects of Clinical Work*, chapter 11. Einsiedeln, Switzerland: Daimon.

———. 2001. *Finding Space: Winnicott, God, and Psychic Reality*. Louisville, Ky.: Westminster John Knox Press.

———. 2001a/2004. After analysis what? In *Spiritual Aspects of Clinical Work*, chapter 17. Einsiedeln, Switzerland: Daimon.

———. 2001b/2004. Hate in the analyst. In *Spiritual Aspects of Clinical Work*, chapter 16. Einsiedeln, Switzerland: Daimon.

Ulanov, B. 1973/2003. Mysticism and negative presence. In *Creative Dissent*, chapter 22. Ed. Alan Roland, Barry Ulanov, and Claude Barbre. Westport, Conn.: Praeger.

Von Franz, M-L. 1980. *Alchemy: An Introduction to the Symbolism and the Psychology*. Toronto: Inner City Books.

———. 1999. *Muhammad ibn Umail's Hall AR-RUMUZ ('Clearing of Enigmas') Historical Introduction and Psychological Comment*. Egg, Switzerland: Fotorotar AG.

Winnicott, D. W. 1962/1965. Ego integration in child development. In *The Maturational Processes and the Facilitating Environment*. New York: International Universities Press.

———. 1963/1965. On communicating and not communicating. In *The Maturational Processes and the Facilitating Environment*. New York: International Universities Press.

———. 1971. *Playing and Reality*. London: Tavistock.

INDEX